A Practical Guide for Scholarly Reading in Japanese

A Practical Guide for Scholarly Reading in Japanese is an innovative reference guide for scholars specializing in Asian studies, with a special focus on Chinese studies. The book aims to prepare those scholars to conduct research with primary sources from a variety of genres from the 20th century.

The book contains concise descriptions of grammar points essential for reading scholarly writings in Japanese and exercises based on excerpts taken from prominent Japanese scholarly texts. Each exercise reading provides a list of vocabulary and explanations of expressions. The reading materials provided mainly cover Chinese history, comparative literature, religion, and culture.

The book can be used as a textbook or self-study guide for scholars of Asian studies, as well as students who have completed two years of basic language learning and need to learn to read scholarly Japanese.

Fumiko NAZIKIAN is a senior lecturer in Japanese at Columbia University, USA. Among her recent publications are *Social Networking Approach to Japanese Language Teaching: The Intersection of Language and Culture in the Digital Age* (co-editor, Routledge, 2021), *Modern Japanese Grammar: A Practical Guide & Modern Japanese Workbook* (co-author, Routledge, 2014), and *Hiyaku* (co-author, Routledge, 2011).

Keiko ONO is a lecturer in Japanese and classical language specialist at Princeton University, USA. Prior to joining Princeton University in 2000, she taught at Columbia University, the University of Cologne, Germany, and Bukkyo University, Japan. Her current research interests and article publications lie in the teaching of both classical and academic Japanese for non-native speakers.

Naofumi TATSUMI is a visiting lecturer of Japanese at Brown University, USA. Prior to joining Brown in 2021, he taught at Illinois Wesleyan University and Columbia University. He has recently been writing a textbook in English collaboratively with four professors from other institutions to broaden cultural awareness of Japan.

Routledge Practical Academic Reading Skills

German Reading Skills for Academic Purposes
By Alexander Burdumy

A Practical Guide for Scholarly Reading in Japanese
By Fumiko Nazikian, Keiko Ono, and Naofumi Tatsumi

A Practical Guide for Scholarly Reading in Japanese

Fumiko NAZIKIAN
Keiko ONO
Naofumi TATSUMI

LONDON AND NEW YORK

Designed cover image: gautier075 via Getty Images

First published 2023
by Routledge
4 Park Square, Milton Park, Abingdon, Oxon OX14 4RN

and by Routledge
605 Third Avenue, New York, NY 10158

Routledge is an imprint of the Taylor & Francis Group, an informa business

© 2023 Fumiko Nazikian, Keiko Ono, and Naofumi Tatsumi

The right of Fumiko Nazikian, and Keiko Ono, Naofumi Tatsumi to be identified as authors of this work has been asserted in accordance with sections 77 and 78 of the Copyright, Designs and Patents Act 1988.

All rights reserved. No part of this book may be reprinted or reproduced or utilised in any form or by any electronic, mechanical, or other means, now known or hereafter invented, including photocopying and recording, or in any information storage or retrieval system, without permission in writing from the publishers.

Trademark notice: Product or corporate names may be trademarks or registered trademarks, and are used only for identification and explanation without intent to infringe.

British Library Cataloguing-in-Publication Data
A catalogue record for this book is available from the British Library

Library of Congress Cataloging-in-Publication Data
Names: Nazikian, Fumiko, author. | Ono, Keiko (Lecturer in Japanese) author. | Tatsumi, Naofumi, author.
Title: A practical guide for scholarly reading in Japanese / Fumiko Nazikian, Keiko Ono, Naofumi Tatsumi.
Description: Abingdon, Oxon ; New York, NY : Routledge, 2023. | Series: Routledge practical academic reading skills | Includes bibliographical references and index.
Identifiers: LCCN 2022028918 (print) | LCCN 2022028919 (ebook) | ISBN 9781032014906 (hardback) | ISBN 9781032014890 (paperback) | ISBN 9781003178842 (ebook)
Subjects: LCSH: Japanese language—Textbooks for foreign speakers. | Reading comprehension—Problems, exercises, etc. | Academic writing—Problems, exercises, etc. | Japanese language—Written Japanese. | Japanese language—Grammar. | Japanese language—Style.
Classification: LCC PL539.3 .N25 2023 (print) | LCC PL539.3 (ebook) | DDC 495.682/421—dc23/eng/20220920
LC record available at https://lccn.loc.gov/2022028918
LC ebook record available at https://lccn.loc.gov/2022028919

ISBN: 978-1-032-01490-6 (hbk)
ISBN: 978-1-032-01489-0 (pbk)
ISBN: 978-1-003-17884-2 (ebk)

DOI: 10.4324/9781003178842

Typeset in Minion Pro
by Apex CoVantage, LLC

Contents

Preface	*ix*
To the Reader	*xii*
List of Abbreviations	*xvi*
Acknowledgements	*xviii*

Chapter 1: "Toolbox": Essential Grammar for Scholarly Reading 1

1. Understanding Written Style 3

2. Finding the Predicate and the Subject 5

2.1 Finding the Predicate: The Ending of a Sentence 5

2.2 Finding the Subject 5

2.2.1 When the Particle が Marks the Subject 6

2.2.2 When the Particle の Marks the Subject 6

2.2.3 When the Particle は Marks the Subject 6

2.2.4 When the Particle も Marks the Subject 7

2.2.5 Other Particles That Mark the Subject 7

2.2.6 Cases in Which the Subject is Omitted 9

3. Separating Sentences Based on Meaning (Chunking) 10

3.1 Compound Sentences: Listing with the て-Form 11

3.1.1 Connecting Verbs 11

3.1.2 Connecting *I*-adjectives 12

3.1.3 Connecting *Na*-adjectives 12

3.1.4 Connecting Nouns 12

3.2 The Suspended Form Method (連用中止法) 14

3.2.1 Verbs 14

3.2.2 *I*-adjectives 14

3.3 〜し 'what's more; not only ~ but also' 16

3.4 X という Y 'Y called X' 17

3.4.1 X (Clause) という Y (Noun) 17

3.4.2 X (Noun) という Y (Noun) 17

3.5 S1 が、S2 'S1, but/and S2' 18

3.5.1 BUT/ 逆接 (Concessive Connection) 18

3.5.2 AND/ 順接 (Simple Connection) 18

v

A Practical Guide for Scholarly Reading in Japanese

3.6 Conditional Expressions 20

3.6.1 S たら, S/N なら, S ば, and S と 'If/When' 20

3.6.2 Other Often-Used Conditional Expressions, 〜場合 'in case of; in the case (of)' and 〜限り 'as long as' 21

3.7 Conditional Expressions with Concessive Conjunctions ても and とも 'even though; even if' 21

3.8 Review Exercises 22

4. Sentence-Ending Expressions 23

4.1 Explaining a Circumstance のだ/のである/のです 23

4.2 Rhetorical Questions 〜(の)ではないか/だろうか 24

4.3 Softening of a Claim/Conclusion 24

4.3.1 〜と思う/考える 24

4.3.2 〜と思われる/考えられる 25

5. Defining Expressions X を Y とする 'regard X as Y' 28

6. Particles 29

6.1 Compound Particles 29

6.2 Particle Equivalent Phrases 30

7. Kanji 37

7.1 国字 (Kanji Made in Japan) 37

7.2 当て字 Chinese Character(s) Used for Its Phonetic Sound 37

7.3 新字体 Simplified Kanji 38

7.4 同形異義語 Japanese-Chinese Homographs 39

7.5 同音異義語 Japanese-Chinese Homophones 40

8. Classical Japanese Grammar (for Reading Academic Articles from the Meiji Era Onwards) 42

8.1 歴史的仮名遣い Historical *Kana* Orthography 42

8.2 Inflected Forms 47

8.3 Verbs 48

8.4 形容詞 Adjectives and 形容動詞 Adjectival Verbs 51

8.4.1 形容詞 Adjectives (*i*-adjectives) 51

8.4.2 形容動詞 Adjectival Verbs (*na*-adjectives) 52

8.5 助動詞 Auxiliary Verbs 54

8.5.1 ず Negative 55

8.5.2 き and けり Recollective 56

8.5.3 なり and たり Copular/Declarative 58

8.5.4 たり, り, and ぬ Perfective 60

8.5.5 べし Advice, Appropriateness, Potential, Intentional, Speculative, and Command 63

vi

Contents

8.5.6 る and らる　Passive, Potential, Honorific, and Spontaneous 64

8.5.7 ごとし　Comparative 65

8.5.8 しむ　Causative 66

8.5.9 む　Speculative, Intentional, and Circumlocution 67

8.5.10 まい　Negative Speculative and Negative Intentional 69

8.6　Conjunctive Particles 71

8.6.1 ば　Hypothetical/Logical Connections 71

8.6.2 とも, ど, ども, and も　Concessive Connections 73

8.6.3 に and を　Causal, Concessive, and Simple Connections 75

8.6.4 して　Causal, Concessive, and Simple Connections 77

8.7　連体形 Attributive Form + Particle 80

9.　The Influence of Chinese Texts in Japanese 85

9.1　Expressions Used for Japanese Readings 85

9.1.1 Causative Expressions 85

9.1.2 所 86

9.2　漢語 Verbification, Adjectivization, and Adverbization 86

Chapter 2 Section 1: What Are Modifiers? (Mechanisms of Modifying Sentences in Japanese) 88

1.1　Modifying Nouns 91

1.2　The Particle は 92

1.3　The て-Form as a Conjunction 93

1.4　Subordinate Clauses: Clauses with Conjunctive Particles 94

1.4.1 Concessive のに 95

1.4.2 Reason Clause から 95

1.4.3 Conjunctive Particle し '(and) what is more' 96

2.　Summary 97

3.　Exercises 97

Chapter 2 Section 2: 中国史の時代区分問題をめぐって—現時点からの省察— 101

Chapter 2 Section 3: 中国古典詩のリズム—リズムの根源性と詩型の変遷— 139

Chapter 2 Section 4: 封建制度と家族道徳 151

Chapter 2 Section 5: 概括的唐宋時代觀 165

Chapter 2 Section 6: 格調・神韻・性靈の三詩說を論ず 199

Chapter 2 Section 7: 兩漢文學考 213

Chapter 2 Section 8: 文人畫の原理 227

練習問題回答　Answers 238

vii

A Practical Guide for Scholarly Reading in Japanese

Bibliography 254

Index Chapter 1 255

Index (Expressions) 259

Auxiliary Verb Conjugations 261

Preface

Li Feng

Columbia University

There was once a time when Western, especially American, sinologists customarily acquired their essential training in Japan. This was not only because of the political reality that after the Korean war, China was completely closed to the West in an America-centered new Asia-Pacific world order, but also because Japan had such a long tradition and rich legacy in the study of China. A good indication of Japanese influence on American Sinology is the introduction, in the time of Edwin O. Reischauer and John K. Fairbank, of NAITŌ Konan's theory of China's early modernity in the 10th century (*kinsei* 近世), which then evolved into the proposition of the so-called "Tang-Song transition" that has attracted scholarly devotion ever since. For those of us who dwell in the early period, few could have failed to acknowledge David N. Keightley's 1982 extensive "Review: Akatsuka Kiyoshi and the Culture of Early China: A Study in Historical Method." In *Early China*, the journal founded by Keightley, an annual summary of Japanese scholarship has long been included as an essential component, echoing distantly Harvard's early bibliographies of *Japanese Studies of Modern China*. Without going back to the earliest time when Japan first substantially encountered China and developed a vision of its history and culture that can somehow be seen in such works as FUJIWARA no Sukeyo's (847–897) surviving bibliography of Chinese texts in Japan, it can be said that in the rise of Chinese history as a modern academic discipline, Japan stood firmly on the frontline. Not only did Japan modernize her reading and commentaries of Chinese texts in the hands of classicists like IKEDA Suetoshi; in areas that have come to represent the core of modern studies of ancient China such as oracle bone and bronze inscriptions, Japan also produced scholars like SHIMA Kunio at about the same time as China produced her first generation of scholars, not to mention Japan's long-standing leading role in more international fields such as Dunhuang Studies.

To those of us who had arrived from China to study in Japan in the late 1980s and early 1990s, Japanese historical scholarship was apparently at a higher level than that of China both in terms of its conceptual frameworks and of professional practice. While China just emerged from the prolonged political-social turmoil during which academic studies were suspended until near the end of the Cultural Revolution in 1976, in the thirty years of enduring peace and prosperity since World War II, Japanese Sinology had maintained its high academic quality and produced some of the finest works in Sinology across various fields of history and literature. Good examples are NISHIJIMA Sadao's studies on the economy of rural societies under China's early empires or works on the commercial and economic history of southern China under the Song by SHIBA Yoshinobu. Studies of oracle bone and bronze inscriptions from the Shang and Zhou periods that served as the basis for interpreting political and social institutions, such as the works by MATSUMARU Michio and ITŌ Michiharu, enjoyed high international recognition. They were complemented by HAYASHI Minao's erudition about almost any type of material objects from early China. Over the course of this postwar development, Japanese Sinology also achieved a better regional balance between western and eastern Japan.

It is also true that Japanese scholars were heavily influenced by the Marxist theory of social-historical development; from this arose the issue of periodization of Chinese history and the argument for slave or feudal society in China (see TANIGAWA in Chapter 2). Ultimately these remained discourses within the tradition of Marxist historiography. In China, the question of the periodization of Chinese

A Practical Guide for Scholarly Reading in Japanese

history was highly political and the answer to it determined the goal of the Chinese revolution, thus providing the ideological foundations of both the nationalist Kuomintang and the Communist Party of China. After 1949, any study of particular historical issues was expected, ultimately, to contribute to the grand narrative of social evolution endorsed by the Communist Party. Yet in Japan, the debates remained by and large academic discourses. Japanese scholars benefited from the global perspectives and emphasis on activities of production inherent in Marxist historiography, but they were also free to develop new paradigms about Chinese history without having to prove that ancient China had been either slave-based or feudal. This background knowledge is essential to understand the success of postwar Japanese historiography.

Japan has much to offer as one of the three birth places (in addition to Europe and China) of modern Sinology and has produced an enormous inventory of scholarly literature on China. To fully understand and benefit from this legacy requires knowledge about the history of Japanese Sinology as well as the mastery of the Japanese language. Therefore, in the United States all Ph.D. programs in East Asian Studies require two or three years of modern Japanese as the second East Asian language for students whose research focus is on China (or, to a lesser extent, on Korea). Columbia University has traditionally insisted on a three-year curriculum with exemptions only granted to students working on the Qing and modern periods. However, unless a student had the chance to attend years of school in Japan, even a three-year curriculum is insufficient to achieve the proficiency to freely read and utilize Japanese academic works in research. Without changing the mandated schedule for progress, the only solution to the problem is pedagogical. In this regard, Columbia students were lucky enough to have been offered a course specially designed for the China and Korea fields, "Third-year Scholarly Reading in Japanese" (parallel to the regular-track third-year Japanese), established in 2009 by the department's Japanese language program under its director, Fumiko NAZIKIAN. A yearlong course of the same nature, "Readings in Japanese Academic Style," was already offered at Princeton University since 2002 by Keiko ONO, herself a Sinologist and Comparatist by training and a specialist in both Classical Chinese and Japanese literature. Thus, members of the two Japanese language programs regularly exchanged their ideas and teaching materials and collaborated closely to enrich the content of these courses at both universities. At Columbia, the course was first taught in 2009 by Shinji SATO, then by NAZIKIAN herself, and recently by Naofumi TATSUMI, all of them experienced lecturers of the Japanese language; at Princeton, the course has been continuously offered by ONO for twenty years. Thus, it is a wonderful surprise that these instructors at both universities have decided to jointly publish the fruits of their research and teaching in the present book, so that it can benefit students and scholars in East Asian Studies around the world.

I would be out of my depth trying to evaluate this volume. However, as a life-long learner of the Japanese language, I can perhaps make some recommendations about the strengths of the book to the readers. First, this book defines academic Japanese as a special field of knowledge through a meticulous account of its grammar and features at the level of writing style and expression (see primarily Chapter 1). Although not all points analyzed in this book are strictly relevant to academic Japanese alone, even a skilled reader will appreciate this introductory chapter together with its large number of tables and illustrative charts. As a result, the book serves as both a textbook and a useful reference work. Second, on the methodological level, I completely agree with the authors that the key to correctly reading academic Japanese lies in the analysis of the often lengthy sentences by isolating the *predicates*; in order to do so successfully, it is important to first identify what is the *modifier* and what the *modified* (Chapter 2, Section 1). The authors provide long discussions on how to achieve these critical steps. Another strength of the book lies in its concise introduction to the essential grammar of Classical Japanese.

As is true also with Chinese, the modern form of a language can always serve as the depository of the remnants of its classical form that are sometimes employed to achieve higher aesthetic standards. Academic Japanese is no exception, if not more so especially in works by prewar authors such as NAITŌ Konan and SUZUKI Torao (Chapter 2). Although such Classical elements as *beshi* べし or *tari* たり that a student often encounters can be treated as special usage and historical *kana* such as *fu* ふ (for *u* う) and *e* ゑ (for *e* え) can be learned by heart one by one, the systematic discussion of such features is doubtlessly very helpful to readers of academic Japanese. Finally, from my own experience of teaching Classical Chinese for many years, no matter how deeply one studies a text, what matters most are the unique *language patterns* that students can memorize and apply independently to future texts. The authors of the present book fully understand the importance of *language patterns*, which they call "expressions." From the texts presented, they have extracted a total of forty-three such *expression* patterns that, if fully learned, will enable the students to deal successfully with most works in academic Japanese.

Finally, I should like to emphasize that the selection of texts in this volume strikes a good balance between prewar and postwar authors, that the disciplinary coverage is broad, and that the level of technicality is appropriate. All this is based on the substantial understanding of Chinese history and culture as presented in Japanese scholarship, from where the subtleties of grammar and expression are then explained within the logic and conventions of the English language.

In sum, I congratulate the authors on their most impressive work! While beginners will find it deeply informative and inspiring, experienced readers of academic Japanese will find it refreshing and entertaining.

March, 2022

To the Reader

Introduction

A Practical Guide for Scholarly Reading in Japanese is an innovative reference guide for scholars specializing in Asian studies, with a special focus on Chinese studies. The book aims to help prepare those scholars to conduct research with primary sources from a variety of genres from the 20th century. The book contains concise descriptions of grammar points essential for reading scholarly writings in Japanese and exercises based on excerpts taken from prominent Japanese scholarly texts. Each exercise reading provides a list of vocabulary and explanations of expressions. The reading materials provided mainly cover Chinese history, comparative literature, religion, and culture. The book can be used as a textbook or self-study guide for successful scholarly reading in Japanese.

Features of This Book

This book includes:

- Concise and comprehensive explanations of grammar points* including classical Japanese grammar that is useful for reading scholarly texts
- Translation exercises on those grammar points
- Reading comprehension exercises of authentic reading materials and answer keys
- Lists of useful vocabulary and expressions for each scholarly text

* These explanations and exercises are designed to help you develop your reading comprehension skills. Excessive details about nuances and implications, although useful for language production, are left out so you can learn to read the materials efficiently.

You can:

- Select and start with any reading material depending on your needs and interests
- Do exercises and check your answers on your own
- Use the "Toolbox" as a reference when reading scholarly texts

Organization of This Book/Structure and Content

Chapter 1

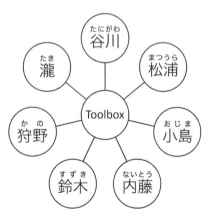

> "Toolbox": Essential Grammar for Scholarly Reading

Chapter 1 introduces a "toolbox," or set of tools necessary for successful scholarly reading. Such tools include but are not limited to written styles, particles, kanji, classical grammar, and how to find the predicate and subject of a sentence. This chapter also provides example sentences and practice questions with model answers, so that you can study on your own.

To the Reader

Chapter 2

Section 1: Modifying Sentences

One of the most important—yet challenging—aspects of reading complex scholarly texts is finding the relationship between the modifier and the modified. In this section, we discuss some key points of identifying the modifying–modified relationships of sentences, especially placing emphasis on noun modifying sentences.

Sections 2–8: Scholarly Texts and Practice Questions

Sequence and Script of Each Text

Sections 2–8 provide seven scholarly texts with practice questions for each. We handpicked authentic reading materials from a variety of genres. They were all written by prominent Japanese scholars in the 20th century.

Based on the difficulty of sentence structures and the use of classical Japanese grammar, our suggested order of the texts is as follows:

Section	Author	Field of Study	Kana	Kanji
2	谷川 (1987)	History	Modern *kana* system 現代仮名遣い Ex. おもう	Simplified *kanji* 新字体 Ex. 学問
3	松浦 (1986)	Literature		
4	小島 (1943/1988)	Intellectual history		
5	内藤 (1922)	History	Historical *kana* system 歴史的仮名遣い Ex. おもふ	Traditional characters 旧字体 Ex. 學問
6	鈴木 (1940)	Literature		
7	狩野 (1964, 78, 88)	Intellectual history /Literature		
8	瀧 (1922)	Art history		

The first three texts are written in the modern *kana* system (現代仮名遣い) and simplified kanji (新字体), while the rest of them are written in the historical *kana* system (歴史的仮名遣い) and traditional characters (旧字体). You can select and start with any of these articles depending on your needs and interests.

xiii

A Practical Guide for Scholarly Reading in Japanese

Layout and Contents

Each section contains a text, practice questions, vocabulary, and expressions. As illustrated in the picture below, the text is placed on the left page while the questions are on the right page for ease of readability. Whenever questions contain quotes from the text, the corresponding question numbers and alphabet letters are added to the text. The answer keys for the questions are included in the appendices.

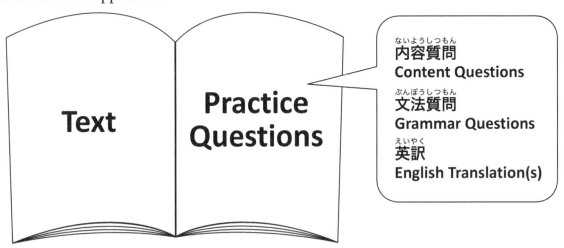

Vocabulary

We handpicked useful words and phrases for reading the text, such as vocabulary commonly used in scholarly texts, 当て字 (phonetic borrowing), and proper nouns. However, if an item is listed in Expressions, it is not included in Vocabulary, and vice versa.

As shown in the table below, each vocabulary comes with the kanji (if applicable), the reading in hiragana (the modern *kana* system), and the English equivalent.

Verbs are listed in the dictionary form. If a verb in the text is conjugated, we added its dictionary form along with its English meaning.

ページ番号	本文の語彙	辞書形・漢字	読み方 (現代語表記)	英語
P. xx	からんで	絡む	からむ	to be involved
P. yy	尚ほ		なお	still

Expressions

From each text, we selected expressions that are commonly used in scholarly texts and added two example sentences with English translations. Below is an example of Expressions and its detailed explanations.

To the Reader

〜に他[外]ならず / ならない nothing but 〜 　cf. Kano, Tanigawa

　　　　　　①　　　　　②　　　　　　③　　　　　④

◆箇人につきていへるものに外ならず。

⑤ They are none other than [terms] referring to individuals.

　　　　　　　　　　　　　　⑥

1) 成功とは日々の努力の成果に外ならず。

⑦ Success is nothing other than the result of daily hard work.

2) 互いに関係が良好であったのは、共通の敵がいたからに他ならない。

Their relationship was good precisely because they had a common enemy.

① [ ] indicates an alternative kanji

② / indicates an alternative ending

③ the English meaning

④ cross-references

⑤ an excerpt from the text

⑥ [ ] indicates an omission

⑦ example sentences

Readings of Kanji

For your convenience, we added readings in hiragana to all kanji used in Chapter 1, Modifying Sentences, Vocabulary, Expressions, and also to some kanji in the scholarly texts that may be difficult to read. The readings we added to the texts are all written in the modern *kana* system regardless of the type of kanji, be it simplified or traditional. However, the readings added by the original authors may be written in the historical *kana* system. There are two articles where the authors added readings to some kanji on their own as explained below.

Matsuura: We only added readings to 詩経, 桃夭, 寿和, 贈鄭曼季, and 答陸士龍. The rest of the readings are added by Matsuura himself.

Taki: 舒情詩的 is the only reading added by Taki. The rest of the readings are ours.

Others

• Names of books are italicized

• Names of authors: surname in upper case + given name in lower case: Eg. NAITŌ Konan

• For the ease of readability, Japanese words are written in Japanese where appropriate:

Eg. The auxiliary verb たり has two meanings (copular and perfective)

XV

A Practical Guide for Scholarly Reading in Japanese

Appendices

Answer Keys

The answer keys for the practice questions are available in both Japanese and English, except for English translations and questions that require answers in Japanese (e.g., "本文の言葉を使って答えなさい" and "修飾部分はどこからですか。最初の三文字を答えなさい")

Auxiliary Verb Conjugations

Conjugation tables of classical auxiliary verbs are included in the appendices for your quick reference. The explanations of each auxiliary verb are available in Chapter 1.

List of Abbreviations 1

Part of Speech		Abbreviations used in Vocabulary	
V	verb	NP	the name of a person
ADJ	adjective	NB	the name of a book
ADJ-V	adjectival verb	PB	phonetic borrowing (当て字)
ADV	adverb		
N	noun/nominal		
P	particle		
CONJ-P	conjunctive particle		
AUX	auxiliary verb		
Vpot	potential verb		
S	sentence		

xvi

List of Abbreviations 2

Classical Japanese verbs		Classical Japanese verb conjugations	
Yodan	四段活用 （よだんかつよう）	*MIZEN*	未然形 （みぜんけい）
Shimo ichidan	下一段活用 （しもいちだんかつよう）	*RENYŌ*	連用形 （れんようけい）
Nahen	ナ行変格活用 （ぎょうへんかくかつよう）	*SHŪSHI*	終止形 （しゅうしけい）
Rahen	ラ行変格活用 （ぎょうへんかくかつよう）	*RENTAI*	連体形 （れんたいけい）
Shimo nidan	下二段活用 （しもにだんかつよう）	*IZEN*	已然形 （いぜんけい）
Kami ichidan	上一段活用 （かみいちだんかつよう）	*MEIREI*	命令形 （めいれいけい）
Kami nidan	上二段活用 （かみにだんかつよう）	Others	
Kahen	カ行変格活用 （ぎょうへんかくかつよう）	MJ	modern Japanese
Sahen	サ行変格活用 （ぎょうへんかくかつよう）	CJ	classical Japanese

About the Name 支那 *Shina*

As this book contains essays which refer to China as *Shina*, we wish to use this opportunity to explain the name. Throughout modern times, many illustrious sinologists have exchanged a variety of debates regarding the name *Shina*. Joshua Fogel's "New Thoughts on an Old Controversy: *Shina* as a Toponym for China" (*Between China and Japan*, Boston: Brill, 2015) discusses all the main debates and adds its own profound insights.

Numerous theories exist for the name's origin, but it first came into frequent use in Japan during the 19th century. During the time period when the essays in this book were written, imperial universities in Tokyo, Kyoto, and elsewhere used names such as "*Shina* philosophy/history," "*Shina* literature," and "*Shina* linguistics," for their courses of study, and "*Shina* studies" referred to the research of China's thought, culture, language, history, etc.

It is a fact that this name can be interpreted as derogatory and that it offended the people of China throughout modern history. It is therefore impossible to disregard the distasteful impression the name may give even in the present day. However, the sinologists whose work this book includes devoted themselves to the development of "*Shina* studies" as a purely academic topic of study, and it is clear that their use of the name "*Shina*" contains no derogatory intent whatsoever. Moreover, in consideration of the book's purpose of fostering reading comprehension of sources, the names used by the original texts must not be altered. Therefore, we left the name "*Shina*" as is throughout the book. We hope that readers will understand our decision.

Acknowledgements

This project owes its completion to the strong support we received from many colleagues.

We owe an immense debt to Mary HUE, Keiko ONO and Shinji SATO who taught the course and inspired us to write this book. In particular, Keiko ONO's teaching of this course for two decades at Princeton founded and molded the basis of this book. We also wish to thank Haruo SHIRANE and Tomi SUZUKI for their useful comments on the course in spring 2015. We would like to thank Wesley JACOBSEN, the director of the Japanese language program at Harvard, for kindly allowing us to sit in on his class and sharing his ideas.

The book also benefited from the feedback we received from our colleagues at Columbia and Princeton. Our sincere thanks to Benjamin A. ELMAN, Dorothy KO, Eugenia LEAN, Feng LI and Stephen F. TEISER who offered valuable comments on the book proposal and contents. Their feedback shaped and refined our thoughts. The ideas deployed in this book also benefited tremendously from the valuable comments of the four anonymous reviewers of the manuscript.

We would like to express our deep gratitude to Brian R. STEINGER, John KIESCHNICK, Matthias L. RICHTER, and Yuri PINES who helped us with strong support and helpful feedback.

We have received the generous support of several divisions within Columbia University and Princeton University: the department of East Asian Languages and Cultures (EALAC), the Tang Center for Early China, the Donald Keene Center of Columbia University; the program for East Asian Study (EAS) and the EAS department of Princeton University. We would particularly like to thank Shang WEI, the chair of the of EALAC of Columbia University, and Anna SHIELDS, the department chair of East Asian Studies of Princeton University, for their generous and strong support of this project.

We are grateful to the Japan Foundation for a 2020 Japanese-language Education grant for a project, "A Practical Guide for Scholarly Reading in Japanese." We are particularly grateful to Mami NAKAI of the Japan Foundation for her empathy and wonderful professional attention. We would also like to express our special gratitude to Kaitlin R. Collins-Palmer for assisting us through the procedure of the grant application.

Special thanks to Rieko RADOMSKI, Nestor SERRANO, Yusuke TSUZUKI, and Kevin H. WOOLSEY for their generous assistance and thorough proofreading and editing. A vow of thanks to Andrea HARTILL and Iola ASHBY of Routledge who shepherded this to production with patience and understanding.

It has been almost seven years since this book project began in 2015. We hope the book can contribute to the education of scholars in Asian studies in the years to come.

April, 2022

Chapter 1
"Toolbox": Essential Grammar for Scholarly Reading

A Practical Guide for Scholarly Reading in Japanese

We will be introducing a toolbox for academic reading in this section. The table below displays the nine goals for successful scholarly reading and the tools necessary for each goal. We will proceed to explain each tool in order.

Goals and Tools

Goal		Tool
1. Understanding Written Style		である style だ style
2. Finding the Predicate and the Subject	Predicate	Locations and parts of speech of predicates
	Subject (marked)	1. The nominative particle が 2. (Potentially) nominative particles の, は, and も 3. Other particles だけ, こそ, さえ, etc.
	(unmarked/ implied)	1st person, 2nd person, 3rd person, or previously mentioned word
3. Separating Sentences Based on Meaning (Chunking)		1. Compound Sentences: Listing with the て-Form 2. The Suspended Form Method 3. 〜し 'what's more; not only 〜 but also' 4. X という Y 'Y called X' 5. S1 が、S2 'S1, but/and S2' 6. Conditional Expressions 7. Conditional Expressions with Concessive Conjunctions ても and とも 8. Review Exercises
4. Sentence-Ending Expressions		1. Explaining a Circumstance のだ 2. Rhetorical Questions 〜のではないか/だろうか 3. Softening of a Claim/Conclusion
5. Defining Expressions		X を Y とする 'regard X as Y'
6. Particles		1. Compound Particles 2. Particle Equivalent Phrases
7. Kanji (Chinese Characters)		1. *Kokuji*: Kanji made in Japan 2. *Ateji*: Chinese Character(s) Used for Its Phonetic Sound 3. Simplified Kanji 4. Japanese-Chinese Homographs 5. Japanese-Chinese Homophones

2

8. Classical Grammar	1. Historical *Kana* Orthography 2. Inflected Forms 3. Verbs 4. Adjectives and Adjectival Verbs 5. Auxiliary Verbs 6. Conjunctive Particles 7. Attributive Form + Particle
9. Japanese Expressions for *Kanbun*	1. Expressions Used for Japanese Readings 2. *Kango*: Verbification, Adjectivization, and Adverbization of Chinese words

1. Understanding Written Style

The styles of written Japanese are the です/ます (polite) form, the だ (plain) form, and the である (expository) form. The following table summarizes these three styles. The です/ます form is mainly used for formal lectures and speeches, but academic texts are typically written using the だ form and the である form.

Summarization of Written styles

	Tense	だ	である	です・ます
Noun/ Adjectival Verb	Present affirmative	学生（がくせい）だ 元気（げんき）だ	学生（がくせい）である 元気（げんき）である	学生（がくせい）です 元気（げんき）です
	Present negative	学生（がくせい）ではない 元気（げんき）ではない	○	学生（がくせい）ではありません 元気（げんき）ではありません
	Past affirmative	学生（がくせい）だった 元気（げんき）だった	学生（がくせい）であった 元気（げんき）であった	学生（がくせい）でした 元気（げんき）でした
	Past negative	学生（がくせい）ではなかった 元気（げんき）ではなかった	○	学生（がくせい）ではありませんでした 元気（げんき）ではありませんでした
Adjective	Present affirmative	高（たか）い	○	高（たか）いです
	Present negative	高（たか）くない	○	高（たか）くないです
	Past affirmative	高（たか）かった	○	高（たか）かったです
	Past negative	高（たか）くなかった	○	高（たか）くなかったです
Verb	Present affirmative	読（よ）む	○	読（よ）みます
	Present negative	読（よ）まない	○	読（よ）みません
	Past affirmative	読（よ）んだ	○	読（よ）みました
	Past negative	読（よ）まなかった	○	読（よ）みませんでした
Other	Conjecture	〜だろう	〜であろう	〜でしょう
	Explanation	〜のだ	〜のである	〜のです

Chapter 1 – "Toolbox": Essential Grammar for Scholarly Reading

2. Finding the Predicate and the Subject

In academic papers, the probability of coming across long sentences is very high. In order to understand the structure of a sentence accurately, you first need to identify the predicate and subject. The following are the means of finding them.

2.1 Finding the Predicate: The Ending of a Sentence

2.2 Finding the Subject

    2.2.1 When the Particle が Marks the Subject

    2.2.2 When the Particle の Marks the Subject

    2.2.3 When the Particle は Marks the Subject

    2.2.4 When the Particle も Marks the Subject

    2.2.5 Other Particles That Mark the Subject

    2.2.6 Cases in Which the Subject is Omitted

2.1 Finding the Predicate: The Ending of a Sentence

Japanese predicates consist of verbs (including auxiliary verbs), adjectives (*i*-adjectives), adjectival verbs (*na*-adjectives), and nouns + copulas (だ, である, です) and they are typically placed at the end of sentences. English predicates are always accompanied by a verb, but Japanese predicates can potentially consist only of adjectives (as in the sentence, "Xは難しい" [X is difficult]). The underlined portions in the following sentences are the predicates.

▶*Example Sentences*

① 我が国の学会には中国史の時代区分に関する二つの有力な説が<u>ある</u>。(verb)

    (There are two influential theories in Japanese academia regarding the division of the eras in Chinese history.)

② 今ではそのような議論は<u>稀である</u>。(noun + copular)

    (These days, that type of argument is rare.)

③ 唐代には李白、杜甫など有名な詩人が<u>多い</u>。(adjective)

    (There are many famous poets such as Li Bai and Du Fu during the Tang Dynasty.)

2.2 Finding the Subject

The subject must be a noun, but in Japanese, there are many instances in which it is either omitted, or if present, is difficult to discern. Students should thus learn the method for finding the predicate and the subject without depending on context. In order to find the subject, one must first pay special attention to the particle that marks it.

5

A Practical Guide for Scholarly Reading in Japanese

2.2.1 When the Particle が Marks the Subject

If the sentence is in the form "noun + が" there is a high probability that the noun is the subject.

▶ *Example Sentences*

① 我が国の学会には中国史の時代区分に関する二つの有力な説<u>が</u>ある。

(There are two influential theories in Japanese academia regarding the division of the eras in Chinese history.)

② 歴史をいかに発展的にとらえるか<u>が</u>重要なモチーフであった。

(How progressive we perceive history to be was an important motif.)

The interrogative sentence 歴史をいかに発展的にとらえるか, which uses the interrogative sentence-ending particle か, can be the subject of the sentence.

③ このような豪族勢力の意見を官人候補者の選挙に利用しようとしたの<u>が</u>、九品中正制度の一面である。

(That [people] tried to use these types of opinions from influential noble families for elections of official candidates was one side of the nine-rank system.)

2.2.2 When the Particle の Marks the Subject

There are cases in which the particle の is used to mark the subject of a sentence instead of が. However, it should be noted that の can only express the subject when it is inside of a noun modifier clause.

▶ *Example Sentences*

① 雪<u>の/が</u>降る夜に車を運転しない方がよい。

(One shouldn't drive a car on nights when it snows.)

② 弟 <u>の/が</u>卒業した大学は東京にある。

(The university that my younger brother graduated from is in Tokyo.)

③ これは間違いなく日本政府、文化庁<u>の/が</u>発表した公式の数字である。

(These are unmistakably the public figures that were presented by the Japanese government's Agency for Cultural Affairs.)

2.2.3 When the Particle は Marks the Subject

は is the topic marker that introduces the topic of the sentence. The following sentences show instances in which the topic marked by は functions as the subject.

6

Chapter 1 – "Toolbox": Essential Grammar for Scholarly Reading

▶*Example Sentences*

① 谷川先生<u>は</u>優しい。(Professor Tanigawa is nice.)

② 谷川さん<u>は</u>先生だ。(Tanigawa-san is a teacher.)

③ 谷川さん<u>は</u>来るでしょう。(Tanigawa-san will probably come.)

Note: It should be noted that the topic is not necessarily the subject. It can also be the object or various other parts of speech.

▶*Example Sentences*

④ フランス語<u>は</u>話せます。([I] can speak French [as opposed to other languages].)

⑤ 金曜日<u>は</u>忙しい。([I] am busy on Friday.)
金曜日 is the topic of the sentence, but isn't the subject. 私 is the subject.

2.2.4 When the Particle も Marks the Subject

As in the particle は , も "also/too" can mark the subject as well.

▶*Example Sentences*

① 鈴木先生は優しい。谷川先生<u>も</u>優しい。

(Professor Suzuki is nice. Professor Tanigawa is nice, too.)

② 鈴木さんは先生だ。谷川さん<u>も</u>先生だ。

(Suzuki-san is a teacher. Tanigawa-san is also a teacher.)

③ 鈴木さんは来るでしょう。谷川さん<u>も</u>来るでしょう。

(Suzuki-san will probably come. Tanigawa-san will also probably come.)

▶*Example Sentences*

④ フランス語<u>も</u>話せます。([I] can also speak French.)

⑤ 金曜日<u>も</u>忙しい。([I] am also busy on Friday.)
金曜日 is the topic of the sentence, but isn't the subject. 私 is the subject.

2.2.5 Other Particles That Mark the Subject

Other particles can mark the subject of a sentence as well. These particles can inherently include meanings such as limitation, degree, or emphasis.

7

A Practical Guide for Scholarly Reading in Japanese

▶*Example*: The particle だけ (meaning 'limitation')

① 田中さん**だけ**（が）来た。（が : subject marker)

(Only Tanaka-san came.)

Here, the particle が can be omitted, with だけ serving as the subject marker. Particles that can serve to mark the subject have been summarized below.

Other particles that can mark the subject

Particle	English Meaning	Example Sentence
こそ	very	この説**こそ**正しかった。 (It was this very theory that was correct.)
さえ	even	唐代には、このような諺**さえ**出来た。 (Even this type of proverb was made during the Tang Dynasty.)
でも	even	有名な先生**でも**言い間違えた。 (Even the famous teacher said it incorrectly.)
しか	only	この方法**しか**問題を解決できない。 (This is the only way to solve the problem.)
まで	even	親しい友人**まで**私の結婚に反対した。 (Even my close friend was against my marriage.)
ばかり	only	最後は、実力の無い官吏**ばかり**残ってしまった。 (At the end, only incapable officials remained.)
だけ	only (as opposed to others)	天子の権力**だけ**強大になっていった。 (Only the emperor's authority was becoming more powerful.)
ほど	approximately	三十人**ほど**手伝いに来てくれた。 (Approximately 30 people came to help.)
など	such as	その店では青銅器**など**売られていた。 (Things such as bronze artifacts were sold at that store.)

8

Chapter 1 – "Toolbox": Essential Grammar for Scholarly Reading

2.2.6 Cases in Which the Subject is Omitted

In Japanese, when the subject is obvious from the context, it is often omitted. When the subject is omitted, it is usually one of the following four options:

1. 1st person

2. 2nd person

3. 3rd person

4. A word that was previously mentioned

▶ *Example Sentences*

① 世界平和のために貢献しなければならない。

([We] must make contributions for world peace.)

Since this is a general statement, the subject is either 私たち (1st person), 人々 (3rd person), or あなた (2nd person).

② 美しい自然を守りたい。

([I] want to protect the beautiful environment.)

It is in the たい (desire) form, so the subject is the 1st person.

③ もう少しゆっくり話してください。 (Please speak a little slower.)

Since this is a request, the subject is the 2nd person.

④ 田中さんが昨日欠席した。風邪をひいたらしい。

(Tanaka-san was absent yesterday. Apparently, [Tanaka-san] caught a cold.)

The subject is 田中さん from the previous sentence.

✤ Practice Questions

Find the subject and predicate for each of the following sentences.

(1) 中央政府には最高の機関として中書と枢密院がある。

(2) 宋政府の統治形態は、太祖、太宗の二代の間に基礎が置かれた。

(3) 文官の仕事は裁判であるが、その権限は極めて限られた。

(4) 王も親征して戦った。しかし遂に敗退した。

(5) 時代区分は歴史を大局的に、また普遍性においてとらえる方法の一つである。

A Practical Guide for Scholarly Reading in Japanese

★ Answers and English Translations

(1) Predicate: ある

Subject: 中書と枢密院が

English translation: The Central Government has the Imperial Secretariat and the Bureau of Military Affairs as its highest institutions.

(2) Predicate: 置かれた

Subject: 基礎が

English translation: The foundation for the Song regime's governmental structure was laid between the two generations of Taizu and Taizong.

(3) Predicate: 限られた

Subject: 権限は

English translation: The job of the civil official is to judge trials, but that authority was highly limited.

(4) Predicate: 戦った and 敗退した

Subject: 王も

English translation: The king led his troops into battle. However, (the king) ultimately lost.

(5) Predicate: 一つである

Subject: 時代区分は

English translation: Dividing time periods is one method of understanding history in a holistic and universal way.

3. Separating Sentences Based on Meaning (Chunking)

In this section, we will learn how to understand sentences with one or more parts or clauses, such as simple sentences (単文), compound sentences (重文), and complex sentences (複文).

A **simple sentence** contains only one predicate.

▶ *Example Sentences*

① きのう田中さんは授業に遅れた。(Yesterday, Tanaka-san was late to class.)

② 北京の夏は暑い。(Beijing's summers are hot.)

③ 兄は学者になった。(My older brother became a scholar.)

10

Chapter 1 – "Toolbox": Essential Grammar for Scholarly Reading

A **compound sentence** combines two or more independent clauses.

▶ *Example Sentences*

① きのう田中さんは授業に遅刻して、山田さんは欠席した。

(Yesterday, Tanaka-san was late to class, and Yamada-san was absent.)

② 北京の夏は暑いが、札幌の夏は涼しい。

(Beijing's summers are hot, but Sapporo's summers are cool.)

③ 兄は学者になり、弟は医者になった。

(My older brother became a scholar, and my younger brother became a doctor.)

A **complex sentence** is constructed from one main clause and one or more dependent (subordinate) clauses. The subordinate clause functions as a cause, reason, intention, condition, and time, among other things.

▶ *Example Sentences*

① きのう電車が遅れたので、田中さんは授業に遅れた。

(Since the train was late yesterday, Tanaka-san was late to class.)

② 北京の緯度は高いのに、北京の夏は暑い。

(Although the latitude of Beijing is high, its summers are hot.)

③ きれいな海を守るために、努力しなければならない。

(In order to protect the beautiful sea, [we] must work hard.)

④ よく勉強した学生だけが留学できる。

(Only students who study a lot can study abroad.)

3.1 Compound Sentences: Listing with the て-Form

The て-form means 'and' and connects parts of speech such as verbs, *i*-adjectives, and *na*-adjectives. The て-form itself doesn't indicate the tense.

3.1.1 Connecting Verbs

① 魯迅は仙台に行った。(Lu Xun went to Sendai.) AND

（魯迅は）医学を学んだ。([Lu Xun] studied medicine.)

➡ 魯迅は仙台に行って、医学を学んだ。

(Lu Xun went to Sendai and studied medicine.)

11

A Practical Guide for Scholarly Reading in Japanese

② 魯迅は仙台に行った。(Lu Xun went to Sendai.) AND

周作人は東京へ行った。(Zhou Zuoren went to Tokyo.)

➡ 魯迅は仙台に行って、周作人は東京へ行った。

(Lu Xun went to Sendai and Zhou Zuoren went to Tokyo.)

3.1.2 Connecting *I*-adjectives

① この桃は甘い。(This peach is sweet.) AND

（この桃は）おいしい。([This peach,] It is delicious.)

➡ この桃は甘くておいしい。(This peach is sweet and delicious.)

② 空は青い。(The sky is blue.) AND 雲は白い。(The clouds are white.)

➡ 空は青くて、雲は白い。(The sky is blue, and the clouds are white.)

3.1.3 Connecting *Na*-adjectives

① この事件は不思議だ。(This incident is mysterious.) AND

（この事件は）難解だ。([This incident] is baffling.)

➡ この事件は不思議で、難解だ。 (This incident is mysterious and baffling.)

② この事件は不思議である。(This incident is mysterious.) AND

（この事件は）難解である。([This incident] is baffling.)

➡ この事件は不思議であって、難解である。

(This incident is mysterious, and it is baffling.)

③ 姉は英語が得意だ。(My older sister is good at English.) AND

妹はピアノが上手だ。(My younger sister is good at playing the piano.)

➡ 姉は英語が得意で、妹はピアノが上手だ。

(My older sister is good at English and my younger sister is good at playing the piano.)

3.1.4 Connecting Nouns

Connecting two or more [Noun + Copular (だ/である/です)] phrases

① 彼女は教師だ。(She is a teacher.) AND

（彼女は）三人の子供の母親だ。([She is] a mother of three children.)

➡ 彼女は教師で、三人の子供の母親だ。

(She is a teacher and a mother of three children.)

12

Chapter 1 – "Toolbox": Essential Grammar for Scholarly Reading

② 彼女は教師である。(She is a teacher.) AND

(彼女は) 三人の子供の母親である。([She is] a mother of three children.)

➡ 彼女は教師であって、三人の子供の母親である。

(She is a teacher, and she is a mother of three children.)

③ 兄は医者です。(My older brother is a doctor.) AND

弟はシェフです。(My younger brother is a chef.)

➡ 兄は医者で、弟はシェフです。

(My older brother is a doctor and my younger brother is a chef.)

✛ Practice Questions

Divide the following sentences into two simple sentences. Also, translate the original sentence into English.

(1) 貴族政治の最も盛行した時代は六朝・隋唐時代であって、この時代の貴族政治はそれ以前の貴族政治とは段階を異にしている。

(2) 仮作制は国家的奴隷制度の均田制に転化して、豪族階級は官僚として国家権力に寄生する。

(3) 貴族の官界における地位を保証するものは、その郷里社会における実力であって、皇帝権力にあるのではない。

★ Answers and English Translations

(1) 貴族政治の最も盛行した時代は六朝・隋唐時代である。AND この時代の貴族政治はそれ以前の貴族政治とは段階を異にしている。

六朝・隋唐時代であって is the て-form of 六朝・隋唐時代である.

English translation: The aristocracies during the Six Dynasties Period and the Sui and Tang Periods were most prosperous, with the aristocracy of these periods differing in (shifting) stages from the previous ones.

(Lit. The periods when the aristocracy was the most prosperous were the Six Dynasties, and the Sui and Tang periods; (and) the aristocracy of these periods differs in (shifting) stages from the previous aristocracies.)

13

A Practical Guide for Scholarly Reading in Japanese

(2) 仮作制は国家的奴隷制度の均田制に転化する。AND 豪族階級は官僚として国家権力に寄生する。

転化して is the て-form of 転化する.

English translation: The provisional system converts into a form of national slavery known as the equal-field system; (and) the baronial class lives off of national authority as a bureaucrat.

(3) 貴族の官界における地位を保証するものは、その郷里社会における実力である。AND 皇帝権力にあるのではない。

English translation: The factor that guarantees status in the official realm of aristocrats is the tangible power of the local community; (and) it does not lie in the imperial authority.

3.2 The Suspended Form Method (連用中止法)

When a sentence is combined using the continuative form, the suspended form method is employed. It means 'AND' like the て-form. It is often used in written Japanese. However, the suspended form method only applies to *i*-adjectives and verbs.

3.2.1 Verbs

In the case of verbs, the continuative form is the so called, ます-form stem.

① 魯迅は仙台に行った。(Lu Xun went to Sendai.) AND

（魯迅は）医学を学んだ。([Lu Xun] studied medicine.)

➡ 魯迅は仙台に行き、医学を学んだ。(Lu Xun went to Sendai and studied medicine.)
行き is the continuative form of 行く.

3.2.2 *I-adjectives*

In the case of *i*-adjectives, the continuative form is the て-form without the て.

① 空は青い。(The sky is blue.) AND 雲は白い。(The clouds are white.)

➡ 空は青く、雲は白い。(The sky is blue and the clouds are white.)
青く is the continuative form of 青い.

Chapter 1 – "Toolbox": Essential Grammar for Scholarly Reading

✥ Practice Questions

First, separate the following sentences into simple sentences. Then, translate the original sentence into English.

(1) 我が国の学会には中国史の時代区分に関する二つの有力な説があり、それが平行線をなしたまま今日に至っている。

(2) 十世紀以後を、A説は近世と呼び、B説は中世と見なしている。

(3) ここは夏は蒸し暑く、冬はとても寒い。

(4) 西嶋の奴隷制説は前田のそれのように単純ではなく、これを中国型奴隷制と名付けた。

★ Answers and English Translations

(1) 我が国の学会には中国史の時代区分に関する二つの有力な説がある。AND それが平行線をなしたまま今日に至っている。

English translation: There are two influential theories regarding the division of eras in Chinese history within our country's academic society; (and) they (the two theories) continue to run parallel to each other to this day.

あり is the continuative form of ある.

Note: Be aware of the difference between 山である (copular) and 山がある (to exist).
これは山である。This is a mountain.
ここに山がある。There is a mountain here.

(2) 十世紀以後を、A説は近世と呼ぶ。AND （十世紀以後を）B説は中世と見なしている。

English translation: Theory A refers to the period from the 10th century onward as the modern age; (and) Theory B considers it (the period from the 10th century onward) the Middle Ages.

呼び is the continuative form of 呼ぶ.

(3) ここは夏は蒸し暑い。AND 冬はとても寒い。

English translation: Here, the summers are hot and humid; (and) the winters are cold.

暑く is the continuative form of 暑い.

(4) 西嶋の奴隷制説は前田のそれのように単純ではない。AND これを中国型奴隷制と名付けた。

English translation: Nishijima's slavery theory is not as simple as that of Maeda's; (and) he named this (system) the Chinese-model slavery system.

（単純では）なく is the continuative form of （単純では）ない.

15

A Practical Guide for Scholarly Reading in Japanese

3.3 〜し 'what's more; not only ~ but also'

し is a conjunctive particle that connects sentences and lists activities and states. The し clause mainly uses the plain form.

▶ *Example Sentences*

① Listing activities (with verbs)

鈴木さんはタバコを吸う。(Suzuki-san smokes cigarettes.) AND

（鈴木さんは）お酒も飲む。([Suzuki-san] also drinks alcohol.)

➡ 鈴木さんはたばこを吸う<u>し</u>、お酒も飲む。

(Suzuki-san smokes cigarettes, and also drinks alcohol.)

② Listing states (with *na*-adjectives)

その花はきれいだ。(That flower is beautiful.) AND

（その花は）良いにおいだ。(That flower smells good.)

➡ その花はきれいだ<u>し</u>、良いにおいだ。(That flower is beautiful, and it smells good.)

③ Listing states (with *i*-adjectives)

田中さんはやさしい。(Tanaka-san is kind.) AND

（田中さんは）頭もいい。([Tanaka-san] is also smart.)

➡ 田中さんはやさしい<u>し</u>、頭もいい。(Tanaka-san is kind, and is also smart.)

✥ Practice Questions

Separate the following sentences into simple sentences. Then, translate the original sentence into English.

(1) 勿論、既成の説にとらわれない立場もありうるし、そうした立場が拡大することが学問の発展には望ましい。

(2) 宮廷には新年を祝う習慣があったし、庶民の間にも同様の習慣があった。

★ Answers and English Translations

(1) 勿論、既成の説にとらわれない立場もありうる。AND そうした立場が拡大することが学問の発展には望ましい。

English translation: Certainly, a stance that doesn't adhere to established theories is possible; moreover, the expansion of that type of stance is desirable for the development of academia.

16

(2) 宮廷には新年を祝う習慣があった。AND 庶民の間にも同様の習慣があった。

English translation: There was a customary New Year`s celebration in the Court, and a similar custom existed among commoners.

3.4 X という Y 'Y called X'

3.4.1 X (Clause) という Y (Noun)

When X is a clause, it serves to describe what Y is. In [clause という N] the clause introduces the content of the following noun, which tends to be related to communication (e.g. stories, rumors, reports, notifications, news, and phone calls).

▶ *Example Sentences*

① あの作家が日本で医学を学んだ**という**情報は本当だ。

(The information stating that that author studied medicine in Japan is true.)

The clause before という identifies the content of 情報.

② 人のために家伝を作った**という**非難を受けた。

([They] received criticism for having created a family history for the individuals.)

The clause before という explains the details of 非難.

3.4.2 X (Noun) という Y (Noun)

In the case that X is a noun in X という Y, the author generally modifies Y with information (=X) that is believed to be unknown by the reader.

▶ *Example Sentences*

① 魯迅は仙台**という**町で医学を学んだ。

(Lu Xun went to a city called Sendai to study medicine.)

The author assumes that the reader doesn't know 仙台 (Sendai), and so uses という to introduce the city of 仙台.

Cf. 周作人は東京で英文学を学んだ。

(Zhou Zuoren studied English literature in Tokyo.)

The author assumes that the reader knows 東京 well, and so doesn't use という to introduce Tokyo.

② 昨日、『沈黙』**という**本を借りた。

(Yesterday, I borrowed a book called "Silence.")

The author assumes that the reader doesn't know the book "沈黙 (Silence)," and so uses という to introduce the book titled "沈黙 (Silence)."

A Practical Guide for Scholarly Reading in Japanese

Cf. きのう『源氏物語』を借りた。(Yesterday, I borrowed "The Tale of Genji.")
The author assumes that the reader can identify "源氏物語 (The Tale of Genji)" and so
doesn't use という.

3.5 S1 が、S2 'S1, but/and S2'

が serves as a conjunctive particle that connects two sentences. Although が primarily means
'BUT,' there are some instances in which it means 'AND.'

Note: Nominative particle が (See 2.2.1)

3.5.1 BUT/逆接 (Concessive Connection)

▶ *Example Sentences*

① イタリア語を7年勉強している**が**、なかなか上手にならない。

(Although I have been studying Italian for seven years, I'm not getting much better.)

➡ イタリア語を7年勉強している。(I have been studying Italian for seven years.) BUT
なかなか上手にならない。(I am not getting much better.)

② 今日は雨だ**が**、ニューヨークシティマラソンは予定通り行われる。

(It is raining today, but the New York City Marathon will be held as scheduled.)

➡ 今日は雨だ。(It is raining today.) BUT ニューヨークシティマラソンは予定通り行われ
る。(The New York City Marathon will be held as scheduled.)

3.5.2 AND/順接 (Simple Connection)

The antecedent of が serves as an 'introduction' and loosely connects it with the consequent. In
English, it is similar to the word 'but' in the phrase "Excuse me, but…."

▶ *Example Sentences*

① コンサートのチケットが二枚あるんです**が**、一緒に行きませんか。

(I have two concert tickets, so won't you join me?)

➡ コンサートのチケットが二枚あるんです。(I have two concert tickets.) AND
一緒に行きませんか。(Won't you join me?)。
The antecedent コンサートのチケットが二枚あるんです introduces the speech act of
invitation 一緒に行きませんか.

18

Chapter 1 – "Toolbox": Essential Grammar for Scholarly Reading

② あの議員の汚職が大きな問題になっている<u>が</u>、過去十年間にわたる政治家の汚職の例を挙げてみよう。

(That senator's corruption is becoming a big issue, and so let's look at examples of political corruption from the last 10 years.)

➡ あの議員の汚職が大きな問題になっている。(That senator's corruption is becoming a big issue.) AND 過去十年間にわたる政治家の汚職の例を挙げてみよう。 (Let's look at examples of political corruption from the last 10 years.)

✥ Practice Questions

Determine whether the conjunctive particle が means BUT or AND. Then, translate the sentence.

(1) 現在学生社より刊行中の『中世史講座』全十二巻は、世界各地域の中世史を網羅するものであり、そこには当然中国の中世史に関する論考を収載する<u>が</u>、ここでの中世は、宋代以後を中世とする一方の説を採用している。

(2) 以下、前者をA説、後者をB説とよぶことにする<u>が</u>、この両説が古代・中世・近世等々の時代名称で中国史をどう区別しているかを、ごく大まかに対照表示すれば、左図のごとくである。

(3) A説ではこれを近世的小作制と考えた<u>が</u>、B説では、中世的封建農奴制の本質をそなえるものとした。

★ Answers and English Translations

(1) AND—English translation: The 12 book series, "Lecture on the History of the Middle Ages," which is currently being published by Gakuseisha, covers the history of the Middle Ages in various regions of the world. The series necessarily includes a discussion regarding China during the Middle Ages, and they adopt a theory stating that the Middle Ages here is from the Song Dynasty and thereafter.

(2) AND—English translation: The following text will refer to the former as Theory A and the latter as Theory B, and the way in which both theories divide the period names such as ancient times, the Middle Ages, and the modern era is roughly contrasted as seen on the left chart.

(3) BUT—English translation: Theory A considered this to be a modern tenant system, but in Theory B, it has the qualities of a Middle Age feudal serfdom system.

19

A Practical Guide for Scholarly Reading in Japanese

3.6 *Conditional Expressions*

3.6.1　S たら, S/N なら, S ば, and S と 'If/When'

These expressions make the supposition that events that may or may not occur, or events that haven't occurred, have actually happened. They can also suppose that something different from the actual events of the past actually happened. From now on, we will translate it as, "if/when." There are times when adverbs such as もし（も）, 仮_{かり}に, and 万_{まん}（が）一_{いち} are included, and they function to inform the reader that a supposition will be mentioned. When the event described in the たら clause is certain to happen, たら means "when" (i.e., Example ②). Moreover, たら and と can mean "when" when referring to events in the past (i.e., Example ③).

▶*Example Sentences*

① もし来年日本に行っ**たら**、寿司をたくさん食べるつもりだ。

(If [I] go to Japan next year, I intend to eat a lot of sushi.)

② 1 時になっ**たら**、電話してください。

(When it becomes one o'clock, please call me.)

③ 図書館に行っ**たら**、弟がいた。

(When [I] went to the library, [my] younger brother was there.)

④ 仮に来年就職するとし**たら**、どんな会社に入りたいですか。

(Supposing that you start working next year, what type of company would you like to join?)

⑤ 一年日本に行く**なら**、ビザが必要である。

(If [you] are going to Japan for a year, you need a visa.)

⑥ 今これを買え**ば**、30％安いですよ。

(If you buy this now, it will be 30% cheaper.)

⑦ 日本に留学すれ**ば**、日本語が上手になります。

(If you study abroad in Japan, your Japanese will get better.)

⑧ 図書館に行け**ば**、眠くなる。

(Whenever [I] go to the library, [I] get sleepy.)

⑨ お酒を飲む**と**、顔が赤くなります。

(Whenever [I] drink sake, my face gets red.)

20

Chapter 1 – "Toolbox": Essential Grammar for Scholarly Reading

⑩ 窓を開けると、海が見えます。

(If [you] open the window, [you] can see the ocean.)

⑪ 翼があれば、飛んでいける。(If [you] had wings, [you] could fly away.)

⑫ もしあの時大学に合格しなかったら、留学はできなかっただろう。

(If, let's say, you didn't get into a university that time, you probably would not have been able to study abroad.)

There are instances when ば expresses "because" in classical grammar. (See 8.6.1)

3.6.2 Other Often-Used Conditional Expressions, 〜場合 'in case of; in the case (of)' and 〜限り 'as long as'

▶ *Example Sentences*

① 火事になった場合は、ここに電話をかけてください。

(In case of a fire, please call this number.)

② この教室を使う場合は、許可が必要である。

(In the case that you use this classroom, you will need permission.)

③ この説に従う限り、それは不可能である。

(As long as you conform to this theory, that is not possible.)

④ 話し合いをしない限り、解決はできない。

(Unless [you] discuss it, [you] can't come to a solution.)

(Lit. As long as [you] don't discuss it, [you] can't come to a solution.)

3.7 Conditional Expressions with Concessive Conjunctions ても and とも 'even though, even if'

When two clauses contrast in meaning or when the second clause expresses what is not expected from the first clause, the two clauses may be connected by concessive conjunctions such as ても, とも.

Note that とも(ども)、といえども、とはいえ, and ものの are the written forms of ても.

▶ *Example Sentences*

① お金がなくても、幸せです。(Even if I don't have money, I am happy.)

② 練習が辛くとも、あきらめずに続けた。

(Even though the practice was hard, he continued without giving up.)

21

A Practical Guide for Scholarly Reading in Japanese

3.8 *Review Exercises*

✥ Practice Questions

Separate the underlined sentence into simple sentences (単文) using "/." Then, translate the following passage into English.

(1) 孔子は、為政者が徳治主義で人民の道徳心に訴えてその自由に任すと、かえって不法行為がなくなるから、徳治主義の方が法治主義にまさっていると考えた。

★ Answers and English Translations

(1) 為政者が徳治主義で人民の道徳心に訴えて / その自由に任すと /、かえって不法行為がなくなるから /、徳治主義の方が法治主義にまさっていると / 考えた。

English translation: Confucius thought that if the ruler appeals to the ethics of citizens and allows them the freedom (of acting at their own discretion) using the principle of virtuous government, then unlawful practices would contrarily diminish, so the principle of a virtuous government is thus superior to the principle of a legalistic government.

❖*Explanation*

① 為政者が徳治主義で人民の道徳心に訴えて (The て-form of the verb 訴える ➡ 'and')

Subject: 為政者

Predicate: 訴える

② その自由に任すと (The conditional conjunctive particle と ➡ when, if)

Subject: 為政者 (任す is conjoined with 訴えて, so the subject is the same as in ① .)

Predicate: 任す

③ かえって不法行為がなくなるから (The conjunctive particle for reason から ➡ because)

Subject: 不法行為 (The particle/subject marker が is used.)

Predicate: なくなる

④ 徳治主義の方が法治主義にまさっていると (と is the citation particle ➡ that)

Subject: 徳治主義の方 (The particle/subject marker が is used.)

Predicate: まさっている

⑤ 考えた。

Subject: 孔子

Predicate: 考えた

Chapter 1 – "Toolbox": Essential Grammar for Scholarly Reading

4. Sentence-Ending Expressions

The following are sentence-ending expressions that are often used in academic texts.

	Sentence-Ending Expression	Meaning (Function)
1	の + copular だ	Emphasizing an Explanation or Reason
2	〜のであろう／〜のだろうか 〜（の）ではないだろうか 〜（の）ではなかろうか（と思う）	Genuine or Rhetorical Question
3	〜と思う・〜と思われる 〜と考える・〜と考えられる 〜と言える	Softening of an Emphasis or Conclusion

4.1 *Explaining a Circumstance* のだ/のである/のです

When のだ is at the end of the sentence, the の functions to explain something or provide a reason. This ending doesn't affect the meaning of the sentence itself, so it does not need to be translated. [ ] indicates a contextual meaning that may not require translation.

▶*Example Sentences*

① 新しい証拠が発見された<u>のである</u>。 ([And so,] New evidence was discovered.)

➡ 新しい証拠が発見された。 (New evidence was found.)

② 先日の火事は寝たばこが原因だった<u>のだ</u>。

([Let me explain to you that] Smoking in bed was the cause of the fire the other day.)

➡ 先日の火事は寝たばこが原因だった。

(Smoking in bed was the cause of the fire the other day.)

③ 次の資料を皆さんに是非見ていただきたい<u>のです</u>。

([Let me tell you,] I would certainly like everyone to take a look at the following documents.)

➡ 次の資料を皆さんに是非見ていただきたいです。

(I would certainly like everyone to take a look at the following documents.)

23

A Practical Guide for Scholarly Reading in Japanese

4.2 Rhetorical Questions 〜(の)ではないか/だろうか

As in English, rhetorical questions are often used in academic Japanese as well; they have the same structures as genuine questions. Rhetorical expressions function to express the author's thoughts strongly. It is thus one way to emphasize an opinion.

▶ *Example Sentences*

① 当時の外交政策は失敗だった**のではないか**。

(Wasn't the foreign policy at the time a failure?)

➡ 当時の外交政策は失敗だった。(The foreign policy at the time was a failure.)

② そんな話、誰が信じる**だろうか**。(Who will believe such a story?)

➡ そんな話、誰も信じない。(No one will believe such a story.)

Questions in academic reading are frequently used when the author wants to raise an issue by involving the reader, and then precedes to offer an opinion. Take a look at the following example.

① この影響はどこから来ているのだろうか。私は清代の異民族支配から来ていると考える。

(Where can this influence be coming from? I think that it comes from the control by the different ethnic group during the Qing Dynasty.)

It is possible to omit だろう/でしょう and to only include the sentence-ending particle か at the end of the sentence.

② この影響はどこから来ているの(だろう/でしょう)か。

(Where is this influence coming from?)

4.3 Softening of a Claim/Conclusion

Various softening expressions are used in academic texts at the end of sentences.

4.3.1 〜と思う/考える

Sentence-ending expressions such as 〜と思う/考える tend to be used in academic Japanese to soften the tone of the speaker's opinion, assessment, or evaluation. There is no need to translate this part.

▶ *Example Sentences*

① この問題は再考すべきだ**と考える**。

(I think that) This problem should be reconsidered.

② 日本経済は今後も発展していくはずだ**と思う**。

(I think that) The Japanese economy should develop further.

24

Chapter 1 – "Toolbox": Essential Grammar for Scholarly Reading

③ 今後も研究を続けていきたい<u>と思っている</u>。

(I have been thinking that) I would like to continue further with my research.

In spoken Japanese, と思う is also used when one is uncertain about something mentioned. In this case it can be replaced with 多分〜だろう as a conjecture.

▶*Example Sentences*

① 明日は雨が降る<u>と思う</u>。(I think it will rain tomorrow. [General Information])

＝多分降るだろう。(It will probably rain tomorrow.)

② A: あした行ける？ (Can you go tomorrow?)　B: 行ける<u>と思う</u>。(I think I can go.)

＝多分行けるだろう。(I can probably go.)

4.3.2 〜と思われる/ 考えられる

In academic Japanese, the sentence-ending expressions 〜と思われる/ 考えられる are frequently used. These are used to soften the tone of the speaker's own opinions and thoughts. Thus, there is no need to translate 〜と思われる and 〜と考えられる.

▶*Example Sentences*

① この問題を避ける傾向が生まれた<u>と思われる</u>。

(A tendency to avoid the problem has emerged.)

② 日本経済は今後も発展していくはずだ<u>と思われるのである</u>。

(The Japanese economy should develop further.)

③ 平安時代の文学は中国の六朝文学の多大なる影響を受けている<u>と考えられる</u>。

(The literature of the Heian Period was greatly influenced by that of China's Six Dynasty's period.)

✥ Practice Questions

Part A

Underline the parts that don't need to be translated in the following sentences.

(1) X は間違っていると思う。

(2) X は間違っているのではないかと思う。

(3) X は間違っていると思われる。

(4) X は間違っているのではないかと思われる。

(5) X は間違っているのではないかと思われるのである。

A Practical Guide for Scholarly Reading in Japanese

(6) Ｘは間違っているのではないかと考えられる。

(7) Ｘは間違っているのではなかろうかと考えられる。

★ Answers

(1) Ｘは間違っていると思う。

(2) Ｘは間違っているのではないかと思う。

(3) Ｘは間違っていると思われる。

(4) Ｘは間違っているのではないかと思われる。

(5) Ｘは間違っているのではないかと思われるのである。

(6) Ｘは間違っているのではないかと考えられる。

(7) Ｘは間違っているのではなかろうかと考えられる。

Part B The author's claim

As mentioned above, many sentence-ending expressions in academic Japanese are indirect expressions that are used in a variety of ways. Once it is accurately understood that these expressions are used to avoid sounding too assertive, one can learn the important technique of shortening sentences by cutting the sentence-ending portions.

Underline the parts that don't need to be translated and translate the author's claim.

(1) 学問における根本的なくいちがいが、時代区分上の亀裂として発現したと考えられるのである。

(2) この凝固した状態に生きた血流を通わす必要があるのではなかろうか。

(3) 中国史の時代区分法はかれによって一挙に原理的なレベルにまで高められ、それじたいが歴史学の一分野となったのであった。

(4) 要するに、時代区分は中国史研究者のなかに潜在的、顕在的に生きていると思われるのである。

(5) 言語に内在している相反する特徴が例外自体の存在を容認せざるを得ない要因を生み出すのではないかと思われるのである。

(6) これは南北朝時代の実際状態が無意識の裡に歴史の上に現れたのである。

(7) あくまでも両者の相違点をできるだけ深く見つめたいと思うのである。

(8) この方面の一歩前進を期したいのである。

(9) それは、六朝の国家に対する理解の相違ではなかろうか。

Chapter 1 – "Toolbox": Essential Grammar for Scholarly Reading

★ Answers and English Translations

(1) 学問における根本的なくいちがいが、時代区分上の亀裂として発現した<u>と考えられる</u><u>のである</u>。

English translation: There are fundamental discrepancies in the academic fields.

(2) この凝固した状態に生きた血流を通わす必要がある<u>のではなかろうか</u>。

English translation: It is necessary to have living blood flow through this solidified state.

(3) 中国史の時代区分法はかれによって一挙に原理的なレベルにまで高められ、それじたいが歴史学の一分野となった<u>のであった</u>。

English translation: Because of him, the method of periodization in Chinese history was raised to the level of principal in one big effort, making the method itself a field of historical studies.

(4) 要するに、時代区分は中国史研究者のなかに潜在的、顕在的に生きている<u>と思われる</u><u>のである</u>。

English translation: To put it briefly, periodization lives latently and overtly within the researchers of Chinese history.

(5) 言語に内在している相反する特徴が例外自体の存在を容認せざるを得ない要因を生み出すのではないか<u>と思われるのである</u>。

English translation: This characteristic that exists within languages gives rise to factors that necessitate the acceptance of exceptions.

(6) これは南北朝時代の実際状態が無意識の裡に歴史の上に現れた<u>のである</u>。

English translation: The actual circumstances of the Northern and Southern Dynasties period appeared in history without anyone's realization.

(7) あくまでも両者の相違点をできるだけ深く見つめたい<u>と思うのである</u>。

English translation: I would like to look as deeply as I can into the differences between the two groups.

(8) この方面の一歩前進を期したい<u>のである</u>。

English translation: I hope for this theory to progress one step forward.

(9) それは、六朝の国家に対する理解の相違<u>ではなかろうか</u>。

English translation: That is a difference in the understanding of the concept of a nation.

A Practical Guide for Scholarly Reading in Japanese

5. Defining Expressions　Ｘ を Ｙ とする　'regard X as Y'

する in the form of Ｘ を Ｙ とする carries the meaning of conveying a definition. Verbs such as 見なす, なす, 見る, 考える, 定義する and 仮定する can be used in place of する. There are instances when the part Ｘ を is omitted.

▶ *Example Sentences*

① Ａ説を正しい<u>とする</u>と、Ｂ説の主張は間違っていることになる。

If Theory A is deemed correct, then that would mean that the claim for Theory B is incorrect.

② 少子化問題をテーマ<u>とした</u>討論会が開かれた。

A debate regarding the problem of a declining birthrate was held.

③ この店では、お客様は神様<u>として</u>丁寧に応対している。

In this store, customers are treated courteously as if they are deities.

④ Ａ説は十世紀以後を中世となし、Ｂ説は近代<u>としている</u>。

Theory A classifies the period from the 10th century onward as the Middle Ages, while Theory B places it in the modern era.

✛ Practice Questions

Translate the following into English:

(1) 貴族政治は六朝から唐の中世までを最も盛んなる時代とした。

(2) 佃戸制をＢ説では中世的封建農奴制の本質を備えるものとした。

(3) そのことを無下に虚妄として否定し去るわけにはゆかない。

(4) 従来の方法は史学的には不正確であるとされている。

(は serves as a substitute for を.)

(5) 十世紀以後をＢ説では中世と見なしている。

(6) Ｂ説は、六朝の国家権力を貴族階級から自立した権力とみなし、小農民の対極にある一種の階級と考えた。

★ Answers

(1) The aristocracy from the Six Dynasties period to the middle of the Tang Dynasty is considered the most prosperous period.

(2) Under Theory B, the tenant farmer system is seen as containing the essential characteristics of a feudal serfdom like in the Middle Ages.

28

Chapter 1 – "Toolbox": Essential Grammar for Scholarly Reading

(3) [You] can't flatly deny that as a falsehood.

(4) The methods thus far are thought to be historically inaccurate.

(5) The period from the 10th century onward is considered the Middle Ages under Theory B.

(6) Theory B considered the state powers of the Six Dynasties as an authority that was independent from the nobility and was thought of as its own class in contrast with small farmers.

6. Particles

6.1 Compound Particles

Compound particles such as には and では are often used in Japanese, with は being a topic marker that conveys emphasis, but it doesn't have much of an effect on the meaning of the sentence so it doesn't necessarily need to be translated.

▶*Example Sentences*

① ニューヨーク**には**行く。(I will go [specifically] to New York.)

➡ ニューヨークに行く。(I will go to New York.)

② 母**からは**手紙が来た。(A letter came [specifically] from my mother.)

➡ 母から手紙が来た。(A letter came from my mother.)

③ この建物**では**タバコを吸ってはいけない。

([You] are not allowed to smoke [specifically] in this building.)

➡ この建物でタバコを吸ってはいけない。

([You] are not allowed to smoke in this building.)

When the particles が and を are combined with は, が and を are omitted, leaving only は, as in examples 1 and 2.

▶*Example Sentences*

① Incorrect: 私**がは**行く。

Correct: 私は行く。(I will go. [I don't know about you.])

② Incorrect: この小説**をは**読む。

Correct: この小説は読む。([I] will read this book [specifically].)

29

A Practical Guide for Scholarly Reading in Japanese

However, there are instances in academic texts when the old form をば is used.

③ とうとう国家の統一<ruby>国家<rt>こっか</rt></ruby>の<ruby>統一<rt>とういつ</rt></ruby><u>をば</u>果たした。

(The unification of the state [specifically] was achieved at last.)

➡ とうとう<ruby>国家<rt>こっか</rt></ruby>の<ruby>統一<rt>とういつ</rt></ruby>を<ruby>果<rt>は</rt></ruby>たした。(The unification of the state was finally carried out.)

6.2 *Particle Equivalent Phrases*

In written Japanese, so called "particle equivalent phrases" are used often. This term refers to two or more words that are joined to create a set phrase that serves the same role as a particle. Why is it that "particle equivalent phrases" are often used in academic texts? There are many particles that carry several meanings, so these particle equivalents are used to avoid any ambiguity in the meaning.

As an example, let's take a look at the case for the particle で.

Meaning	Particle で	Particle Equivalent
Place	学校で勉強する	学校に於いて勉強する。 [I] study at school.
Tool/Means	ペンで書く	ペンで以て書く。[I] write using a pen.
Criteria	成績でクラスを分ける	成績に拠って（に拠り）クラスを分ける。 [We] will divide the class based on grades.

The main particle equivalents are listed below.

	Particle Equivalent	Meaning	Example
1	において におけるN においてのN	Expresses a place or time and qualifies the sentence.	1) 文学研究に於いて言語の分析は重要だ。 It is important to analyze the language for literary research. (Lit. In the area of literary research, linguistic analysis is important.) 2) 江戸時代に於ける食文化はどのような特色があるのだろうか。 What type of features does the food culture of the Edo period have?

30

Chapter 1 – "Toolbox": Essential Grammar for Scholarly Reading

2	として としての N	Indicates someone's or something's qualification, stance, or category.	1) 学者<u>として</u>発言する。 To speak as a scholar. 2) 日本はすべてが東京を中心<u>として</u>動いている。 In Japan, everything moves with Tokyo at its center. 3) 別府市は温泉地<u>として</u>有名だ。 Beppu is famous for being a natural hot spring. 4) 市長<u>としての</u>責任をとって辞任した。 [S/he] took responsibility as the mayor and resigned.
3	にとって にとっての N	States what/whose viewpoint the evaluation or decision is made from.	1) 私<u>にとって</u>北京は第二の故郷である。 Beijing is a second home to me. 2) 地球温暖化は我々<u>にとっての</u>重大な課題だ。 Global warming is a grave issue to us all.

31

4	をもって	Expresses a means, method, cause, reason, time of an occurrence, or limit.	1) 誠意<u>をもって</u>交渉した。 [We] engaged in negotiations with sincerity. 2) 品不足<u>をもって</u>販売を停止した。 Sales were stopped due to supply shortage. 3) 8月15日<u>をもって</u>終戦記念日とした。 August 15th marks the anniversary of the end of World War II. (Lit. We marked August 15th as the anniversary of the end of World War II.) 4) 本日<u>をもって</u>営業を終了する。 Today will be the last day of business. (Lit. As of today, business will be closed.)
5	でもって	Expresses a reason and cause, method and means, occasion and criterion.	1) 津波<u>でもって</u>すべてを失った。 [I] lost everything due to the tsunami. 2) 明日の会議<u>でもって</u>決定することになっている。 It will be decided at tomorrow's meeting.

6	に対して に対する N に対しての N	Indicates an object of an action/comparison, or a ratio.	1) 質問に対して答える。 [I] answer the question asked. 2) 男子30人に対して女子は10人しかいない。 Compared to 30 males, there were only 10 females. 3) このインスタントコーヒーはティースプーン一杯に対して140mlのお湯を注いで作る。 This instant coffee is made with one teaspoon for every 140ml of hot water poured. 4) 今のご質問に [対しての/対する] 私の考えを述べます。 I will state my thoughts regarding the current question.
7	に反して に反する N に反しての N	Expresses a situation that is incongruent with existing rules or one's expectations.	1) カンニングは学校の規則に反することだ。 Cheating means going against school rules. 2) この店は、前評判に反して客が入らなかった。 Contrary to their prior reputation, this store didn't attract customers. 3) その候補者は我々の予想に反し当選した。 That candidate won the election against our expectations. 4) 予想に [反する/反しての] 結果に皆が驚いた。 Everyone was surprised by the unexpected results.

8	によって による N	Expresses the basis for occurrences such as causes, reasons, criteria, means, and methods. In passive sentences, it expresses an agent of historical events.	1) 環境汚染**によって**、たくさんの動植物が絶滅してしまった。 Many living things went extinct due to environmental pollution. 2) 地域**によって**生活習慣が異なる。 Lifestyles differ based on the region. 3) 運動をすること**によって**体力をつける。 By exercising, [I] can gain physical strength. 4) 兄は会社の命令**による**転勤を余儀なくされた。 [My] older brother was inevitably relocated on company orders. 5) 電話はアレクサンダー・グラハム・ベル**によって**発明された。 The telephone was invented by Alexander Graham Bell. 6) 食習慣は地域**による**違いがある。 Eating habits are based on regional differences. (Lit. Regarding eating habits, there are differences among regions.)
9	のもとで のもとでの N	Expresses something under a specific condition.	1) 有名な書道家**のもとで**修行をすることになった。 [I] can now practice under the guidance of a famous calligrapher. 2) 大自然**のもとでの**生活は、心も体も健康にしてくれる。 Living under Mother Nature brings health of both body and mind.

Chapter 1 – "Toolbox": Essential Grammar for Scholarly Reading

10	をめぐって をめぐる N をめぐっての N	Expresses the problematic matter, or something related to it, at the center.	1) 輸入制限<u>をめぐる</u>協議が二国間で行われた。 A conference regarding import restrictions was held between the two nations. 2) 亡くなった父の遺産<u>をめぐって</u>、兄弟で争いが始まった。 A feud between siblings broke out regarding their deceased father's inheritance.
11	にあたって にあたっての N	Places importance on a specific/special event or occasion at a certain time/place. At or during a designated time	1) 日本に留学する<u>にあたって</u>、特に注意すべきことを教えてください。 Please tell me what to especially watch out for when studying abroad in Japan. 2) 新年<u>にあたっての</u>抱負を述べる。 [I] will state my New Year's resolution. (Lit. I will state my resolution of this coming New Year.)

✛ Practice Questions

Pay attention to the particle equivalent phrases and translate the following sentences.

(1) (a) 日本の歴史において仏教の役割は少しずつ変化してきた。

(b) 日本の歴史における仏教の役割の変化について以下で述べる。

(2) (a) 政府は、日本は経済大国としてもっと責任を果たすべきだとして、途上国援助予算を増額した。

(b) 日本は経済大国としての責任を果たすべきだ。

(3) (a) 太郎にとって問題を一人で解決することは難しい。

(b) 太郎にとっての問題は睡眠時間が足りないことである。

(4) (a) その商品は期待に反して売上高がかなり低調だった。

(b) その商品は期待に反する売上高となった。

35

A Practical Guide for Scholarly Reading in Japanese

(5) (a) 知事の見解に対して、アメリカで長く日本経済を研究している鈴木教授は、反対意見を述べた。

(b) 環境問題に対する見解の相違から、各国の対策が異なる。

(6) (a) 地域によって食習慣は顕著に違っている。

(b) 地域による食習慣の違いは顕著であった。

(7) (a) 大空のもとでピクニックを楽しんだ。

(b) 大空のもとでのピクニックは楽しかった。

(8) (a) 学会では、この言葉の意味をめぐって議論が起こった。

(b) 学会では、この言葉の意味をめぐる議論が起こった。

(9) (a) 新製品の開発にあたって社長の記者会見が行われた。

(b) 新製品の開発にあたっての社長の判断は正しかった。

★ Answers

(1) (a) The role of Buddhism gradually changed throughout Japanese history.

(b) [We] will describe the change in the role of Buddhism in Japanese history below.

(2) (a) The government, deciding that Japan should take more responsibility as an economic power, increased the budget allotted for providing aid to developing countries.

(b) Japan should carry out its responsibility as an economic power.

(3) (a) For Taro, it is difficult to solve the problem on his own.

(b) The problem for Taro was his lack of sleep.

(4) (a) Contrary to expectations, the sales for that product were quite subdued.

(b) That product had unexpected sales results.

(5) (a) In response to the governor's stance, Professor Suzuki, who has been studying Japan's economy for a long time in America, stated an opposing opinion.

(b) From differences in opinion on environmental problems, the measures taken in each country differ.

(6) (a) Eating habits differ notably based on region.

(b) The difference of regional eating habits was notable.

(7) (a) [I] enjoyed the picnic under the skies.

(b) The picnic under the skies was enjoyable.

36

Chapter 1 – "Toolbox": Essential Grammar for Scholarly Reading

(8) (a) An argument broke out regarding the meaning of this word at the conference.

(b) A discussion regarding the meaning of this word was held at this conference.

(9) (a) A press conference with the president of the company was held regarding the development of a new product.

(b) The company president's decision regarding the development of the new product was correct.

7. Kanji

There are differences in the usage of Chinese characters and Japanese kanji, so if you rely too much on your knowledge of Chinese characters, there is a chance that you will make an error in your translation. In this chapter, we will provide you with basic knowledge that you should know regarding the usage of Japanese kanji.

7.1 国字 (Kanji Made in Japan)

Kokuji refers to kanji that was made by the Japanese. There are more than 2,600 known kanji of this type, but only some of them are being used presently (e.g. 匂, 働, 塀, 峠, 込, 枠, 栃, 搾, 畑, 腺, 辻). However, it should be noted that some *kokuji* are frequently used as basic Japanese kanji, and they are also often used for proper nouns such as names of people and places.

▶*Examples*

1) 働（はたらく、ドウ） to work: In Chinese, it is either 動 or 动. In Japanese, it is one of the most basic kanji.

2) 畑（はたけ） field; garden: Originally meant "burnt field." (In Chinese, 田 meant both paddy field and field.)

3) 鱈（たら） cod fish: Because it is a winter fish that is white in color, people say that 魚＋ 雪 were combined to form this kanji. In Japan, where a wide variety of fish are eaten, many *kokuji* that express the names of fish were created.

It should be noted that during and after the Meiji period, some *kokuji* were exported back to China and used there. For example, the kanji 腺 was a medical term made in Japan during the Meiji period, and it is now used in China as well. Other examples include 鱈 (cod) and 膵 (臓) (pancreas).

7.2 当て字 *Chinese Character(s) Used for Its Phonetic Sound*

Ateji refers to a Chinese character which is used to mark Japanese sounds.

Note that the meaning of the Japanese words cannot be inferred from the meaning of the original Chinese characters in this case.

37

A Practical Guide for Scholarly Reading in Japanese

The following words are frequently used examples of *ateji*:

➤*Examples*

1) 沢山: たくさん (a lot)

2) 多分: たぶん (probably)

3) 素敵: すてき (nice)

4) Proper nouns such as 亜米利加(アメリカ), 独逸(ドイツ), 仏蘭西(フランス), and 欧羅巴(ヨーロッパ): These location names are now typically written in *katakana*, but parts of the original kanji such as 米国 (America), 独国 (Germany), 仏国 (France), and 欧州 (Europe) are still used often in written Japanese.

   Western proper nouns may be written differently in Chinese.

   America: 亜美利加 or 美国

   Germany: 徳意志 or 徳国

   France: 法蘭西 or 法国

5) Foreign loan words such as 浪漫(ロマン) and 珈琲(コーヒー) are transliterated.

6) 子供: 供 is a suffix that expresses the plural in Japanese.

   The phonetically borrowed words mentioned above appear in a separate section in the Chinese-Japanese character dictionary (漢和辞典) .

7.3 新字体 *Simplified Kanji*

There are fewer 'simplified kanji' in Japanese than in Chinese. Chinese and Japanese simplified characters can differ in shape as in:

➤*Examples*

Meaning	Traditional Character	Simplified Chinese	Simplified Japanese
broad; wide	廣	广	広
swamp	澤	泽	沢
diagram; chart	圖	图	図

38

There are some traditional characters which are simplified in Chinese, but not in Japanese. For example, 機 'opportunity' or 'machinery' and 葉 'leaf' are simplified in Chinese as 机 and 叶, respectively. It should be noted that these simplified characters in Chinese have different meanings in Japanese (i.e., 机 means 'desk'; 叶 means '(dream/wish) coming true'). Here are some examples:

Meaning	Traditional Character	Simplified Chinese	Japanese Kanji
machinery; opportunity	機	机	機
leaf	葉	叶	葉
behind	後	后	後
cloud	雲	云	雲
rear	裏	里	裏
dry	乾	干	乾

7.4 同形異義語 *Japanese-Chinese Homographs*

These are words that exist both in Japanese and Chinese, but differ in nuance and usage.

➤*Examples*

	Japanese	Chinese
差別	discrimination	to discern; difference
招待	to invite	to entertain
期待	to expect good things	to expect (can be used for both good and bad things)
発現	to emerge	to discover
故人	a deceased person	an old friend
以 + X	As a general principle, X is included, but there are some times when it is excluded. 十六世紀以後 includes the 16th century and everything after it.	X is not included. 十六世紀以後 doesn't include the 16th century. It starts from the 17th century onwards.
的	孔子的言論 (A saying that sounds like something Confucius would say, but actually isn't.)	孔子的言論 (Words that were uttered by Confucius)

Note that there are many other words of this variety such as 結束, 工作, 告訴, 小心, 湯, 鬼, 勉強, 読書, and 手紙.

A Practical Guide for Scholarly Reading in Japanese

✣ Practice Questions

Take the meaning of the kanji combinations into consideration and translate the following sentences:

(1) このような学問（がくもん）の根本（こんぽん）におけるくいちがいが、時代区分（じだいくぶん）上（じょう）の亀裂（きれつ）として発現（はつげん）したと考（かんが）えられるのである。

(2) 魯迅（ろじん）は日本（にほん）で医学（いがく）を学（まな）んでいたが、中国人（ちゅうごくじん）としての差別（さべつ）を感（かん）じていた。

(3) Ａ説（せつ）は十世紀以後（じゅっせいきいご）を近世（きんせい）と呼（よ）ぶ。

(4) 貴族政治（きぞくせいじ）は、秦漢（しんかん）の統一帝国時代（とういつていこくじだい）に至（いた）って一種（いっしゅ）の君主独裁政治的傾向（くんしゅどくさいせいじてきけいこう）を帯（お）びた。

★ Answers

English Translation

(1) This type of discrepancy in the foundation of the academic fields is thought to manifest itself as a fissure in periodization.

(2) Lu Xun was learning medicine in Japan, but he felt discriminated against as a Chinese person.

(3) Theory A refers to the period after the 10th century as the Modern Ages.

(4) The aristocracy assumed a type of dictatorship role during the period of the unified Qin-Han empire.

7.5 同音異義語（どうおんいぎご） *Japanese-Chinese Homophones*

The Japanese words また and すなわち carry several meanings. Pay attention to the meanings of また and すなわち when they are written in *hiragana*. With regard to Chinese, the following meanings differ based on the kanji.

▶*Examples*

	Meaning	Example Sentence
又	その上（うえ）　moreover	私（わたし）は英語（えいご）を話（はな）す。**また**フランス語（ご）も話（はな）す。 I speak English. Moreover, I speak French.
亦	同様（どうよう）に　also; as well	私（わたし）は英語（えいご）を話（はな）す。**また**弟（おとうと）も英語（えいご）を話（はな）す。 I speak English. My younger brother also speaks English.
復	再（ふたた）び　once more; again	昨日英語（きのうえいご）を話（はな）した。**また**今日（きょう）も英語（えいご）を話（はな）す。 I spoke English yesterday. I will speak English again today.

40

Chapter 1 – "Toolbox": Essential Grammar for Scholarly Reading

However, when the Japanese word また is written in kanji, the meaning does not coincide with the Chinese characters mentioned above. Therefore, if you see the kanji 又, for example, the meaning could be either 亦, 還, or 復. The same is true for すなわち. In Chinese, the following kanji have different meanings.

➤*Examples*

	Meaning	Example Sentence
乃	その結果、そこではじめて、やっと As a result; It was then that ~ (it was not until ~ that); finally	2年間寺で修行し、**すなわち**悟った。 [I] trained myself at a temple for two years, whereupon I came to a spiritual awakening.
則	～すれば、(その時は)……となる If X, then Y.	戦えば、**すなわち**勝つ。 If [I] fight, then [I] will surely win.
即	～は(とりもなおさず)……だ X, namely Y.	戦いは、**すなわち**勝負をつけることだ。 A battle is, namely, a matter of winning or losing.

✢ Practice Questions

Think about the following meanings of すなわち and write the English translations.

(1) 信じれば、すなわち救われる。

(2) 生きることは、すなわち挑戦の連続である。

(3) 三度行きて、すなわち見ることができたのである。

★ Answers and English Translations

(1) If you believe, then you will be saved.

(2) Living is, namely, a succession of challenges.

(3) [I] went thrice, whereupon [I] was finally able to see it.

41

8. Classical Japanese Grammar (for Reading Academic Articles from the Meiji Era Onwards)

In Japan, due to the 言文一致 (reconciliation of speech and writing) movement which started in the Meiji period (1868–1912), the style of written language up until then changed, and, furthermore, due to the national language reforms after World War II, written language became even closer to spoken language, which continues to the present day. That is to say, the academic Japanese used up through the first half of the 20th century contains many classical Japanese expressions not currently in use. In addition, given the primarily formal style of academic Japanese, many classical expressions can still be seen in the present. Because of this, this section will systematically cover the classical expressions needed to read academic Japanese from the Meiji period to the present.

8.1 歴史的仮名遣い *Historical Kana Orthography*

Japanese *kana* orthography has taken on various forms in addition to the current *hiragana* and *katakana*. Contemporary *hiragana* uses a single character to express each syllable, but from the Heian period until modern times, multiple characters had been used to express the same syllable.

➤ *Examples*

/i/: い　 ゐ (以)

い (意)

い (移)

伊 (伊) ……

This changed to the current system of one character per syllable with the 1900 (Meiji 33) Elementary School Order, which selected a unique *hiragana* for each syllable. As a result, the rest of the characters (those not selected) came to be called *hentaigana* (deviant *kana*). Accordingly, documents from before 1900 use *hentaigana* (see the first edition of 学問のすすめ "An Encouragement of Learning").

On the other hand, *katakana* are said to have been created in the Heian period (794–1185) as supplementary marks for reading 漢文 *kanbun* (literary Chinese). Starting from that time, official and scholarly documents were, as a rule, written in *kanbun*. In other words, *katakana* were traditionally viewed as characters to be used in scholarly texts. Accordingly, when official and scholarly documents began to be written in the mixed kana style in the Meiji period, they often used *katakana* instead of *hiragana* (see the Meiji 6 reprinting of 学問のすすめ "An Encouragement of Learning").

Chapter 1 – "Toolbox": Essential Grammar for Scholarly Reading

The following is a summary of historical *kana* orthography.

1) The w-row (of the Japanese syllabary table) is written as:

a. *hiragana*: わ、ゐ、う、ゑ、を /wa/ /i/ /u/ /e/ /o/

b. *katakana*: ワ、ヰ、ウ、ヱ、ヲ /wa/ /i/ /u/ /e/ /o/

2) When NOT appearing at the beginning of a word, h-row *kana* are pronounced /wa/ /i/ /u/ /e/ /o/ instead of /ha/ /hi/ /fu/ /he/ /ho/.

Ex. おも<u>ふ</u>(思^{おも}う) /omou/, い<u>へ</u>ば(言^いえば) /ieba/, あるひ<u>は</u>(或^{ある}いは) /aruiwa/

3) When an a-vowel is followed by either u or hu, it is pronounced as おう /ō/

a. Ex. あふ /au/ ➡ おう /ō/

b. When an i-vowel is followed by either u or hu, it is pronounced as ゆう /yū/.

Ex. いふ /iu/ ➡ ゆう /yū/

c. When an e-vowel is followed by either u or hu, it is pronounced as よう /yō/.

Ex. えう /eu/ ➡ よう /yō/

4) The double/geminate consonant *kana* (っ) and contracted sound *kana* (や、ゆ、よ) are not necessarily written smaller.

Ex. すつかり (すっかり)、いつてゐる (いっている)、

しやれた (しゃれた)、きやう (きょう)

Until the end of World War II kanji was sometimes used with *katakana*, rather than *hiragana*, in academic/official Japanese.

43

Imperial Rescript of Education (教育勅語 きょういくちょくご)

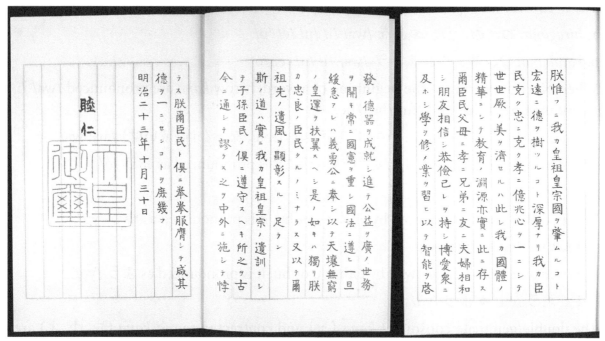

The Tokyo University Archives

Our Imperial Ancestors have founded Our Empire on a basis broad and everlasting and have deeply and firmly implanted virtue.

Our subjects ever united in loyalty and filial piety have from generation to generation illustrated the beauty thereof. This is the glory of the fundamental character of Our Empire, and herein also lies the source of Our education.

Ye, Our subjects, be filial to your parents, affectionate to your brothers and sisters; as husbands and wives be harmonious, as friends true; bear yourselves in modesty and moderation; extend your benevolence to all; pursue learning and cultivate arts, and thereby develop intellectual faculties and perfect moral powers; furthermore advance public good and promote common interests; always respect the Constitution and observe the laws; should emergency arise, offer yourselves courageously to the State; and thus guard and maintain the prosperity of Our Imperial Throne coeval with heaven and earth.

So shall ye not only be Our good and faithful subjects, but render illustrious the best traditions of your forefathers.

The Way here set forth is indeed the teaching bequeathed by Our Imperial Ancestors, to be observed alike by Their Descendants and the subjects, infallible for all ages and true in all places.

It is Our wish to lay it to heart in all reverence, in common with you, Our subjects, that we may all thus attain to the same virtue.

The 30th day of the 10th month of the 23rd year of Meiji (1890)

Authorized Translation by Ministry of Education, 1907

学問ノススメ　An Encouragement of Learning

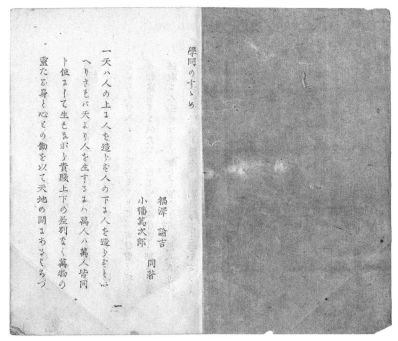

First edition (1872, Meiji 5): written mixed with *hentaigana*

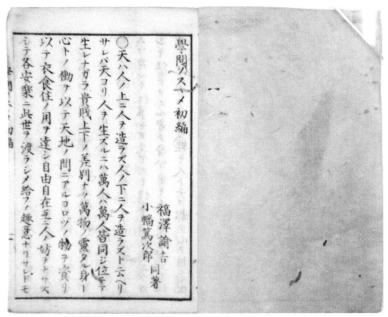

Noda City Library

Kana reprinting (1873, Meiji 6): written mixed with *katakana*

Heaven, it is said, does not create one person above or below another. This signifies that when we are born from Heaven we all are equal and there is no innate distinction between high and low. It means that we humans, who are the highest of all creation, can use the myriad things of the world to satisfy our daily needs through the labors of our own bodies and minds...

Translated by David A. Dilworth, *An Encouragement of Learning*, Columbia University Press, New York, 2012

Practice Questions

Change the historical kana system to modern Japanese.

① ゐなか　　　➡

② こゑ　　　　➡

③ けふ　　　　➡

④ とふ　　　　➡

⑤ いへ　　　　➡

⑥ かほ　　　　➡

⑦ あふぎ　　　➡

⑧ うつくしう　➡

⑨ とほす　　　➡

⑩ からうじて　➡

★ Answers and English Translations

① ゐなか	➡	いなか（田舎）	countryside
② こゑ	➡	こえ（声）	voice
③ けふ	➡	きょう（今日）	today
④ とふ	➡	とう（問う）	ask; inquire
⑤ いへ	➡	いえ（家）	house
⑥ かほ	➡	かお（顔）	face
⑦ あふぎ	➡	おうぎ（扇）	folding fan
⑧ うつくしう	➡	うつくしゅう（美しゅう）	beautifully
⑨ とほす	➡	とおす（通す）	let (someone, something) through
⑩ からうじて	➡	かろうじて	barely

Chapter 1 – "Toolbox": Essential Grammar for Scholarly Reading

8.2 Inflected Forms

Verbs, adjectives (*i*-adjectives), adjectival verbs (*na*-adjectives), and auxiliary verbs have six inflected forms as shown in the following table.

Inflected Form	Function or Feature
未然形 MIZEN or Imperfective form	**MIZEN is similar to the *nai*-form in modern Japanese.** Followed by auxiliary verbs of negation ず, the passive forms る and らる, the conjunctive particle ば (hypothesis), etc. Ex. 言はず。 (I) do not say. (See 8.5.1)
連用形 RENYŌ or Continuative form	**RENYŌ is similar to the *masu*-form in modern Japanese.** Followed by declinable words (e.g., verbs, adjectives, and adjectival verbs), auxiliary verbs in the past (perfect) tense (e.g., き, けり, たり, and り), the conjunctive particle て, etc. Ex. 言ひ始める。 (I) start to say.　　言ひて… (I) say and…
終止形 SHŪSHI or Final form	**SHŪSHI is similar to the dictionary form in modern Japanese. Marks the end of the sentence.** Followed by an auxiliary verb of firm expectation べし. Ex. 言ふ。 (I) say.　　言ふべし。 (I) should say.
連体形 RENTAI or Attributive form	**RENTAI is similar to the plain/prenominal form in modern Japanese. Modifies a nominal (noun, pronoun).** Followed by copular auxiliary verbs なり and たり. Ex. 言ふ時　　When (I) say [Lit. the time I say] 言ふなり。 (I) say.
已然形 IZEN or Perfective form	**IZEN is similar to the *ba*-form in modern Japanese.** Followed by the perfect tense auxiliary verb り, the particle ば ('because; when'), and the concessive particles ど, ども ('although'). Ex. 言へば　because (I) say　　言へども　though (I) say
命令形 MEIREI or Imperative form	**MEIREI is similar to the imperative form in modern Japanese.** Indicates a command. Ex. 言へ。 Say!

Note: Henceforth, "-形 *kei* (form)" is omitted as in *MIZEN* (未然), *RENYŌ* (連用), *SHŪSHI* (終止), *RENTAI* (連体), *IZEN* (已然), and *MEIREI* (命令) in both English and Japanese.

The detailed explanation for each part of speech is given in 8.3.

47

A Practical Guide for Scholarly Reading in Japanese

8.3 Verbs

While modern Japanese verbs are divided into three conjugation types (e.g., *U*-verb, *Ru*-verb, and Irregular verb), classical Japanese verbs have nine conjugations. Five are regular (四段 *yodan*/fourth grade, 上一段 *kami ichidan*/upper one-grade, 上二段 *kami nidan*/upper two-grade, 下一段 *shimo ichidan*/lower one-grade, 下二段 *shimo nidan*/lower two-grade) and four are irregular (ナ行変格 *nahen*/*n*-row irregular, ラ行変格 *rahen*/*r*-row irregular, 力行変格 *kahen*/*k*-row irregular, サ行変格 *sahen*/*s*-row irregular).

Classical Japanese	Modern Japanese
四段活用 *Yodan* 下一段活用 *Shimo ichidan* ナ行変格活用 *Nahen* ラ行変格活用 *Rahen*	*U*-verb
下二段活用 *Shimo nidan*	*Ru*-verb
上一段活用 *Kami ichidan* 上二段活用 *Kami nidan*	
力行変格活用 *Kahen*	Irregular verbs （する/来る）
サ行変格活用 *Sahen*	

The following table summarizes the rules for each regular verb.

四段動詞 *Yodan* conjugation	Four different vowel grades in the stem: *a*, *i*, *u* and *e* Ex. 書く 書か → 書き → 書く → 書く → 書け → 書け (kak*a*)→(kak*i*)→(kak*u*)→(kak*u*)→(kak*e*)→(kak*e*)
上一段活用 *Kami ichidan* conjugation	Conjugates with one vowel (*i*) Ex. 見る み → み → みる → みる → みれ → みよ (m*i*)→(m*i*)→(m*i*ru)→(m*i*ru)→(m*i*re)→(m*i*yo)

48

Chapter 1 – "Toolbox": Essential Grammar for Scholarly Reading

かみにだんかつよう 上二段活用 *Kami nidan* conjugation	Conjugates with two vowels (*i* and *u*) Ex. 落ちる 落ち → 落ち → 落つ → 落つる → 落つれ → 落ちよ (och*i*)→(och*i*)→(ots*u*)→(ots*u*ru)→(ots*u*re)→(och*i*yo)
しもいちだんかつよう 下一段活用 *Shimo ichidan* conjugation	Conjugates with one vowel (*e*) Ex. 蹴る け → け → ける → ける → けれ → けよ (k*e*)→(k*e*)→(k*e*ru)→(k*e*ru)→(k*e*re)→(k*e*yo)
しもにだんかつよう 下二段活用 *Shimo nidan* conjugation	Conjugates with two vowels (*u* and *e*) Ex. 受ける 受け → 受け → 受く → 受くる → 受くれ → 受けよ (uk*e*)→ (uk*e*)→ (uk*u*)→ (uk*u*ru)→ (uk*u*re)→ (uk*e*yo)

The table below summarizes the conjugations of the nine old verb types.

Inflection	*Yodan*[2]	*Kami ichidan*	*Kami nidan*	*Shimo ichidan*	*Shimo nidan*	*Nahen*	*Rahen*[3]	*Kahen*	*Sahen*
Example	書く	見る	落つ	蹴る	受く	死ぬ	有り	来	す
MIZEN 未然	書か	見	落ち	蹴	受け	死な	有ら	こ	せ
RENYŌ 連用	書き	見	落ち	蹴	受け	死に	有り	き	し
SHŪSHI[1] 終止	書く	見る	落つ	蹴る	受く	死ぬ	有り	く	す
RENTAI 連体	書く	見る	落つる	蹴る	受くる	死ぬる	有る	くる	する
IZEN 已然	書け	見れ	落つれ	蹴れ	受くれ	死ぬれ	有れ	くれ	すれ
MEIREI 命令	書け	見よ	落ちよ	蹴よ	受けよ	死ね	有れ	こ/ こよ	せよ

Notes

1. *SHŪSHI* (dictionary form) and *RENTAI* (plain form) are the same in modern Japanese. In classical Japanese, however, this rule applies only for 四段 *yodan* verbs, 上一段 *kami ichidan* verbs, and 下一段 *shimo ichidan* verbs.

   Ex. *kahen* verb

   Classical Japanese (CJ)：来 (*SHŪSHI*)—来る (*RENTAI*)

   Modern Japanese (MJ)：来る (*SHŪSHI*, dictionary form)—来る (*RENTAI*, plain form)

49

A Practical Guide for Scholarly Reading in Japanese

2. All *yodan* 四段 verbs are included in the modern "*u*-verb." In modern languages, the vowel "o" is also included, as in "書こ（う）let us write," so they are sometimes referred to as *godan* 五段 verbs.

3. In both modern and classical Japanese, all *SHŪSHI* (dictionary) forms of the verb end with the vowel *u*, with the exception of the *nahen* verb, 有り／在り in Classical Japanese.

   Ex. 落ちる *ochiru* (MJ)—落つ *otsu* (CJ)　有る *aru* (MJ)—有り *ari* (CJ)

✢ Practice Questions

Give the conjugation type (*yodan, kami ichidan, shimo ichidan, kami nidan, shimo nidan*) and the inflected form (*MIZEN, RENYŌ, SHŪSHI, RENTAI, IZEN, MEIREI*) of the underlined verbs. Then translate each sentence into English.

Ex. 日記を書かず。　　（　　*yodan, MIZEN*　　）　　(I) don't write a diary.

① 父が死ぬる時、　　（　　　　　　　）

② 木の葉が落つ。　　（　　　　　　　）

③ 正義は我にあり。　（　　　　　　　）

④ 君主の命を受くれば、（　　　　　　　）

⑤ 賊を追ひ払ふ。　　（　　　　　　　）

⑥ 出陣せよ！　　　　（　　　　　　　）

★ Answers and English Translations

① (*nahen, RENTAI*) The verb is *RENTAI* because it is followed by a nominal, 時.

   When my father dies,

② (*kami nidan, SHŪSHI*) The verb is *SHŪSHI* because it is at the end of the sentence.

   Tree leaves fall.

③ (*rahen, SHŪSHI*) The sentence ends with the verb. This is the exceptional verb in which the *SHŪSHI* ends with the vowel *i*, not *u*.

   Justice is on my side. (I have justice.)

④ (*shimo nidan, IZEN*) The verb is followed by the conjunctive particle, *ba*.

   Because (I) receive the order of the monarch,

⑤ (*yodan, RENYŌ*) The verb is followed by another verb, 払う.

   (I) drive away the bandits.

⑥ (*sahen, MEIREI*) The verb is sahen in *MEIREI*.

   Depart for the front!

50

Chapter 1 – "Toolbox": Essential Grammar for Scholarly Reading

8.4 形容詞 *Adjectives and* 形容動詞 *Adjectival Verbs*

8.4.1 形容詞　Adjectives (*i*-adjectives)

In modern Japanese the *SHŪSHI* (dictionary) form of *i*-adjectives end with い, as in 清い (pure) and 美しい (beautiful), whereas in classical Japanese it ends with し as in 清し and 美し. While there is one type of conjugation form in modern Japanese, there are two types in classical Japanese, *ku*-type ク活用 and *shiku*-type シク活用.

Ku-type: ク活用：清い (MJ) ➡ 清し (CJ)

Shiku-type: シク活用：美しい (MJ) ➡ 美し Ø (CJ)

The respective conjugations are as follows:

Conjugation	*Ku*-type		*Shiku*-type	
Example	清し		美し	
MIZEN 未然	清く	清から	美しく	美しから
RENYŌ 連用	清く	清かり	美しく	美しかり
SHŪSHI 終止	清し	○	美し	○
RENTAI 連体	清き	清かる	美しき	美しかる
IZEN 已然	清けれ	○	美しけれ	○
MEIREI 命令	○	清かれ	○	美しかれ

✤ Practice Questions

Conjugate the adjective (*i*-adjective) 高し and provide the inflected form (*MIZEN, RENYŌ, SHŪSHI, RENTAI, IZEN, MEIREI*). Then translate each sentence into English.

Ex. (　高き　) 山に登る。　　　　(*RENTAI*)　I climb the high mountain.

① 雪 (　　　　) 積もる。　　　(　　　　)

② この山は (　　　　)。　　　(　　　　)

③ あの山は (　　　　) ず。　　(　　　　)

④ この山 (　　　　) ば、登らず。(　　　　)

51

A Practical Guide for Scholarly Reading in Japanese

★ Answers and English Translations

Ex. 高き, *RENTAI*: Followed by the nominal 山.　I climb the high mountain.

① 高く, *RENYŌ*: Followed by the verb 積もる.　Snow piles high.

② 高し, *SHŪSHI*: Ends the sentence.　This mountain is high.

③ 高から, *MIZEN*: Followed by the negative auxiliary verb ず. (See 8.5.1)
That mountain is not high.

④ 高けれ, *IZEN*: Followed by the conjunctive particle ば.
As this mountain is high, I do not climb.

8.4.2 形容動詞　Adjectival Verbs (*na*-adjectives)

Adjectival verbs are descriptive nouns that are converted into adjectives when followed by inflective endings such as なり and たり. The following table shows the respective conjugations.

Conjugation	*Nari*-type	*Tari*-type
Example	静かなり	堂々たり
MIZEN 未然	静かなら	堂々たら
RENYŌ 連用	静かなり/ 静かに	堂々たり/堂々と
SHŪSHI 終止	静かなり	堂々たり
RENTAI 連体	静かなる	堂々たる
IZEN 已然	静かなれ	堂々たれ
MEIREI 命令	静かなれ	堂々たれ

① ナリ活用 *Nari*-type conjugation

This type consists of *SHŪSHI* conjugations with adjectival verbs that end in なり. There are two *RENYŌ* forms: –なり and –に .
Ex. 静かなり―静かに quietly

② タリ活用 *Tari*-type conjugation

This type consists of *SHŪSHI* conjugations that end with たり. There are two *RENYŌ* forms: –たり and –と .
Ex. 堂々たり―堂々と dignified

Chapter 1 – "Toolbox": Essential Grammar for Scholarly Reading

❖ Practice Questions

Conjugate the adjectival verb (*na*-adjective) 静かなり *shizukanari* and provide the inflected form (*MIZEN, RENYŌ, SHŪSHI, RENTAI, IZEN, MEIREI*). Then translate each sentence into English.

Ex. (　静かなる　) 山に登る。　　　(　*RENTAI*　)　I climb the quiet mountain.

① 雪、(　　　　　　) 降る。　　　(　　　　　　)

② この山は (　　　　　)。　　　(　　　　　　)

③ あの山は (　　　　　) ず。　　　(　　　　　　)

④ この山 (　　　　　) ば、うれし。(　　　　　　)

★ Answers and English Translations

Ex. 静かなる, *RENTAI:* Followed by a nominal 山.

I climb the quiet mountain.

① 静かに, *RENYŌ:* Followed by a verb 降る.

It snows quietly.

② 静かなり, *SHŪSHI:* Ends the sentence.

This mountain is quiet.

③ 静かなら, *MIZEN:* Followed by a negative auxiliary verb ず.

That mountain is not quiet.

④ 静かなれ, *IZEN:* Followed by a conjunctive particle ば.

As this mountain is quiet, I am happy.

53

A Practical Guide for Scholarly Reading in Japanese

8.5 助動詞 *Auxiliary Verbs*

Auxiliary verbs represent tense, mood, voice, aspect, etc. The classical auxiliary verbs that are frequently used in academic papers are as follows:[1]

Function	AUX	Follows	*MIZEN*	*RENYŌ*	*SHŪSHI*	*RENTAI*	*IZEN*	*MEIREI*
Negative (8.5.1)	ず [2-A]	*MIZEN*	ざら	ず ざり	ず	ぬ ざる	ね ざれ	ざれ
Recollective (8.5.2)	き	*RENYŌ*	○	○	き	し	しか	○
	けり [3]		○	○	けり	ける	けれ	○
Copular (8.5.3)	なり [2-B]	Nominal *RENTAI* Adverb Particle	なら	なり に	なり	なる	なれ	なれ
	たり [2-C][4-A]	Nominal	たら	たり と	たり	たる	たれ	たれ
Perfective (8.5.4)	たり [4-B]	*RENYŌ*	たら	たり	たり	たる	たれ	たれ
	り	*MIZEN* for *sahen* verbs *IZEN* for *yodan* verbs	ら	り	り	る	れ	れ
	ぬ	*RENYŌ*	な	に	ぬ	ぬる	ぬれ	ね
Advice Appropriateness Potential Intentional Speculative Command (8.5.5)	べし [2-D]	*SHŪSHI* *RENTAI* for *rahen* type[5] conjugation words	べから	べく べかり	べし	べき べかる	べけれ	○
Passive Potential Honorific Spontaneous (8.5.6)	る	*MIZEN*	れ	れ	る	るる	るれ	れよ
	らる		られ	られ	らる	らるる	らるれ	られよ
Comparative (8.5.7)	ごとし	Nominal *RENTAI* Particle (が/の)	ごとく	ごとく	ごとし	ごとき	○	○
Causative (8.5.8)	しむ	*MIZEN*	しめ	しめ	しむ	しむる	しむれ	しめよ
Speculative Intentional and Circumlocution (8.5.9)	む	*MIZEN*	○	○	む (ん)	む (ん)	め	○
Negative speculative Negative intentional (8.5.10)	まい [6]	*SHŪSHI* for *Yodan*, *rahen* type[5] conjugation words *MIZEN* for the others	○	○	まい	まい	(まいけれ)	○

54

Chapter 1 – "Toolbox": Essential Grammar for Scholarly Reading

Notes

1. There are 28 main auxiliary verbs, some with more than one meaning, but this table only shows those which frequently appear in academic Japanese from the Meiji period onward and their meanings. For a complete table, see the appendix.

2. ず, なり, たり, and べし have primary (top line) and supplementary (bottom line) conjugations. It is common to use supplementary type when followed by an auxiliary verb (see the description for each type).

3. In addition to the past tense (recollective), けり has the meaning of exclamatory, but since it is hardly seen in academic Japanese, it is not dealt with here.

4. The auxiliary verb たり has two meanings (copular and perfective). The meaning can be distinguished based on the inflected form which it follows.

5. *Rahen* type conjugation words are those which conjugate in the same way as *rahen* verbs. Those include all adjectives, all adjectival verbs, some auxiliary verbs, and *rahen* verbs (e.g. あり).

6. まい is the same as the auxiliary verb まじ. Sound change (音便^{おんびん}) occurred for the easier pronunciation in history. Here it shows the inflected forms in the written language.

8.5.1 ず Negative

Function	Follows	*MIZEN*	*RENYŌ*	*SHŪSHI*	*RENTAI*	*IZEN*	*MEIREI*
Negative	*MIZEN*	ざら	ず ざり	ず	ぬ* ざる	ね ざれ	ざれ

* There are cases where the *RENTAI* form ぬ ends a sentence instead of the *SHŪSHI* ず. In this construction, it is thought that のだ, where の is a nominal, is abbreviated after the ぬ.

(1) まかぬ種^{たね}は生^はえぬ。 (Seeds not planted do not grow.)

(2) この非常事態^{ひじょうじたい}、どうにかせねばならぬ。 (Something must be done about this emergency situation.)

➤ *Examples*

	SHŪSHI	*MIZEN*	＋ず	MJ
Verb (V)	言^いふ	言^いは	言^いはず	言^いわない
Adjective (ADJ)	高^{たか}し	高^{たか}から	高^{たか}からず	高^{たか}くない
Adjectival verb (ADJ-V)	静^{しず}かなり	静^{しず}かなら	静^{しず}かならず	静^{しず}かではない
Auxiliary verb (AUX)	(言^いふ) べし	(言^いふ) べから	(言^いふ) べからず	(言^いう) べきではない

55

A Practical Guide for Scholarly Reading in Japanese

✥ Practice Questions

Translate the following sentences.

① その男日記を書かず。

② 日記を書かぬ男

③ つぎに、B説について語らねばならない。

★ Answers and Explanations

① That man does not write a diary.

書か	ず
V 書く *MIZEN*	AUX ず (Negative) *SHŪSHI*

② The man who does not write a diary.

書か	ぬ	男
V 書く *MIZEN*	AUX ず (Negative) *RENTAI*	N

③ Next, we must discuss Theory B.

語ら	ね	ば
V 語る *MIZEN*	AUX ず (Negative) *IZEN*	CONJ-P

Note: ね is AUX ず (Negative) *IZEN*, thus is the same as なけれ in modern Japanese, 語らなければならない.

8.5.2 き and けり　Recollective

Function	AUX	Follows	*MIZEN*	*RENYŌ*	*SHŪSHI*	*RENTAI*	*IZEN*	*MEIREI*
Recollective	き	*RENYŌ*	○	○	き	し	しか	○
	けり		○	○	けり	ける	けれ	○

The verbs, adjectives, adjectival verbs, and auxiliary verbs that precede き and けり are in the *RENYŌ* form.

56

Chapter 1 – "Toolbox": Essential Grammar for Scholarly Reading

➤*Examples*

	SHŪSHI	*RENYŌ*	AUX	＋き/けり	MJ
V	言^いふ	言^いひ	き	言^いひき	言^いった
			けり	言^いひけり	
ADJ	高^{たか}し	高^{たか}かり	き	高^{たか}かりき	高^{たか}かった
			けり	高^{たか}かりけり	
ADJ-V	静^{しず}かなり	静^{しず}かなり	き	静^{しず}かなりき	静^{しず}かだった
			けり	静^{しず}かなりけり	
AUX	ず	ざり	き	ざりき	〜なかった
			けり	ざりけり	

✥ Practice Questions

Translate the following sentences into English.

① 京^{きょう}に男^{おとこ}ありき。

② 昔^{むかし}、男^{おとこ}ありけり。

③ 日記^{にっき}を書^かきし人。

④ 日記^{にっき}を書^かきける人。

⑤ 我^わが国^{くに}にはかかる(このような)場合^{ばあい}なかりしために、…

★ Answers and Explanations

① There was a man in the capital.

あり	き
V あり *RENYŌ*	AUX き (Recollective) *SHŪSHI*

② There was once a man.

あり	けり
V あり *RENYŌ*	AUX けり (Recollective) *SHŪSHI*

57

③ The person who wrote a diary.

書き	し	人
V 書く *RENYŌ*	AUX き (Recollective) *RENTAI*	N

④ The person who wrote a diary.

書き	ける	人
V 書く *RENYŌ*	AUX けり (Recollective) *RENTAI*	N

⑤ Because in our country there were not such cases,...

なかり	し	ため
ADJ なし *RENYŌ*	AUX き (Recollective) *RENTAI*	N

8.5.3 なり and たり Copular/Declarative

Function	AUX	Follows	*MIZEN*	*RENYŌ*	*SHŪSHI*	*RENTAI*	*IZEN*	*MEIREI*
Copular Declarative	なり	N P ADV *RENTAI*	なら	なり に	なり	なる	なれ	なれ
	たり	N	たら	たり と	たり	たる	たれ	たれ

Chapter 1 – "Toolbox": Essential Grammar for Scholarly Reading

➤ *Examples*

	Example	＋なり/たり	MJ
V	言^いふ	言^いふなり	言^いうのだ
ADJ	高^{たか}し	高^{たか}きなり	高^{たか}いのだ
ADJ-V	静^{しず}かなり	静^{しず}かなるなり	静^{しず}か(なの)だ
AUX	はず 言^いふべし 静^{しず}かならず	言^いはざるなり 言^いふべきなり 静^{しず}かならざるなり	言^いわないのだ 言^いうべきだ 静^{しず}かではないのだ
N	学者^{がくしゃ}	学者^{がくしゃ}なり 学者^{がくしゃ}たり	学者^{がくしゃ}である
ADV	さ	さなり	そうである
P	ばかり	九^{ここの}つばかりなり	九^{ここの}つぐらいである

Note: なり has four functions.

The meaning of なり depends on what comes before it.

	Part of speech	How to distinguish	Functions	Example
1	The *RENYŌ* of V なる	N ＋ に ＋ なり (なる) N ＋ と ＋ なり (なる) The *RENYŌ* of inflected form ＋ なり (なる)	(〜に)なる	1) 宋代^{そうだい}は近世^{きんせい}の発端^{ほったん}となりて… The Song Dynasty marked the beginning of the early modern period… 2) 領土^{りょうど}が大^{おお}きくなる時^{とき}… When territory increases…
2	Ending of an ADJ-V	N that describes things + *nari*	〜だ/である	静^{しず}かなり It is quiet.
3	AUX (Copular)	The *RENTAI* of inflected form + *nari* N + *nari*	〜だ/である	これは普通^{ふつう}に用^{もち}ふる語^ごなるが… This is a word which is commonly used, but…
4	AUX (Hearsay)*	The *SHŪSHI* of inflected form + *nari*	〜だそうだ	男^{おとこ}もすなる日記^{にっき}といふものを… The diaries which I hear men keep…

* From the Meiji period onward, なり (hearsay) was used less frequently in academic texts.

A Practical Guide for Scholarly Reading in Japanese

✥ Practice Questions

Translate the following sentences into English.

① われ、日記を書くなり。

② その子、美しかるなり。

③ 君主の位置は貴族階級中の一の機関たり。

★ Answers and Explanations

① I write a diary.

書く	なり
V 書く *RENTAI*	AUX なり (Copular) *SHŪSHI*

② That child is pretty.

美しき	なり
ADJ 美し *RENTAI*	AUX なり (Copular) *SHŪSHI*

③ The monarch's position is one organ of the aristocratic class.

機関	たり
N	AUX たり (Copular) *SHŪSHI*

8.5.4 たり, り, and ぬ   Perfective

Function	AUX	Follows	*MIZEN*	*RENYŌ*	*SHŪSHI*	*RENTAI*	*IZEN*	*MEIREI*
Perfective Resultative	たり	*RENYŌ* of V	たら	たり	たり	たる	たれ	たれ
	り	*MIZEN* of *sahen* V, *IZEN* of *yodan* V	ら	り	り	る	れ	れ
	ぬ	*RENYŌ*	な	に	ぬ	ぬる	ぬれ	ね

60

> *Examples*

	SHŪSHI	Conjugation	AUX	+ AUX	MJ
V	言ふ	言ひ *RENYŌ*	たり	言ひたり	言った
			ぬ	言ひぬ	
		言へ *IZEN*	り	言へり	
ADJ	高し	高かり	たり	高かりたり	高かった
			ぬ	高かりぬ	
ADJ-V	静かなり	静かなり	たり	静かなりたり	静かだった
			ぬ	静かなりぬ	

✛ Practice Questions

Translate the following sentences into English.

① 君主独裁政治が起こりたり。

② 異なりたる点があり。

③ 唐太宗が天子になれる時、…

★ Answers and Explanations

① The autocracy has emerged.

起こり	たり
V 起こる *RENYŌ*	AUX たり (Perfective) *SHŪSHI*

② There was a point which has been different. (There was a different point.)

異なり	たる	点
V 異なる *RENYŌ*	AUX たり (Perfective) *RENTAI*	N

③ When Taizong of Tang had become an Emperor...

なれ	る	時
Yodan V なる *IZEN*	AUX り (Perfective) *RENTAI*	N

A Practical Guide for Scholarly Reading in Japanese

Note: The meaning of auxiliary verb たり depends on what comes before it.

Part of speech	How to distinguish	Function	Example
AUX (Perfective)	*RENYŌ* + たり	〜した 〜であった	君主独裁政治が起こりたる事は、… The rise of an absolute monarchy… [Lit. The fact that an absolute monarchy rose, …]
AUX (Copular)	N + たり	だ、である	絶対的権力者たる領主は… The lord who holds absolute power… [Lit: The lord who is the absolute authority…]

✥ Practice Questions

Pay attention to the use of たり and translate the following sentences into English.

① 梅の花咲きたり。

② 当時は君主独裁政治たれば、貴族の勢力は強いとは言いがたかった。

★ Answers and Explanations

① The plum blossom has bloomed.

梅	の	花	咲き	たり
N	P	N	V 咲く *RENYŌ*	AUX たり (Perfective) *SHŪSHI*

Since たり follows the *RENYŌ* of the verb 咲く, it is "perfective."

② It was an autocracy at the time so the influence of the nobility could not be said to be powerful.

当時	は	君主独裁政治	たれ	ば
N	P	N	AUX たり (Copular) *IZEN*	CONJ-P

Since たり follows the nominal 君主独裁政治, it is "copular."

62

Chapter 1 – "Toolbox": Essential Grammar for Scholarly Reading

8.5.5 べし Advice, Appropriateness, Potential, Intentional, Speculative, and Command

Function	Follows	MIZEN	RENYŌ	SHŪSHI	RENTAI	IZEN	MEIREI
Advice Appropriateness Potential Intentional Speculative Command	SHŪSHI (except rahen types*) RENTAI (all rahen types)	べから	べく べかり	べし	べき べかる	べけれ	○

* Words which conjugate in the same way as rahen verbs, adjectives, etc.

➤ Examples

		Example	＋べし	MJ
RENTAI	Rahen V	あり	あるべし	あるべきだ
	Rahen type AUX	たり	たるべし	〜であるべきだ
	ADJ	高<ruby>高<rt>たか</rt></ruby>し	高<ruby>高<rt>たか</rt></ruby>かるべし	高<ruby>高<rt>たか</rt></ruby>くあるべきだ
	ADJ-V	静<ruby>静<rt>しず</rt></ruby>かなり	静<ruby>静<rt>しず</rt></ruby>かなるべし	静<ruby>静<rt>しず</rt></ruby>かであるべきだ
SHŪSHI	Non-rahen V	言<ruby>言<rt>い</rt></ruby>ふ	言<ruby>言<rt>い</rt></ruby>ふべし	言<ruby>言<rt>い</rt></ruby>うべきだ

✥ Practice Questions

Translate the following sentences into English.

① 男<ruby>男<rt>おとこ</rt></ruby>は文<ruby>文<rt>ふみ</rt></ruby>を書<ruby>書<rt>か</rt></ruby>くべし。

② 男<ruby>男<rt>おとこ</rt></ruby>は文<ruby>文<rt>ふみ</rt></ruby>を書<ruby>書<rt>か</rt></ruby>くべからず。

③ 文<ruby>文<rt>ふみ</rt></ruby>を書<ruby>書<rt>か</rt></ruby>くべき人<ruby>人<rt>ひと</rt></ruby>なし。

④ ペリーは日本<ruby>日本<rt>にほん</rt></ruby>が開国<ruby>開国<rt>かいこく</rt></ruby>を進<ruby>進<rt>すす</rt></ruby>めるべく提案<ruby>提案<rt>ていあん</rt></ruby>したり。

★ Answers and Explanations

① Men should write letters.

書<ruby>書<rt>か</rt></ruby>く	べし
V 書く SHŪSHI	AUX べし (Appropriateness) SHŪSHI

63

A Practical Guide for Scholarly Reading in Japanese

② Men should not write letters.

書かく	べから	ず
V 書く *SHŪSHI*	AUX べし (Appropriateness) *MIZEN*	AUX ず (Negative) *SHŪSHI*

③ There is no person who should write letters.

書かく	べき	人
V 書く *SHŪSHI*	AUX べし (Appropriateness) *RENTAI*	N

④ Perry made a suggestion that Japan proceed with opening itself up to the world.

進すめる	べく	提案ていあんし	たり
V 進める *SHŪSHI*	AUX べし (Appropriateness) *RENYŌ*	V [提案] す *RENYŌ*	AUX たり (Perfective) *SHŪSHI*

8.5.6 る and らる   Passive, Potential, Honorific, and Spontaneous

Function	AUX	Follows	*MIZEN*	*RENYŌ*	*SHŪSHI*	*RENTAI*	*IZEN*	*MEIREI*
Passive Potential Honorific Spontaneous	る	*MIZEN*	れ	れ	る	るる	るれ	れよ
	らる		られ	られ	らる	らるる	らるれ	られよ

Note: The types of verbs that precede る and らる differ.

る follows the *MIZEN* of *yodan, rahen,* and *nahen* verbs.

らる follows the *MIZEN* of all other verb types mentioned above.

✦ Practice Questions

Translate the following sentences into English.

① そのありさま、目めも当あてられず。

② 太宗たいそう、即位そくいせられたり。

③ この時代じだいの貴族きぞくは、天子てんしから領土人民りょうどじんみんを与あたえられたり。

64

Chapter 1 – "Toolbox": Essential Grammar for Scholarly Reading

★ Answers and Explanations

① You can't look at such a mess.

当て	られ	ず
V 当てる *MIZEN*	AUX らる (Potential) *MIZEN*	AUX ず (Negative) *SHŪSHI*

② The emperor acceded to the throne.

Note: らる is used as an honorific in this case because the subject is 太宗 (Tai Zong).

即位せ	られ	たり
V [即位] す *MIZEN*	AUX らる (Honorific) *MIZEN*	AUX たり (Perfective) *SHŪSHI*

③ The nobility of this period was allotted territory and people by the emperor.

与え	られ	たり
V 与う *MIZEN*	AUX らる (Passive) *RENYŌ*	AUX たり (Perfective) *SHŪSHI*

8.5.7 ごとし Comparative

Function	AUX	Follows	*MIZEN*	*RENYŌ*	*SHŪSHI*	*RENTAI*	*IZEN*	*MEIREI*
Similitude Similarity	ごとし	N, *RENTAI*, P (が / の)	ごとく	ごとく	ごとし	ごとき	◯	◯

➤ *Examples*

踊る	が	ごとし	MJ
V 踊る *RENTAI*	P	AUX ごとし (Comparative) *SHŪSHI*	(まるで)踊っているようだ As if they were dancing

花	の	ごとし		MJ
N	P	AUX ごとし (Comparative) *SHŪSHI*		(まるで)花のようだ　As if it were a flower

✜ Practice Questions

Translate the following sentences into English.

① あって無きがごとし。

② 過ぎたるは及ばざるがごとし。

③ 次のごとく決定せり。

65

A Practical Guide for Scholarly Reading in Japanese

★ Answers and Explanations

① It is non-existent (= useless) [Lit. It exists, but it is as if it is non-existent].

無^なき		が	ごとし
ADJ 無し *RENTAI*		P	AUX ごとし (Comparative) *SHŪSHI*

② Too much is just as bad as too little.

及^{およ}ば	ざる	が	ごとし
V 及ぶ *MIZEN*	AUX ず (Negative) *RENTAI*	P	AUX ごとし (Comparative) *SHŪSHI*

③ [We] have decided as follows.

次^{つぎ}	の	ごとく	決定^{けってい}せ	り
N	P	AUX ごとし (Comparative) *RENYŌ*	V [決定] す *MIZEN*	AUX り (Perfective) *SHŪSHI*

8.5.8 しむ Causative

Function	Follows	*MIZEN*	*RENYŌ*	*SHŪSHI*	*RENTAI*	*IZEN*	*MEIREI*
Causative	*MIZEN*	しめ	しめ	しむ	しむる	しむれ	しめよ

▶*Examples*

	SHŪSHI	*MIZEN*	＋しむ	MJ
V	言^いふ	言は	言はしむ	言わせる To make something/someone say
ADJ	高^{たか}し	高から	高からしむ	高くさせる To make something/someone high
ADJ-V	静^{しず}かなり	静かなら	静かならしむ	静かにさせる To make something/someone quiet

66

Chapter 1 – "Toolbox": Essential Grammar for Scholarly Reading

✥ Practice Questions

Translate the following sentences into English.

① 吾子に論語を読ましむ。

② 吾子に論語を読ましめず。

③ 吾子に論語を読ましむる人

④ この状況は研究者をして躊躇せしむ。

★ Answers and Explanations

① [I] let/make my child read the Analects of Confucius.

読ま	しむ
V 読む *MIZEN*	AUX しむ (Causative) *SHŪSHI*

② [I] do not let/make my child read the Analects.

読ま	しめ	ず
V 読む *MIZEN*	AUX しむ (Causative) *MIZEN*	AUX ず (Negative) *SHŪSHI*

③ A person who lets/makes children read the Analects.

読ま	しむる	人
V 読む *MIZEN*	AUX しむ (Causative) *RENTAI*	N

④ This situation makes researchers hesitate.

研究者をして	躊躇せ	しむ
Indirect object	V [躊躇] す *MIZEN*	AUX しむ (Causative) *SHŪSHI*

Note: "〜をして" is a written expression that functions to mark the direct marker of causatives. It is equivalent to the direct object marker を, or the indirect object marker に.

8.5.9 む   Speculative, Intentional, and Circumlocution

Function	Follows	*MIZEN*	*RENYŌ*	*SHŪSHI*	*RENTAI*	*IZEN*	*MEIREI*
Speculative Intentional	*MIZEN*	○	○	む (ん)	む (ん)	め	○

Note: In scholarly writing, む is not often used in its circumlocution meaning.

67

A Practical Guide for Scholarly Reading in Japanese

➤ *Examples*

	SHŪSHI	*MIZEN*	+む	MJ
V	言<ruby>言<rt>い</rt></ruby>ふ	言<ruby>言<rt>い</rt></ruby>は	言<ruby>言<rt>い</rt></ruby>はむ	言<ruby>言<rt>い</rt></ruby>おう/言うだろう
ADJ	高<ruby>高<rt>たか</rt></ruby>し	高<ruby>高<rt>たか</rt></ruby>から	高<ruby>高<rt>たか</rt></ruby>からむ	高<ruby>高<rt>たか</rt></ruby>いだろう
ADJ-V	静<ruby>静<rt>しず</rt></ruby>かなり	静<ruby>静<rt>しず</rt></ruby>かなら	静<ruby>静<rt>しず</rt></ruby>かならむ	静<ruby>静<rt>しず</rt></ruby>かだろう
AUX	(言<ruby>言<rt>い</rt></ruby>ひ) たり	(言<ruby>言<rt>い</rt></ruby>ひ) たら	(言<ruby>言<rt>い</rt></ruby>ひ) たらむ	(言<ruby>言<rt>い</rt></ruby>っ) ただろう

✥ Practice Questions

Translate the following sentences into English.

① 我<ruby>我<rt>われ</rt></ruby>は必<ruby>必<rt>かなら</rt></ruby>ず文<ruby>文<rt>ふみ</rt></ruby>を書<ruby>書<rt>か</rt></ruby>かむ。

② 来月<ruby>来月<rt>らいげつ</rt></ruby>、出発<ruby>出発<rt>しゅっぱつ</rt></ruby>せんとす。

③ その男<ruby>男<rt>おとこ</rt></ruby>、隠<ruby>隠<rt>かく</rt></ruby>し事<ruby>事<rt>ごと</rt></ruby>あらむ。

★ Answers and Explanations

① I will definitely write a letter.

書<ruby>書<rt>か</rt></ruby>か	む
V 書く *MIZEN*	AUX む (Intentional) *SHŪSHI*

② We intend to leave next month.

出発<ruby>出発<rt>しゅっぱつ</rt></ruby>せ	ん	と	す
V［出発］す *MIZEN*	AUX む (Intentional) *RENTAI*	P	V す *SHŪSHI*

③ That man may have something to hide.

隠<ruby>隠<rt>かく</rt></ruby>し事<ruby>事<rt>ごと</rt></ruby>	あら	む
N	V あり *MIZEN*	AUX む (Speculative) *SHŪSHI*

Chapter 1 – "Toolbox": Essential Grammar for Scholarly Reading

8.5.10 まい Negative Speculative and Negative Intentional

Function	Follows	MIZEN	RENYŌ	SHŪSHI	RENTAI	IZEN	MEIREI
Negative speculative Negative intentional	SHŪSHI (yodan, nahen) MIZEN (other type of V)	○	○	まい	まい	(まいけれ)	○

➤ *Examples*

見^み	まい	MJ
Kami ichidan V 見る *MIZEN*	AUX まい (Negative speculative) *SHŪSHI*	見ないだろう (Someone) won't probably see. 見るつもりはない (I/We) won't see.
落ち^お	まい	MJ
Kami nidan V 落つ *MIZEN*	AUX まい (Negative speculative) *SHŪSHI*	落ちないだろう (Someone/Something) won't probably fall. 落ちるつもりはない (I/We) won't fall.
受け^う	まい	MJ
Shimo nidan V 受く *MIZEN*	AUX まい (Negative speculative) *SHŪSHI*	受けないだろう (Someone) won't probably take. 受けるつもりはない (I/We) won't take.
行く^い	まい	MJ
Yodan V 行く *SHŪSHI*	AUX まい (Negative speculative) *SHŪSHI*	行かないだろう (Someone/Something) won't probably go. 行くつもりはない (I/We) will never go.

69

A Practical Guide for Scholarly Reading in Japanese

⊹ Practice Questions

Translate the following sentences into English.

① 本稿のタイトルを見て、いまさら時代区分問題でもあるまいと、大方の読者はお考えであろう。

② 日本経済は今後も成長を続ける可能性はあるまい。

③ 会社は今回、給料を上げてくれたのだから、これ以上我々は文句を言うまい。

Note: まい indicates the will of the speaker when the subject of the sentence is the first person subject 'I' or 'we.'

Example: （私/私たちは）決して行くまい。(I/We) will never go again. ➡ (I/We) have no intention to go again. (The subject is expressing a will to "not go.")

★ Answers and Explanations

① (Upon looking at the title of this article, many readers may be wondering why we are now discussing the classification of historical periods (what is the point of discussing classification of historical periods now).

ある	まい
V (MJ) ある *SHŪSHI*	AUX まい (Negative speculative) *SHŪSHI*

Note: Because the sentence subject is not the first person 'I' or 'we,' まい is a negative conjecture here.

② There is no possibility that the Japanese economy will continue to grow.

可能性	は	ある	まい
N	P	V ある *SHŪSHI*	AUX まい (Negative speculative) *SHŪSHI*

Note: Because the sentence subject is not the first person 'I' or 'we,' まい is a negative conjecture here.

③ We will no longer complain, since the company raised our salary this time.

我々	は	文句	を	言う	まい
N	P	N	P	V 言う *SHŪSHI*	AUX まい (Negative intentional) *SHŪSHI*

Note: Because the sentence subject is the first person 'we,' まい expresses a negative volition here.

Chapter 1 – "Toolbox": Essential Grammar for Scholarly Reading

8.6 *Conjunctive Particles*

Many of the conjunctive particles in classical Japanese grammar have the same meaning as those of modern Japanese. Below, we will explain some classical conjunctive particles, which are especially important when reading scholarly documents from the Meiji Period onwards.

8.6.1 ば Hypothetical/Logical Connections

The meaning of the conditional connector ば varies depending on whether it follows a *MIZEN* or *IZEN* verb. It refers to a hypothetical situation when it follows *MIZEN*, while it refers to an existing situation when it follows *IZEN*.

降ら	ば	MJ
V 降る *MIZEN*	CONJ-P	もし降ったとしたら/もし降ったら　If it rains

降れ	ば	MJ
V 降る *IZEN*	CONJ-P	降るので/降ったので　Because it is going to rain/ Because it rained

➤ *Examples*

① 雨降らば、花散らむ。

(Hypothetical)　If it rains, cherry blossom petals will probably scatter.

② 雨降れば、花散りぬ。

(Logical connection)　Because it rained, the cherry blossom petals have scattered.

Note: ば is no longer combined with the *MIZEN* form in modern Japanese, as it is now attached to the *IZEN* to express both 仮定 'hypothetical' and 確定 'existing' situations.

✢ Practice Questions

Translate the following sentences into English.

① 風吹かば、船出でず。
② 風吹けば、船出でられず。
③ 天子は、言はば救世主なり。

71

A Practical Guide for Scholarly Reading in Japanese

★ Answers and Explanations

① If the wind blows, the ship will probably not set sail.

風	吹か	ば	船	出で		ず
N	V 吹く *MIZEN*	CONJ-P (Hypothetical)	N	V 出づ *MIZEN*		AUX ず (Negative) *SHŪSHI*

Note: 吹かば is the combination of the verb 吹く 'to blow' in *MIZEN* and ば, indicating a conditional sentence. The sentence would thus be translated as 'if the wind blows.'

② Because the wind is blowing/blew, the boat cannot set sail.

風	吹け	ば	船	出で	られ	ず
N	V 吹く *IZEN*	CONJ-P (Logical connection)	N	V 出づ *MIZEN*	AUX らる (Potential) *MIZEN*	AUX ず (Negative) *SHŪSHI*

Note: 吹けば is the combination of the verb 吹く 'to blow' in *IZEN* and ば, indicating an existing situation. The sentence would thus be translated as 'because the wind blows.'

③ The Emperor is, what I would call, [Lit. if I say], a savior.

天子	は	言は	ば	救世主	なり
N	P	V 言ふ *MIZEN*	CONJ-P (Hypothetical)	N	AUX なり (Copular) *SHŪSHI*

Note: 言はば is the combination of the verb 言う 'to say' in *MIZEN* and ば, indicating a conditional sentence that would be translated as 'if you say.' It is an idiom that is still used in modern written Japanese to mean 言ってみれば (so to speak: Lit. if we try to speak).

Chapter 1 – "Toolbox": Essential Grammar for Scholarly Reading

8.6.2 とも, ど, ども, and も   Concessive Connections

とも is a hypothetical concessive, meaning 'even if.' ど/ども/も, on the other hand, is a direct concessive, meaning 'even though,' which is based on an actual (existing) situation. The conjugation for とも differs depending on the part of speech of the attached word (e.g., verb, adjective, and adjectival verb). とも follows inflected verbs in *SHŪSHI* and inflected adjectives in *RENYŌ*.   も follows inflected words in *RENTAI*, except for inflected adjectives, which it follows in *RENYŌ*.

Verbs

降る	とも	MJ
V 降る *SHŪSHI*	CONJ-P	たとえ降っても/たとえ降ったとしても Even if it rains

Adjectives

無く	とも	MJ
ADJ 無し *RENYŌ*	CONJ-P	たとえ無かったとしても/たとえ無かったとしても Even if it won't be there

Adjectival verbs

静かなり	とも	MJ
ADJ-V 静かなり *RENYŌ*	CONJ-P	たとえ静かだとしても/たとえ静かだったとしても Even if it is quiet/Even if it was quiet

ど/ども/も, however, always follows an inflected word in the *IZEN* form. も follows inflected words in *RENTAI*, except for inflected adjectives, which it follows in *RENYŌ*.

Verbs

降れ	ども/ど	MJ
V 降る *IZEN*	CONJ-P	降ったけれども/降っているけれども Even though it rained/Even though it is raining
降る	も	
V 降る *RENTAI*	CONJ-P	

73

A Practical Guide for Scholarly Reading in Japanese

Adjectives

無_なけれ	ども	MJ
ADJ 無し *IZEN*	CONJ-P	無いけれども/無かったけれども Even though it is not there/Even though it was not there
無く	も	
ADJ 無し *RENYŌ*	CONJ-P	

Adjectival verbs

静_{しず}かなれ	ども	MJ
ADJ-V 静かなり *IZEN*	CONJ-P	静かだけれども/静かだったけれども Even though it is not there/Even though it was not there
静かなる	も	
ADJ-V 静かなり *RENTAI*	CONJ-P	

✣ Practice Questions

Translate the following sentences into English.

① 風_{かぜ}吹_ふくとも、行_いかむ。

② 風_{かぜ}吹_ふけども、行_いかむ。

③ 難_{むずか}しくとも、諦_{あきら}めるな。

④ 失敗_{しっぱい}は明_{あき}らかなれども、特_{とく}に咎_{とが}め無_なし。

⑤ 宰相_{さいしょう}は相當_{そうとう}の權力_{けんりょく}を有_{ゆう}したるも、…

★ Answers and Explanations

① Even if the wind blows, (I) will not go.

風_{かぜ}	吹_ふく	とも	行_いか	ず
N	V 吹く *SHŪSHI*	CONJ-P (Hypothetical concessive)	V 行く *MIZEN*	AUX ず (Negative) *SHŪSHI*

Note: 吹_ふくとも is the combination of the verb 吹_ふく 'to blow' in *SHŪSHI* and the conjunctive particle とも. It is a concessive conjunction (hypothetical) and means 'even if it blows.'

74

Chapter 1 – "Toolbox": Essential Grammar for Scholarly Reading

② Even though the wind is blowing, (I) will go.

風	吹け	ども	行か	む
N	V 吹く *IZEN*	CONJ-P (Direct concessive)	V 行く *MIZEN*	AUX む (Intentional) *SHŪSHI*

Note: 吹けども is the combination of the verb 吹く 'to blow' in *IZEN* and the concessive conjunctive particle ども. The combined phrase means 'although it blows.'

③ Do not give up even if it is hard.

難しく	とも	諦める	な
ADJ 難し *RENYŌ*	CONJ-P (Hypothetical concessive)	V 諦める *SHŪSHI*	P

Note: 難しくとも is the combination of the adjective 難し(い) 'difficult' in *RENYŌ* and とも. The phrase means 'even if it is difficult.'

④ Although it was clearly a failure, no one in particular was blamed.

失敗	は	明らかなれ	ども	特に	咎め	無し
N	P	ADJ-V 明らかなり *IZEN*	CONJ-P (Direct concessive)	ADV	N	ADJ 無し *SHŪSHI*

Note: 明らかなれども is the combination of the adjectival verb 明らかなり 'clear' in *IZEN* and the concessive conjunctive particle ども. The phrase means 'although it is clear.'

⑤ Although the chancellor held considerable authority,

宰相	は	相當	の	權力	を	有し	たる	も
N	P	N	P	N	P	V 有す *RENYŌ*	AUX たり (Perfective) *RENTAI*	CONJ-P

Note: 有したるも is the combination of the verb 有す 'to hold,' the auxiliary verb たり, and the concessive conjunctive particle も. The phrase means 'although (the chancellor) held.'

8.6.3 に and を   Causal, Concessive, and Simple Connections

The conjunctive particles に and を, which can be used to express 'existing situations,' are frequently used in classical Japanese. The particles may also be used as the causal conjunction 'because,' the simple conditional relationship 'when/if,' and the concessive conjunction 'even if/even though.' The meaning is determined from the context in which the particles are used.

75

A Practical Guide for Scholarly Reading in Japanese

Function	① 〜と If/when/whenever (simple) 〜
	② 〜ので Because/as (logical/causal) 〜
	③ 〜のに Even though (concessive) 〜
Follows	*RENTAI*

The following table summarizes the conjugations and uses of the particles に and を.

言_いふ	に/を	MJ
V 言ふ *RENTAI*	CONJ-P	言うとすると (simple) When you say
		言うので (logical/causal) Because you say
		言うのに (concessive) Although you say

高_{たか}き	に/を	MJ
ADJ 高し *RENTAI*	CONJ-P	高いとすると (simple) When it is high
		高いので (logical/causal) Because it is high
		高いのに (concessive) Although it is high

静_{しず}かなる	に/を	MJ
ADJ-V 静かなり *RENTAI*	CONJ-P	静かだとすると (simple) When it is quiet
		静かなので (logical/causal) Because it is quiet
		静かなのに (concessive) Although it is quiet

✣ Practice Questions

Translate the following sentences into English.

① 態度_{たいど}から察_{さっ}するに、隠_{かく}し事_{ごと}あらむ。

② 雪_{ゆき}の降_ふりたるを、寒_{さむ}からざりけり。

③ 春_{はる}になるに、いまだ花咲_{はなさ}かず。

④ あまり憎_{にく}きに、その法師_{ほうし}をばまづ斬_きれ。

⑤ 日_ひのいとうららかなるに、海_{うみ}の面_{おもて}のいみじうのどかなり。

★ Answers and Explanations

① Judging from [his] attitude, [he] is probably hiding something.

察_{さっ}する	に	隠_{かく}し事_{ごと}	あら	む
V [察] す *RENTAI*	CONJ-P	N	V あり *MIZEN*	AUX む (Speculative) *SHŪSHI*

Chapter 1 – "Toolbox": Essential Grammar for Scholarly Reading

Note: 察するに consists of the verb 察する in the *RENTAI* and に ('supposing/when'). 隠し事 ('secret') is a nominal. あらむ is the combination of the verb あり in the *MIZEN* and the *SHŪSHI* of む, an auxiliary verb for conjectures.

② Although it snowed, it was not cold.

雪[ゆき]	の	降[ふ]り	たる	を
N	P	V 降る *RENYŌ*	AUX たり (Perfective) *RENTAI*	CONJ-P

Note: From context, を indicates the concessive meaning 'although.'

③ Although it is spring, the flowers (cherry blossoms) have not bloomed yet.

春[はる]	に	なる	に
N	P	V なり *RENTAI*	CONJ-P

Note: From context, に (CONJ-P) indicates the concessive meaning 'although.'

④ Because we hate him so much, kill the monk first.

あまり	にくき	に
ADV	ADJ にくし *RENTAI*	CONJ-P

Note: From context, に indicates the causal meaning 'because.'

⑤ Because this is such a lovely day, the sea (surface) is nice and peaceful.

日[ひ]	の	いと	うららかなる	に
N	P	ADV	ADJ-V うららかなり *RENTAI*	CONJ-P

Note: From context, に indicates the causal relationship 'because.'

8.6.4 して Causal, Concessive, and Simple Connections

The conjunctive particle して follows *RENYŌ*, often appearing after adjectives, the negative auxiliary verb ず (*RENYŌ* is ず), and the copular auxiliary verb なり (*RENYŌ* is に). Its meanings include "while (in that condition) (existing condition)," "because of ~ (reason, cause)," and "but ~; despite ~ (concessive)."

Function	① While (in that condition) (existing condition) ② Because of ~ (reason, cause) ③ Even though (concessive)
Follows	*RENYŌ*

77

A Practical Guide for Scholarly Reading in Japanese

The following table summarizes the conjugations and uses of the particle して.

雨	降ら	ず	して	MJ		
N	V 降る *MIZEN*	AUX ず (Negative) *RENYŌ*	CONJ-P	降らなくて　Without raining 降らないので　Because it does not rain 降らないのに　Although it does not rain		

高く			して	MJ		
ADJ 高し *RENYŌ*			CONJ-P	高くて　Being high 高いので　Because it is high 高いのに　Although it is high		

静かに			して	MJ		
ADJ-V 静かなり *RENYŌ*			CONJ-P	静かで　Being quiet 静かなので　Because it is quiet 静かなのに　Although it is quiet		

最初	に		して	最後	の	チャンス	MJ
N	AUX なり (Copular) *RENYŌ*		CONJ-P	N	P	N	最初で Being the first

Note that にして can also mean "to regard X as Y." It must be determined from the context.

例：制度の上に於ては貴族の権力を認めぬ事<u>にして</u>も、實際の政治には尚其形式が殘つて、政治は貴族との協議體となつた。

Example: Even if aristocratic authority was regarded as unrecognizable from the standpoint of the system, in reality the form still remained in the actual politics, and politics became carried out in cooperation with the aristocrats.

✛ Practice Questions

Translate the following sentences into English.

① 戦わずして勝つ。
② 世間小学の数少なからずして至る所就学の便あり…。
③ 人にして人にあらず。

78

Chapter 1 – "Toolbox": Essential Grammar for Scholarly Reading

④ 唐の朋黨は單に權力の爭ひを專らとする貴族中心のものにして、宋代になりては、著しく政治上の主義が朋黨の上に表はれた。

⑤ 典故ある古語を主とせずして、俗語を以て自由に表現するやうに變つた。

⑥ 君主は臣民全體の代表者にあらずして、夫自身が絕對權力の主體となつた。

⑦ 君の説を正しいとして、これが説明できるか。

★ Answers and Explanations

① Win without fighting.

戦わ	ず	して	勝つ
V 戦う *MIZEN*	AUX ず (Negative) *RENYŌ*	CONJ-P	V 勝つ *SHŪSHI*

② There are no small number of elementary schools throughout society, and everywhere you go there are opportunities to enroll.

少なから	ず	して
ADJ 少なし *MIZEN*	AUX ず (Negative) *RENYŌ*	CONJ-P

③ A human but not a human [i.e., biologically a human but lacking humanity].

人	に	して	人	に	あら	ず
N	AUX なり (Copular) *RENYŌ*	CONJ-P	N	AUX なり (Copular) *RENYŌ*	V あり *MIZEN*	AUX ず (Negative) *SHŪSHI*

④ Factions in the Tang were entities centered around aristocrats and simply occupied with struggles over authority, while in the Song stark differences in political beliefs appeared along factional lines.

貴族中心	の	もの	に	して
N	P	N	AUX なり (Copular) *RENYŌ*	CONJ-P

79

A Practical Guide for Scholarly Reading in Japanese

⑤ Rather than primarily using archaic words with well-known sources, it became possible to freely express oneself with slang.

主	と	せ	ず	して
N	P	V する *MIZEN*	AUX ず (Negative) *RENYŌ*	CONJ-P

⑥ The emperor was not the representative of all his subjects but himself the agent of absolute authority.

代表者	に	あら	ず	して
N	P	V ある *MIZEN*	AUX ず (Negative) *RENYŌ*	CONJ-P

⑦ If we suppose your theory is correct, can you explain this?

君	の	説	を	正しい	と	し	て
N	P	N	P	ADJ 正しい *SHŪSHI*	P	V する *RENYŌ*	CONJ-P

Note: Here, we can judge from the context that して is not a particle.

8.7 連体形 *Attributive Form + Particle*

RENTAI is typically a conjugation form that serve as noun modifiers, but there are some cases where the modified noun is omitted. When the omitted noun is not identifiable from context, it tends to be either 'some issue こと/の,' 'someone 人,' 'some time とき,' or 'something もの.'

▶*Examples*

1) 花の咲きたる(こと)を知る。

I realized that flowers are blooming.

花	の	咲き	たる	(こと)	を	知る
N	P	V 咲く *RENYŌ*	AUX たり (Perfective) *RENTAI*	(N)	P	V 知る *SHŪSHI*

2) 負ける(こと)が勝ち。

To lose is to win.

負ける	(こと)	が	勝ち*
V 負ける *RENTAI*	(N)	P	N

*勝ち is the *RENYŌ* of the verb 勝つ which has been nominalized.

80

Chapter 1 – "Toolbox": Essential Grammar for Scholarly Reading

3) 気概ある（人）は少なし。

There are few people who are strong-spirited.

気概	ある	（人）	は	少なし
N	V あり *RENTAI*	N	P	ADJ

4) 之を詩派に名くる（時）に及びて…特別の意義を有するに至る。

When these are given as names to poetic schools, they begin to hold special meanings, …

これ	を	詩派	に	名くる	（時）	に	及び	て
Pronoun	P	N	P	V 名く *RENTAI*	(N)	P	V 及ぶ *RENYŌ*	CONJ-P

It should be noted that there are cases where *RENTAI* is used at the end of the sentence in place of *SHŪSHI*. (See 8.5.1)

In the example below, ぬ (the *RENTAI* of ず) is used at the end of the sentence.

例：説明しなければならぬ。

You must explain.

◆Application Problems

Next, do these classical grammar exercises taken from the NAITŌ Konan text in Chapter 2, Section 5.

1. Out of the list below, choose the correct meaning from A, B, or C for the following なり.

> A. Verb 'to become; to come to'
>
> B. Auxiliary verb (copular) 'to be'
>
> C. Adjectival-verb ending

(1) 普通に用ふる語なるが、……

(2) 宋代は近世の發端となりて、……

(3) 如何なる點に於て、……

(4) 所謂郡望なるものゝ本體がこれである。

(5) 第一流の貴族は必ず天子宰相になるとも限らない。

(6) 唐太宗が天子になれるとき、……

(7) 高い官職につくのにも家柄としての特權がなくなり、……

(8) 明清時代は獨裁政治の完全なる①形式をつくることゝなり②、……

(9) 唐代の宦官は天子の眷族の有力なる部分となつて、……

(10) 黨派を作る主要なる目的となつたのである。

81

A Practical Guide for Scholarly Reading in Japanese

★ Answers and Explanations

> A: Follows the particle と or に, or the *RENYŌ* of a conjugating word.
>
> B: Follows a nominal.
>
> C: Follows a nominal which creates an adjectival verb (a word that expresses a condition).

(1)　　B　　Follows N 語

(2)　　A　　Follows P と

(3)　　C　　Follows N 如何 which creates ADJ-V

(4)　　B　　Follows N 郡望

(5)　　A　　Follows P に

(6)　　A　　Follows P に

(7)　　A　　Follows the *RENYŌ* of ADJ なし

(8)　① C Follows N 完全 which creates ADJ-V　　② A　　Follows P と

(9)　　C　　Follows N 有力 which creates ADJ-V

(10)　　C　　Follows N 主要 which creates ADJ-V

◈ Application Problems

2. Out of the list below, choose the correct meaning and conjugated form for the following たる.

> A. Auxiliary verb たり (Perfective) in *RENTAI* 'has done; has been'
>
> B. Auxiliary verb たり (Copular) in *RENTAI* 'to be'

(1) 著しく異りたる點がある。

(2) 君主獨裁政治が起りたる事で、……

(3) 其家柄が自然に地方の名望家として永續したる關係から生じたるもので、……

(4) これは實力あるものゝ手に歸したるが、……

(5) 貴族階級中の一の機關たる事を免るゝ事が出來ない。

(6) 殆ど祕書官同様となりたるが、……

(7) 宰相は相當の權力を有したるも、……

(8) 君主を擁したる貴族團體

(9) 奴隷小作人たる位置から、……

(10) 幾度も舊說を變じたるも、……

82

Chapter 1 – "Toolbox": Essential Grammar for Scholarly Reading

★ Answers and Explanations

> A: Follows the *RENYŌ* of a conjugating word.
>
> B: Follows a nominal.

(1) A Follows the *RENYŌ* of V 異なる

(2) A Follows the *RENYŌ* of V 起こる

(3) A Follows the *RENYŌ* of V 永続す

(4) A Follows the *RENYŌ* of V 帰す

(5) B Follows N 機関

(6) A Follows the *RENYŌ* of V なる

(7) A Follows the *RENYŌ* of V 有す

(8) A Follows the *RENYŌ* of V 擁す

(9) B Follows N 小作人

(10) A Follows the *RENYŌ* of V 変ず

◈ Application Problems

3. Among る below, choose AUX り (Perfective) in *RENTAI*.

(1) 唐宋時代といふことは普通に用ふる語なるが、……

(2) 唐太宗が天子になれるとき、……

(3) これに代れるものが君主獨裁政治である。

(4) 全く天子の權力によりて任命せらるゝ事となつた。

(5) 支那を征服せるがために、……

(6) 宰相の仕事をとれるものは殿閣大學士であつて、……

(7) 後に明の時にも宦官が跋扈せるも、……

(8) 人民の參政權を認むるといふことは*、……

(9) 單に紙幣のみを流通せしむることゝなつた。

(10) 幾度も舊說を變じたるも、……

★ Answers and Explanations

Follows *yodan* V in *IZEN* or *sahen* V in *MIZEN*.

(1) × Follows N

(2) ○ Follows なれ, *yodan* V なる in *IZEN*

(3) ○ Follows 代れ, *yodan* V 代る in *IZEN*

83

A Practical Guide for Scholarly Reading in Japanese

(4) ☓ Follows (任命せ)らるる, AUX (Passive) らる in *RENTAI*

(5) ◯ Follows 征服せ, *sahen* V 征服す in *MIZEN*

(6) ◯ Follows とれ, *yodan* V とる in *IZEN*

(7) ◯ Follows 跋扈, *sahen* V 跋扈す in *MIZEN*

(8) ☓ Follows 認むる, V 認むる in *SHŪSHI**

(9) ☓ Follows (流通せ)しむる, AUX (Causative) しむ in *RENTAI*

(10) ☓ Follows (変じ)たる, AUX (Perfective) たり in *RENTAI*

* The roughly 80 years from Meiji to the mid-Shōwa were a period of transition from classical Japanese to modern Japanese during which the two existed intermingled with each other. 認むる is *RENTAI*, and its *SHŪSHI* is 認む in the classical Japanese grammar. On the other hand, in the modern Japanese grammar, 認める is a *ru*-verb (下一段 conjugating verb), and both its *SHŪSHI* and *RENTAI* are 認める.

◇ Application Problems

4. Answer with the readings and the meanings of the underlined 当て字 and 国字 below. Examples are taken from the NAITŌ text.

(1) しかし<u>兎も角</u>、……

(2) 其ために當時系譜學が盛んになつた<u>位</u>である。

(3) 貴族でなければ高い官職に就く事が<u>出來</u>なかつたが、……

(4) 後者は君主に<u>不都合</u>あればこれを諫め、……

(5) 若くは責任を全く負擔する古代の宰相の<u>俤</u>はなくなり、……

(6) 然し唐代の科擧は其方法が<u>矢張</u>依然として貴族的なりしが、……

(7) 南宋に至りては<u>餘程</u>盛んになりしものらしく、……

(8) 唐代を通じては新派が舊派を壓倒する<u>譯</u>には行かなかつた、……

(9) 樂律も形式的であり、動作に<u>物眞似</u>などの意味は少くして、……

★ Answers

(1) ともかく in any case (2) ぐらい so...as to ~ (3) でき can (4) ふつごう inconvenience (5) おもかげ trace; vestige (6) やはり still (7) よほど greatly (8) わけ〔わけにはいかない〕 cannot; impossible (9) ものまね mimicry

Chapter 1 – "Toolbox": Essential Grammar for Scholarly Reading

9. The Influence of Chinese Texts in Japanese

There were many instances in the past when academic texts were written in 漢文 *kanbun* (literary Chinese). In order for Japanese people to read these Chinese texts, a type of Japanese reading with a special grammar was created. Since the Meiji era (1868–), the use of *kanbun* has generally decreased; however, its style continues to be used in scholarly texts. There are thus, grammar structures that are characteristic of the Japanese reading of *kanbun* that can still be seen in academic texts. Grammar expressions that are used frequently are listed below.

9.1 Expressions Used for Japanese Readings

9.1.1 Causative Expressions

The Causee Marker for the Causative をして

をして corresponds to を or に in modern Japanese. をして was often used to mark the causee for the Japanese readings of *kanbun*. See p. 67.

▶ *Example Sentences*

① このような状況は、個々の研究者**をして**躊躇させる。

Cf. このような状況は、個々の研究者**を**躊躇させる。 (MJ)

(These types of circumstances cause individual researchers to hesitate.)

The Causative Auxiliary Verb しむ

When reading *kanbun* in Japanese, the particle しむ was generally used for auxiliary verbs in the causative. す and さす are also used as causative auxiliary verbs in classical Japanese, but in academic texts, しむ is often used due to the influence of Japanese *kanbun* readings. Please refer to the auxiliary verb conjugation table (p. 261).

▶ *Example Sentences*

① 唐代の文人は、それまでの暦法に関する知識を集大成し、之を発展せ**しめ**た。

Cf. 唐代の文人は、それまでの暦法に関する知識を集大成し、之を発展さ**せ**た。(MJ)

(Scholars of the Tang Dynasty compiled knowledge regarding calendars of previous eras and were responsible for its development.)

(Lit. allowed it to develop/made it possible to develop)

85

A Practical Guide for Scholarly Reading in Japanese

9.1.2 所

● **9.1.2.1 Verb（連体形 attributive form）＋所：Nominalization**

The ところ in Verb (attributive form) ＋所 has the function of nominalizing the verb. It means
〜すること/もの. This expression was also influenced by the Japanese reading of *kanbun*.

➤ *Examples*

① 欲する所 ➡ 欲すること　　　　　　desiring

② 遵守すべき所である　　　　　　　　something that should be obeyed

➡ 遵守すべきこと（もの）である

● **9.1.2.2 Verb (attributive form) ＋所と為る：Passive Expression**

Due to the fact that 所 is also used for passive expressions in *kanbun*, the form 〜ところとな
る carries with it a passive meaning.

▶ *Example Sentences*

① それは後世の厳しく非難する所と為った。

Cf. それは後世に厳しく非難された。

It was sharply criticized by future generations.

② よき官職は皆これらの人々の占むる所となつた。

Cf. よき官職は皆これらの人々に占められた。

All of the good government posts were occupied by these people.

9.2 漢語 *Verbification, Adjectivization, and Adverbization*

Kango normally means 'Chinese compounds' or 'Chinese words,' and only refers to 音読
み, Chinese derived reading of a kanji. *Kango* are noun phrases that are used to derive verbs,
adjectives, and adverbs. These *kango* expressions are frequently used in academic Japanese texts.

① Verbification

Kango ＋す（る）: attach す or する to the Chinese word

➤ *Examples*

比す/比する　　　　　（=比べる）　　to compare

死す/死する　　　　　（=死ぬ）　　　to die

存す/存する　　　　　（=ある）　　　to exist

有す/有する　　　　　（=持つ）　　　to hold; to own

発展す/発展する　　　（=発展する）　to develop

帰国す/帰国する　　　（=国に帰る）　to return to one's country

86

② Adjectivization

な is attached to the Chinese word.

➤*Examples*

柔軟な〔じゅうなん〕 flexible
簡単な〔かんたん〕 easy
特別な〔とくべつ〕 special
有名な〔ゆうめい〕 famous

Note: In the case of archaic words, なり or たり is used. (See 8.4.2)

③ Adverbization

Chinese word ＋ に/と ➡ Japanese adverbial form

～に	～と	～に and ～と
柔軟に〔じゅうなん〕 (flexibly)	悠々と〔ゆうゆう〕 (easily)	自然に・自然と〔しぜん・しぜん〕 (naturally)
簡単に〔かんたん〕 (easily)	堂々と〔どうどう〕 (confidently)	不思議に・不思議と〔ふしぎ・ふしぎ〕 (strangely)
特別に〔とくべつ〕 (especially)	平然と〔へいぜん〕 (calmly)	意外に・意外と〔いがい・いがい〕 (unexpectedly)
有名に〔ゆうめい〕 (famously)	淡々と〔たんたん〕 (indifferently)	次々に・次々と〔つぎつぎ・つぎつぎ〕 (one after another)

There are some expressions that can function as adverbs without ～に or ～と.

➤*Examples*

相当〔そうとう〕 (quite), 随分〔ずいぶん〕 (very much), 一生懸命〔いっしょうけんめい〕 (with great effort), 段々〔だんだん〕 (more and more),
絶対〔ぜったい〕 (absolutely), 大抵〔たいてい〕 (mostly), 一切〔いっさい〕 (never), 全然〔ぜんぜん〕*([not] at all), 次々〔つぎつぎ〕 (one after another)

*全然, in some cases, can mean "totally" in affirmative sentences. Cf. p. 202, Line 3.

Chapter 2 Section 1
What Are Modifiers?
(Mechanisms of Modifying Sentences in Japanese)

One of the challenges in reading complex texts, such as scholarly texts, is to find the relationship between the modifier and modified. *Modifying* means to qualify or to give additional information about modified elements. Because one single sentence often embeds multiple modified parts within the sentence, identifying the coherent unit of the modifier and the modified is essential for reading the text accurately. This is especially true of complex texts, where nouns are often modified by multiple sentences. For this reason, each reading text in Chapter 2 contains grammar practices to identify the relationship of noun-modifying clauses (i.e. relative clauses) and modified nouns (i.e. head nouns) as coherent units. The question is how we can identify such coherent units. In this section, we discuss some key points of identifying the modifying–modified relationships of sentences, especially placing emphasis on noun-modifying sentences.

As shown in the diagram below, modified elements can be mainly grouped into two types, (A) Noun Type and (B) Non-Noun Type. Noun Type modified elements are basically nouns, including formal nouns and nominalizers (e.g. の, こと). Formal nouns are those which "cannot stand alone and need to be modified by a demonstrative (e.g. そんな) or a clause" (McGloin et al. 2014). Examples include もの, ところ 'particular time or aspect,' わけ 'reason,' はず 'expectation,' つもり 'intention,' ため 'purpose,' etc. Non-Noun Types are non-noun elements such as verbs, adjectives, modals, and conjunctive particles (e.g. から, のに). In this section, we first discuss features of modified elements, then illustrate the modifier and modified relationships, focusing on noun-modifying sentences. Key points are summarized by discussing exemplifying cases such as 1) the particle は, 2) て-forms, and 3) subordinate clauses (e.g. clauses modifying conjunctive particles such as し, から and のに). First, consider the following diagram:

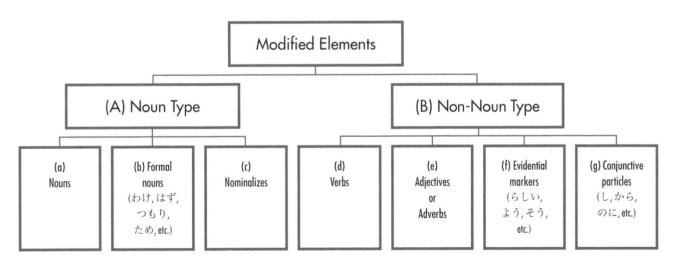

In the diagram above, (a) to (c) belong to Type (A), and (d) to (g) belong to Type (B).

A Practical Guide for Scholarly Reading in Japanese

Here are examples of a) through g). Elements marked by [ ] and elements in bold type indicate modifiers and modified elements, respectively.

Examples of Type (A): [Noun Types]

a) [古い] **本** [adjective][1] + noun
old book

b) [英語がよくできる] **わけ**だ。 [sentence] + formal noun
That explains why (someone) is good at English.

c) [料理をする] **の**が好きだ。 [sentence] + nominalizer
I like cooking.

Examples of Type (B): [Non-Noun Types]

d) [ゆっくり] **歩く** [adverb][2] + verb
walk slowly

e) [とても] **おいしい** [adverb] + adjective
very tasty

[とても] **速く** [adverb] + adverb
very fast

f) [明日、天気が悪化する] **ようだ** [clause] + modal
It looks like the weather will get worse tomorrow.

g) {[今日は日曜だ] **から** }、道が込んでいない {[clause] + conjunctive particle}
Because today is Sunday, the roads are not busy. + sentence

In examples d) to g), 歩く, おいしい, 〜ようだ and 〜から are modified by [ゆっくり], [とても], [明日、天気が悪化する] and [今日は日曜だ], respectively. It should be noted that the sentence with a conjunctive particle itself (i.e. subordinate clause) can be considered as a modifier because the sentence functions to modify the main sentence. In example g), the から reason clause, {今日は日曜だから}, connects to the main sentence 道が込んでいない as a sentence unit of reason and consequence. In the following section we will discuss some features of noun modifiers in more detail.

---

1 Adjectives here include demonstrative adjectives such as このような 'like this,' そのような 'like that' and so on.
2 Adverbs here include demonstrative adverbs such as このように 'in this manner,' そのように 'in that way,' and so on.

Chapter 2 Section 1 – What Are Modifiers? (Mechanisms of Modifying Sentences in Japanese)

1.1   Modifying Nouns

When modified elements belong to Type (A), **all modifiers precede modified nouns.** This is one of the most important points of word order in Japanese. Below, the elements marked by [ ] are modifiers and the elements in bold type are the modified nouns.

1) Noun A *no* Noun B (Noun A modifies Noun B)

   [日本^Aの]**人口**^B

   population [of Japan]

2) [*i*-adjective] noun

   [高い]**車**

   [expensive] car

3) [*na*-adjective] noun

   [静かな]**ところ**

   [quiet] place

4) [sentence] noun

   [電車で通勤する]**人**が多い。

   There are many people [who commute by train].

Case 4) can be the most complex because a noun-modifying sentence may contain elements which are themselves modified by noun-modifying sentences. In other words, **noun-modifying sentences can be nested within each other**. This point is illustrated in example 5):

5) 私が５年前に教えた**学生**が書いた**論文**を読んだ。

   I read **an article** [which **a student** whom I taught 5 years ago wrote].

Here, there are two modified nouns, 学生 'student' and 論文 'article.' The modifiers of 学生 and 論文 are marked by [ ] and { }, respectively.

{[私が５年前に教えた] **学生**が書いた } **論文**を読んだ。

In general, a modified noun is grammatically related to the predicate of the preceding modifying sentence (e.g. sentence subject, (in)direct object). For example, 学生 has a grammatical relationship with (私が５年前に)教えた as the direct object of the verb. 論文 is the direct object of the verb 書いた. 学生 is also the subject of the verb 書いた (the student wrote the article), an element which is part of the modifying sentence of 論文. The modifying sentences of both 学生 and 論文 start from 私, as the modifying sentence of 学生 is included in the modifying sentence of 論文.

91

A Practical Guide for Scholarly Reading in Japanese

One of the reasons why it is difficult to identify the relationships between noun-modifying sentences and head nouns is that, unlike English, **there are no relative pronouns such as 'who,' 'whom,' 'which,' or 'that' in Japanese.** The lack of such relative pronouns may make it difficult to understand the clausal relationships of noun-modifier sentences. For this reason, it is important to find where each noun-modifier sentence begins and which elements are inside or outside the modifying sentence (Makino and Tsutsui 1986). In the following sections, we will discuss general rules to find the relationships between the modifier and modified, focusing on modifying sentences.

1.2   *The Particle* は

The particle は may be used to introduce the topic of a sentence as in example 6) or to express contrast as in example 7) below.

6)　東京は日本の首都だ。
Speaking of Tokyo, it is the capital city of Japan.

7)　魚は嫌いだが、肉は好きだ。
I don't like fish, but I like meat.

The topic of the sentence indicates what the sentence is about. In example 6), the topic is 東京 and the rest of the sentence is about 東京, that is, 'it is the capital city of Japan.' The information marked by the topic marker は is generally assumed to be shared by or 'identifiable' by both the speaker and the listener (Hasegawa 2018).[3] In example 7), は is used to express contrast between 魚 and 肉.

How can we identify whether or not the element marked by は is inside of a noun-modifier sentence? **When the element marked by the topic marker は is the subject of a noun-modifier sentence, it is generally outside of the noun-modifier sentence**[4] as in example 8). Below, the modified noun 車 indicated in bold and the modifying sentence is indicated by [ ].

8)　父は[私が10年前に買った]**車**に乗っている。
My father drives **a car** [which I bought 10 years ago].

---

3 It should be noted that although the element marked by は commonly indicates the sentence subject, this may not always be the case:

きのう市場で桃を買った。桃は友達に分けてあげた。
I bought peaches at the market yesterday. As for the peaches, I shared them with my friends.
Here, 桃, the topic of the second sentence, is the direct object of 分けてあげた.

4 The subject of a noun-modifying sentence is generally marked by が, not は. Hence, は does occur in the following sentence:

[ジョンが/*は買った]**車**は日本の車だ。
The car [which John bought] is a Japanese car.

92

Chapter 2 Section 1 – What Are Modifiers? (Mechanisms of Modifying Sentences in Japanese)

In example 8), the modifier of 車 starts from 私, which is the subject of the modifying sentence. 父 connects to 乗っている, the element which is outside the modifier.

The element marked by the contrastive は, on the other hand, is generally included inside the noun-modifier sentence. In example 9), 刺身 is part of the modifier of 人 because the は is used to contrast 刺身 vs. other dishes.

9) [刺身は食べない]人でも、これは食べられるだろう。

Even for **people** [who don't eat sashimi], this (dish) should be ok.

This rule about the contrastive marker は can also be applied to cases where the modified word is a Non-Noun type. Consider the following:

10) 父は[今日は会社を休む]と言った。

My father said that [he would take a day off <u>today</u>].

The particle と indicates a quotation. It can be used to quote the content of what someone thinks, believes, feels, writes, hears, or explains. In the above sentence, 父 and 今日 are marked by the particle は. 父 is outside the と clause because it indicates the subject of the main sentence and connects to 言った. 今日は, on the other hand, is inside the と clause because the particle は is used to express a contrast between today and other days. This point becomes clearer when 10) is compared with 11). In 11), 今日 is not marked by は.

11) 父は今日会社を休むと言った。

Here, the sentence can be interpreted either as a) or b) below depending on which element the temporal expression 今日 modifies, 言った or 休む.

a) My father said <u>today</u> that he will take a day off.
b) My father said that he will take a day off <u>today</u>.

In a), 今日 modifies the verb, 言った(= 今日言った), while in b), 今日 modifies 休む (= 今日休む). It should be noted that in many cases, the use of punctuation may clarify the interpretation. For example, if 今日 is marked by the Japanese comma, as in (今日、), then the sentence should be interpreted as a) rather than b).

1.3 The て-Form as a Conjunction

The て-form of predicates (verbs, *i*-adjectives, the copula だ) functions as a conjunction and connects two or more clauses. When the て-form is used as a conjunction, the form is

93

commonly used to express the relationship of conjoined clauses such as sequential 'and then,' causal 'and so,' or a coordination 'and' (McGloin et al. 2014). **The clauses connected with the て-form can be either inside or outside the modifying sentence depending on the context.** In the following example, 倒産して is inside the modifying sentence of 人 because it connects to 探し始めた. Here, the clause with the て-form, 倒産して, expresses a causal meaning, while 探し始めた indicates the consequence. Hence, the modifier of 人 starts from 16年勤めた, as indicated in [ ].

12) [16年勤めた会社が倒産して、新しい仕事を探し始めた] 人に会った。

    I met **someone** [who started searching for a new job after the company he worked at for 16 years went bankrupt].

    However, in example 13), the て-form, 倒産して, is not included in the noun-modifying sentence of 会社:

13) 会社が倒産して、[友人が経営している] 会社に勤めることに決めた。

    My company went bankrupt, and (so) I have decided to work at **the company** [which my friend owns].

    In this example, the て-form, 倒産して, is associated with 決めた, not with 経営している. 倒産して expresses the reason for the decision 'to work at the company which my friend owns.' Hence, it is outside the modifying sentence of 会社. **As the examples above show, the key is to identify which predicates the て-form is combined with.**

1.4 Subordinate Clauses: Clauses with Conjunctive Particles

Just like the て-form, it is important to determine which sentences subordinate clauses are combined with.[5] Subordinate clauses are marked with conjunctive particles such as ので, から, けれど, たら, and ば and add to the main sentence the information such as reason 'because,' concession 'although,' condition 'if' (McGloin et al. 2014). In this section, we compare the cases where subordinate clauses are inside a noun-modifier sentence and those where they are outside.

---

5 Hasegawa (2018) explains that subordinate clauses are one of the three types of dependent clauses in Japanese, in addition to noun-modifying clauses and quotative clauses (p. 288).

Chapter 2 Section 1 – What Are Modifiers? (Mechanisms of Modifying Sentences in Japanese)

1.4.1 Concessive のに

In example 14) below, the conjunctive particle, のに is modified by the parts marked by [ ]. The parts which the のに clause modifies is indicated by underline.

14) [一生懸命勉強した] のに全然できなかった。

Even though I studied hard, I did not do well.

Here, the のに clause, 一生懸命勉強したのに modifies 全然できなかった. Example 14) may be an easy case, because it has only one predicate outside the のに clause. How about the cases where the のに clause has more than two or more predicates outside. Compare the following examples:

15) {[大学を卒業した] のに就職できない} 若者が増えている。

The number of **young people** {who cannot get a job [even though they have a college diploma]} is increasing.

16) {[事実を知っている] のに }[報復を恐れた] 兄は何も言わなかった。

My brother [who was afraid of retaliation] did not say anything {even though he knew the truth}.

In example 15), the のに clause is inside the modifying sentence of 若者 because the のに clause is associated with 就職できない, which is inside of the modifying sentence. In example 16), the のに clause is outside the modifying sentence of 兄 because the のに clause connects to 何も言わなかった, which is outside the modifier.

1.4.2 Reason Clause から

Clauses with から or ので causal conjunctive particles modify a predicate. In example 17), the から clause [日本で働きたい] から connects with 専攻している.

17) [日本で働きたい] から、日本語を専攻している。

[Because I want to work in Japan], I am majoring in Japanese.

95

A Practical Guide for Scholarly Reading in Japanese

How about the から clauses in 18) and 19)? Compare the sentences:

18) {[日本で働きたい] から日本語を専攻している } 学生からメールがあった。

I received an email message from **a student** {who is majoring in Japanese [because he wants to work in Japan]}.

19) [日本で働きたい] から [日本語の専攻がある] 大学に入った。

[Because I want to work in Japan] I entered **a college** [which offers Japanese as a major].

In example 18), the から clause 日本で働きたい connects to 専攻している, an element which is inside the noun-modifier sentence of 学生. Hence, the から clause is also inside. In example 19), on the other hand, the から clause 日本で働きたいから connects to the predicate 入った, not ある. The から clause here explains why someone chose a college which offers Japanese as a major. There may be ambiguous cases where a particular subordinate clause can be either inside or outside a noun-modifying sentence. Such cases can often be clarified by the context.

1.4.3 Conjunctive Particle し '(and) what is more'

The conjunctive particle し is used to list states, activities, or events which are connected or grouped together. Hence, in example 20), the clauses with し are inside of the modifier marked by [ ]. The part [頭もいいし、優しいし、信頼できる] lists the attributes of 山田さん and modifies 人 .

20) 山田は [頭もいいし、優しいし、信頼できる] 人だ。

Yamada is **someone** [who is smart, kind, and what is more, reliable].

21) {[物価は上がる] し、[失業する] 人も増えている } 状況が続いている。

The situation {in which prices are going up and the number of **people** [who are unemployed is increasing]}, continues.

The conjunctive particle し in example 21) lists events, (prices are going up) and (the number of people who are unemployed is increasing). The し clause is not inside of the noun-modifier sentence of 人. The conjoined sentences, on the other hand, are inside of the modifying sentence of 状況.

96

Chapter 2 Section 1 – What Are Modifiers? (Mechanisms of Modifying Sentences in Japanese)

2. Summary

In many cases, the relationship of the modifier–modified may depend on the context. However, there are some useful steps for finding the boundary of the modifying sentence:

i. Identify the modified words (i.e. Noun or Non-Noun types).

ii. Identify where a noun-modifying sentence (relative clause) begins.

iii. Determine whether the particle は in the modifying sentence has the meaning of topic or contrast (the element marked by topic marker は tends to be outside the modifier).

iv. For sentences with conjunctive particles (i.e. adverbial sentences), identify which elements they are conjoined with and whether the conjoined parts belong to the inside or outside of the modifying sentence.

v. For the て-form, identify which predicates the て-form is conjoined with and whether the conjoined predicates belong to the inside or outside of the noun-modifying sentence.

vi. To confirm that an element is outside (or inside) the modifying sentence, rearrange the position of the element in the sentence and see whether the sentence still makes sense (see example 24).

vii. When the sentence is ambiguous in terms of the modifying and modified relationship, consider the context.

3. Exercises

Identify where the modifying sentence of the modified word in the box, 説, starts.

22) 我が国の学界には、中国史の時代区分に関する二つの有力な**説**があり…

There are two major theories in our academic field on the periodization of Chinese history, and...

谷川道雄 (1987) 中国史の時代区分問題をめぐって―現時点からの省察―

In example 22), the modifying sentence of 説 starts from 中国史. 我が国の学界には is not inside of the modifying sentence of 説 because it modifies the predicate あり, which is outside the modifier.

97

A Practical Guide for Scholarly Reading in Japanese

我が国の学界には、[中国史の時代区分に関する二つの有力な] 説があり…

It should be noted that if an element modifies a word which is outside the modifier, the element also is outside the modifier. To probe this, you may rearrange the position of the word and see whether the sentence makes sense or not. For example, the following sentence is perfectly ok. if 我が国の学界には is positioned after the modifier:

中国史の時代区分に関する二つの有力な説が我が国の学界にはあり…

There are two major theories in our academic field on the periodization of Chinese history, and...

Example 23) below is a short passage and contains two modified words, ① and ②. Identify the modifier boundaries of each modified word:

23) 戦後しばらくの間は、歴史をいかに発展的にとらえるかが重要なモチーフであった
ために、時代区分問題が大いに論議されたが、そのような、いわば歴史主義的な関
心がうすれた今日では、当然時代区分論への情熱も低下したと考えられる。

For a while after the war, the issue of periodization had been widely discussed because the question of how to view (Chinese) history developmentally was thought to be an important motif, but now that this historical interest has diminished, it can be considered that the passion for periodization has also decreased.

谷川道雄 (1987) 中国史の時代区分問題をめぐって―現時点からの省察―

The modifying sentence of ため starts from 戦後 because 戦後しばらくの間は modifies モチーフであった, which is inside of the modifying sentence. The modifier of 今日 starts from そのような, which is a demonstrative adjective (a demonstrative which modifies nouns) and modifies 関心.

98

Chapter 2 Section 1 – What Are Modifiers? (Mechanisms of Modifying Sentences in Japanese)

　Example 24) also contains two modified words, ① and ②. Identify the modifier boundaries of each:

24) 題名^{だいめい}に示^{しめ}されているように、この番組^{ばんぐみ}は、黄河^{こうが}に象徴^{しょうちょう}される伝統文化^{でんとうぶんか}のために創造^{そうぞう}性^{せい}・発展性^{はってんせい}を圧殺^{あっさつ}されてきた中華民族^{ちゅうかみんぞく}の**悲運**^{ひうん}①を文明論^{ぶんめいろん}（文化哲学^{ぶんかてつがく}）の立場^{たちば}から映像化^{えいぞうか}した**もの**②である。

As suggested by the title, this (TV) program [is something which] displays from the standpoint of civilization theory (cultural philosophy) the misfortune of the Chinese people, whose creativity and development have been suppressed by their traditional culture, symbolized by the Yellow River.

矢内原忠雄^{やないはらただお} (1961)「言論自由の思想的根拠^{げんろんじゆう　しそうてきこんきょ}」

　Here, both the modifiers of 悲運^{ひうん} and もの start from 黄河^{こうが}. 悲運^{ひうん} (misfortune) is modified by 中華民族^{ちゅうかみんぞく} (the Chinese people), which is further modified by 黄河^{こうが}に象徴^{しょうちょう}される伝統文化^{でんとうぶんか}のために創造性^{そうぞうせい}・発展性^{はってんせい}を圧殺^{あっさつ}されてきた 'whose creativity and development have been suppressed by their traditional culture, symbolized by the Yellow River.' この番組^{ばんぐみ}, the topic of the sentence, connects to ものである as a sentence unit. The other elements between them are part of the modifier of もの.

Chapter 2 Section 2

TANIGAWA Michio 谷川道雄 (1925–2013). Scholar of East Asian History.

After graduating from Kyoto Imperial University (presently, Kyoto University), Tanigawa became a professor at Nagoya University before moving to Kyoto University in 1979 and Ryukoku University in 1997.

Tanigawa deepened and further developed NAITŌ Konan's 唐宋変革論 "Tang-Song Transition Theory," expounding his theory of powerful family communities in order to understand the powerful families and aristocrats of the Wei-Jin Northern and Southern Courts period. He took them to be feudal, land-owning powers and argued that this period was medieval. Through this, he raised a question of the traditional view of Chinese history as painted with the singular color of imperial rule throughout the span of 2,000 years beginning with the Qin and Han empires.

The present essay comes from 『中国中世の探求―歴史と人物』 *Exploring China's Medieval Period: History and People* (Japan Editors School Press, 1987). Other representative works include 『隋唐帝国形成史論』 *Historical Theory of the Formation of the Sui and Tang Empires* (Chikuma Shobō, 1971) and 『中国中世社会と共同体』 *Society and Community in China's Medieval Period* (Kokusho Kankōkai, 1976).

中国史の時代区分問題をめぐって
—現時点からの省察—

TANIGAWA Michio 谷川道雄 (1987) Chūgokushi no jidaikubun mondai o megutte

■ はじめに

本稿のタイトルを見て、いまさら時代区分問題でもあるまいと、**大方の読**(2)(1)
者はお考えであろう。周知の通り、我が国の学界には、中国史の時代区分に
関する二つの有力な説があり (その他にも諸説があるが)、それが戦後以来
ちょうど鉄道のレールのように平行線をなしたまま今日に至っている。そし
ておそらくは、今後も同じ状態のまま進んでゆくのではないかと予想される
のである。かつては両説の間にはげしい論戦が交わされたが、今ではもうそ
のようなことも行われなくなった。**その理由**(2)としては、幾つかのことが考え
られる。[A]**戦後しばらくの間は、歴史をいかに発展的にとらえるかが重要なモ
チーフであったために、時代区分問題が大いに論議されたが、そのような、
いわば歴史主義的な関心がうすれた今日**(3)**では、当然時代区分論への情熱も低
下したと考えられる**。第二には、時代区分のような、全時代を見とおすよう
な巨視的な**問題**(4)に関わるよりは、個々の歴史事象をミクロに観察し記述しよ
うとする傾向へと、歴史学の作風が転換してきた**点**(5)が挙げられよう。そして
第三には、中国史の時代区分において、両説は個々の点でたがいに影響しあっ
てきたものの、その原則においては**自らを持してゆずらず**(3)、それぞれの体系
と学派を形づくってきた。

内容質問

(1) 本文で述べられている重要な２つの説の関係は今どのような状態にありますか。

(2) 「大方の読者はお考えであろう」で、読者が「何を」考えているだろうと言っていますか。

(3) 「自らを持してゆずらず」とは、ここではどういう意味ですか。

文法質問

① 「大方の読者はお考えであろう」で、敬語を使っているのはなぜですか。

② 「その理由」は何を指しますか。

③ 「今日」の修飾部分はどこからですか。最初の三文字を答えなさい。

④ 「問題」の修飾部分はどこからですか。最初の三文字を答えなさい。

⑤ 「点」の修飾部分はどこからですか。最初の三文字を答えなさい。

英訳

Ⓐ 戦後しばらくの間は、歴史をいかに発展的にとらえるかが重要なモチーフであったために、時代区分問題が大いに論議されたが、そのような、いわば歴史主義的な関心がうすれた今日では、当然時代区分論への情熱も低下したと考えられる。

①そのため、論戦は一種の膠着状態におちいり、②この問題に触れることを避ける③傾向が生れたようにおもわれる。要するにこのような状況にある中国史の時代区分問題について語ることは、じつは私自身にとっても気の重い作業である。それにもかかわらず、私があえてここに筆をとったのは、つぎに述べ
5 る理由によるのである。

　時代区分問題を正面から論ずることは少なくなったとはいえ、何らかの時代区分によって中国史を理解することは、今日なお個々の研究者のなかで行われているとおもわれる。であるばかりでなく、何らかの時代区分説に対する研究者の④共通理解が前面に出ることさえ、まれではない。少し古い事例で
10 恐縮だが、私自身がメンバーの一人であった、ある共同研究の⑤成果は、『中国中世史研究——六朝隋唐の社会と文化——』(東海大学出版会、一九七〇年)というタイトルで刊行された。最近では、現在学生社より刊行中の『中世史講座』全十二巻(それ以前には『古代史講座』がある)は、世界各地域の中世史を網羅するものであり、そこには当然中国の中世史に関する論考を
15 収載するが、ここでの中世は、宋代以後を中世とする一方の説を採用している。また『史学雑誌』が毎号巻末に附載する文献目録も、同じ説によって「中国一般」「中国古代」「中国中世」「中国近現代」の四つの項目で中国史関係論文を分類し、古代と中世を唐宋の間で区切っていることは②周知の事実である。③要するに、時代区分は中国史研究者のなかに潜在的、顕在的に生きてい
20 るとおもわれるのである。

104

内容質問

(1) なぜ両説の間の論戦が行われなくなったと筆者は考えていますか。以下、正しいものに〇、正しくないものに X をつけなさい。

❶ （　　　）　歴史主義的な関心が少なくなったから
❷ （　　　）　全時代を見通すような問題がもっと大切になったから
❸ （　　　）　両説の論戦が一種の膠着状態になったから
❹ （　　　）　両説は今までも影響しあうことはなかったから

(2) 何が「周知の事実」ですか。

(3) 「要するに〜おもわれるのである」で筆者が言いたいことは何ですか。
次の❶〜❹の中から最も正しいものを選びなさい。

❶　中国史研究者は時代区分に全く関心がなかった。
❷　時代区分の問題は常に歴史家の議論の中心である。
❸　歴史家は何らかの形で時代区分を意識している。
❹　時代区分説に対する研究者の理解は共通している。

文法質問

① 「そのため」は何を指しますか。

② 「この問題」は何を指しますか。

③ 「傾向」の修飾部分はどこからですか。最初の三文字を答えなさい。

④ 「共通理解」の修飾部分はどこからですか。最初の三文字を答えなさい。

⑤ 「成果」の修飾部分はどこからですか。最初の三文字を答えなさい。

時代区分は歴史を大局的に、また普遍性においてとらえる方法の一つである。ひとがいかに個別的事象に関心を集中させようとも、それを全体史の一環として意味づけようとする①意識がはたらいている限り、その意識は時代区分の意識と決して無縁ではないであろう。また、いかに歴史主義的立場を排除しようとも、諸事象がおのずからにして表出する時代的性格を無視する歴史家はいないであろう。このようにして、それぞれの研究者は決して時代区分と無縁に生きているわけでなく、むしろ②それを背後に意識しつつ、それぞれの研究にたずさわっているのではなかろうか。

しかし、実情はさきに述べたごとくである。こころみに日本史や西洋史の場合を考えてみよう。③Aそれらの分野でも、時代区分の実際には諸説があって、なかなか(1)軌を一にすることが難しいのかも知れないが、しかしともかくも、古代といい、中世といえば、ことさらに注釈を加えなくても、そこにほぼ共通した時代観念を想定することができる。だが、中国史ではそうはいかない。後述するように、「中世」は「古代」であるかも知れず、「中世」はまた「近世」であるかも知れないのである。したがって、中国史において、たとえば中世論を展開しようとするならば、(2)つねに二説併記から始めなければならないのである。これを単に時代名称上での相違と片づけるわけにはゆかない。また、中国史の古代、中世等々がいつ始まりいつ終ったかという④問題に止まるものでもない。中国史に対する学問方法の問題、ひいては現代日本人の中国に対する理解方法の問題がからんでいるのである。(3)このような学問の根本におけるくいちがいが、時代区分上の亀裂として発現したと考えられるのである。

内容質問

⑴　「軌を一にする」とは、ここではどういう意味ですか。

⑵　「つねに二説併記から始めなければならない」のは、なぜですか。

⑶　「このような学問の根本におけるくいちがい」とは何を指しますか。

文法質問

①　「意識」の修飾部分はどこからですか。最初の三文字を答えなさい。

②　「それ」は何を指しますか。本文の言葉を使って答えなさい。

③　「それら」は何を指しますか。本文の言葉を使って答えなさい。

④　「問題」の修飾部分はどこからですか。最初の三文字を答えなさい。

英訳

Ⓐ　それらの分野でも、時代区分の実際には諸説があって、なかなか軌を一にすることが難しいのかも知れないが、しかしともかくも、古代といい、中世といえば、ことさらに注釈を加えなくても、そこにほぼ共通した時代観念を想定することができる。

[A] 以上のような意味をもった時代区分説の対立状態が今日凝固したままで あることは、個々の研究の進展にも影響していないであろうか。というのは、 このような状況は、個々の研究者をして事象を自由に、トータルに考えるこ とを躊躇させるおそれなしとしないからである。勿論、既成の説にとらられ ない立場もありうるし、①そうした立場が拡大することが学問の発展には望 ましい。しかしそれと同時に、既成の説の対立点の根拠を問うことで、(1)この 凝固した状態に生きた血流を通わす必要があるのではなかろうか。断ってお くが、私は両説の統一や妥協を計ろうというのではない。またかつての論争 に結着をつけようというのでもない。あくまで両説の相違点をできるだけ深 く見つめたいとおもうのである。これまで説の一方にくみしてきた私にとっ て②この作業を公平に行うことは、(2)至難のわざであるが、あえてこれを試みる ことによって、この方面の一歩前進を期したいのである。

■ 二つの六朝論

　　二つの時代区分説のうち、一つは、いうまでもなく、今世紀の初頭、内 藤湖南によって提唱され、その後継者たちによって今日まで支持されてきた ③学説である。湖南が、中国史の時代区分を唐宋とか明清とか、朝代によっ て行なってきた従来の④方法は史学的には不正確であるとし、「時代を形成す る内容」（『支那近世史』）による区分を⑤主張したことはよく知られている。 中国史の時代区分法はかれによって一挙に原理的なレベルにまで高められ、 ⑥それじたいが歴史学の一分野となったのであった。いまひとつの学説は、戦 後内藤説に対置して提出されたもので、この説の形成には、歴史学研究会 が指導的な役割を果たした。⑦そこには戦中の歴史学に対する反省が契機と なっており、方法的には生産様式の継起的発展を時代区分の原則としている。

内容質問

⑴ 「この凝固した状態に生きた血流を通わす」とはどういう意味ですか。

⑵ 何が「至難のわざ」ですか。また、それはどうしてか説明しなさい。

文法質問

① 「そうした立場」は何を指しますか。本文の言葉を使って答えなさい。

② 「この作業」は何を指しますか。

③ 「学説」の修飾部分はどこからですか。最初の三文字を答えなさい。

④ 「方法」の修飾部分はどこからですか。最初の三文字を答えなさい。

⑤ 「主張した」の主語は何ですか。本文の言葉を使って答えなさい。

⑥ 「それじたい」は何を指しますか。本文の言葉を使って答えなさい。

⑦ 「そこ」は何を指しますか。

英訳

Ⓐ 以上のような意味をもった時代区分説の対立状態が今日凝固したままであることは、個々の研究の進展にも影響していないであろうか。というのは、このような状況は、個々の研究者をして事象を自由に、トータルに考えることを躊躇させるおそれなしとしないからである。

以下前者をＡ説、後者をＢ説とよぶことにするが、この両説が古代・中世・近世等々の時代名称で中国史をどう区分しているかを、ごく大まかに対照表示すれば、下図[1]のごとくである。

	殷	前12世紀	周・秦漢	3世紀	六朝・隋唐	10世紀	宋元・明清	20世紀	
Ａ説	古代（上古）			中世（中古）			近　世		（最近世）
Ｂ説	古　　　　　代					中　　世		近　代	

　これによって明らかなように、両説の間には、二つの大きなちがいがある。一つは、十世紀以後を、Ａ説では近世とよび、Ｂ説では中世と見なしている①<u>こと</u>である。十世紀前後に中国史上決定的な社会変化があったことは湖南によってつとに強調され、Ｂ説もこれを受容したが、しかし②<u>その内容</u>については大きくへだたる結果となった。十世紀前後から盛行するいわゆる佃戸制の③<u>性格理解</u>をめぐって両説の間にはげしい議論がたたかわされ、Ａ説では④<u>これ</u>を近世的小作制と考えたが、Ｂ説では、中世的封建農奴制の本質をそなえるものとした。もう一つの相違点は、三〜十世紀、六朝・隋唐時代の位置づけに関する点で、Ａ説がここに中世時代を設定するのに対し、Ｂ説は、この時代まで古代が延続したとする。すなわち、三世紀前後の時期に中国史上の画期を設けるかどうかという点に両説の見方のちがいがあり、その点では、十世紀がともかくも画期であることでは一致している⑤<u>第一の問題</u>に比べて、一層深刻な対立を生んでいるといえる。以下、⑥<u>この部分</u>に焦点を置いて、両説の差異とその根拠を探ってみよう。

---

1 In original text, the table is illustrated vertically. Hence, 左図 is used.

内容質問

(1) Ａ説、Ｂ説で中心的な役割を担ったのは、それぞれ誰ですか。

(2) Ａ説とＢ説の時代区分に関する相違は、何だと筆者は言っていますか。二つ答えなさい。

文法質問

① 「こと」の修飾部分はどこからですか。最初の三文字を答えなさい。

② 「その内容」は何を指しますか。

③ 「性格理解」の修飾部分はどこからですか。最初の三文字を答えなさい。

④ 「これ」は何を指しますか。本文の言葉を使って答えなさい。

⑤ 「第一の問題」の修飾部分はどこからですか。最初の三文字を答えなさい。

⑥ 「この部分」は何を指しますか。本文の言葉を使って答えなさい。

A説が六朝・隋唐時代を中国における中世と規定するのは、いうまでもなく、この時代に貴族政治が盛行したことに着眼した結果である。貴族政治とは、近世の君主独裁政治の対立概念として、内藤湖南によって設定された<u>概念</u>[①]である。この意味では、貴族政治の時代は、殷周から隋唐までをおおっている。しかし、貴族政治の最も盛行した時代は六朝・隋唐時代であって、この時代の貴族政治はそれ以前の貴族政治とは段階を異にしている。周代、第一次的にピークに達した貴族政治は、秦漢の統一帝国時代に至って一種の君主独裁政治的傾向を帯びた、と湖南は考える。すなわち、中国史全体を貫徹する、貴族政治→君主独裁政治のプロセスが、古代的段階においてまず経過したと見ているようである。しかし古代の君主独裁政治は自らを貫徹できず、後漢中期あたりから第二次的貴族政治の段階へはいる。つまり、古代社会はある種のゆきづまりと屈折を経験するのであって、湖南はまたこの事態を「学問の中毒」という表現でも述べている。**<u>このような時代の変転</u>**[②]を通じて漢代いらいの官僚階級は地方の名望家と化し、この層を基盤として中世貴族政治が成立したと考えるのである。

以上のようにA説における中世とは、古代社会の発展が屈折をよぎなくされたところから出発するものであった。この観点はA説の理解には不可欠のものである。

湖南の中世説は、そのご後継者たちによって発展させられ、さまざまの分野で成果を生んだ。まず岡崎文夫は、複雑をきわめる六朝政治史の底流に、貴族階級と軍閥勢力との二元性がライト・モチーフとしてはたらいている<u>こと</u>[③]を明らかにした。岡崎によれば、**<u>この両者</u>**[④]がたがいに結びついて貴族制国家を形づくったという。このさいに岡崎の強調するところは、貴族階級の軍閥帝王に対する優位性である。

内容質問

⑴　なぜ A 説は六朝・隋唐時代を中世としましたか。

⑵　岡崎は貴族階級と軍閥勢力についてどのような見解を持っていますか。

⑶　P. 112 と P. 114 を読んで、次のことを言ったのは誰か、⒜〜⒠から選びなさい。複数回答あり。

❶（　　　　）漢から六朝に至る時代転換の本質を景気変動であると考えた
❷（　　　　）九品官人法の分析を行った
❸（　　　　）大土地所有の研究を行った
❹（　　　　）「時代格」という用語を用いてそれぞれの時代を特徴づけた
❺（　　　　）中世的集落とされる塢と村の実態を究明した
❻（　　　　）貴族階級と軍閥勢力が互いに結びついて貴族制国家を作ったと考えた

⒜　岡崎文夫　　　　　⒝　宇都宮清吉　　　　　⒞　宮崎市定
⒟　那波利貞　　　　　⒠　宮川尚志

文法質問

①　「概念」の修飾部分はどこからですか。最初の三文字を答えなさい。

②　「このような時代の変転」は何を指しますか。

③　「こと」の修飾部分はどこからですか。最初の三文字を答えなさい。

④　「この両者」は何を指しますか。本文の言葉を使って答えなさい。

A *Practical Guide for Scholarly Reading in Japanese*

　この点はかつて湖南も、六朝の天子が貴族階級の共有物的存在であることを指摘したが、岡崎は湖南のこの見解を、歴史の展開のなかで立証しようとしたといえる。岡崎はまた、六朝時代の社会経済制度についても先鞭をつけたが、以後貴族（あるいはその階級的起点をなす豪族）の経済的基礎としての

5　大土地所有の**研究**①が宇都宮清吉・宮崎市定らによって進められ、一方、中世的集落とされる塢と村の実態が、那波利貞・宮川尚志および宮崎らの手で究明された。Ⓐ宮崎の九品官人法の分析は、学会に多大の影響を与えたが、これもまた六朝の官僚制がその内実においては貴族制であることを実証したものであった。これらの他、思想史・宗教史の分野にいたるまで、湖南の六朝中

10　世説が与えた影響は広汎であり且つ深刻である。**それら**②の一々は省略するが、思想史・宗教史について一言するならば、その主たる担い手が貴族階級であったこと、またそのことによって、貴族階級が当時の価値体系を把握・体現していた**こと**③が、さまざまの論考を通じて説かれてきた。要するに、これら多彩な研究は、漢から六朝に至る時期が中国史上の一大転回点であるという湖

15　南の説を承けた**もの**④であり、そしてその転回の主体を貴族階級と見た結果である。宇都宮・宮崎らは、この時代転換そのものについて論じた。宇都宮は各時代の性格を人格になぞらえて**時代格**⑵なる独特の用語を用い、秦漢時代格を政治性、六朝時代格を自律性と特徴づけた。それは秦漢の外向性の時代から内面的精神の時代への転換を見る**もの**⑤でもあった。宮崎はこの転換の本質

20　を、景気変動という経済学的カテゴリーでとらえ、そこに好況の時代から不況の時代への屈折が生起した**こと**⑥を論じている。

114

内容質問

(1) 岡崎は湖南の見解が正しいことをどのように証明しようとしましたか。

(2) 「時代格」の意味は何ですか。一番近いものを下から選びなさい。
   (A) その時代の特徴　　　　　　　　　(B) その時代の経済的発展段階
   (C) その時代に生きる人達の人格　　　(D) その時代に起きた歴史的出来事

文法質問

① 「研究」の修飾部分はどこからですか。最初の三文字を答えなさい。

② 「それら」は何を指しますか。本文の言葉を使って答えなさい。

③ 「こと」の修飾部分はどこからですか。最初の三文字を答えなさい。

④ 「もの」の修飾部分はどこからですか。最初の三文字を答えなさい。

⑤ 「もの」の修飾部分はどこからですか。最初の三文字を答えなさい。

⑥ 「こと」の修飾部分はどこからですか。最初の三文字を答えなさい。

英訳

A 宮崎の九品官人法の分析は、学会に多大の影響を与えたが、これもまた六朝の官僚制がその内実においては貴族制であることを実証したものであった。これらの他、思想史・宗教史の分野にいたるまで、湖南の六朝中世説が与えた影響は広汎であり且つ深刻である。

つぎに、Ｂ説について語らねばならない。

Ｂ説がこの時代を秦漢時代に連続する古代とみなす<u>の</u>①は、いかなる根拠にもとづくものであろうか。唐代までを古代とする説を最初に提唱したのは、周知の通り前田直典であった。前田におけるその根拠は、六朝期の大土地所有制が主として奴隷制経営にもとづいていたこと（加藤繁の説による）、唐代均田農民の課役負担のうち徭役の<u>それ</u>②がことに過重であったこと、の二点にある。つまり前田は、六朝・隋唐期を奴隷制時代と目して、これを古代と規定したのであったが、この説は西嶋定生に受けつがれた。しかし、西嶋の奴隷制説は前田のそれのように単純ではなく、家父長的家内奴隷制（奴婢制）と共同体農民による仮作制との複合的生産関係が漢代豪族の大土地所有の経営形態であったとし、これを中国型奴隷制と名づけた。そしてその後になると仮作制は国家的奴隷制たる均田制に転化して、豪族階級は官僚として国家権力に寄生する、と展望した。しかしやがて西嶋はこの奴隷制説を撤回し、専制的な皇帝権力と小農民との間を結ぶ直接的関係が、<u>**漢代の基本的階級関係**</u>(2)であるという<u>新説</u>③を提起した。<u>両者</u>④は皇帝の賜与する民爵を媒介として結ばれており、農民の側にもある種の自由が保留されているので、これを単純に奴隷と見ることはできない。[A]しかしまた民の側は、国家権力を媒介として共同体の成員たりえているので、純然たる自由民ではない。このような皇帝権力と人民との支配関係は、個別人身的支配という用語で表現される。皇帝権力は人民のひとりひとりを、何ものをも介在させることなく直接に人身的に支配した、というのである。

内容質問

(1) Ｂ説が３世紀以後を古代とみなす根拠は何ですか。二つ答えなさい。

(2) 西島は、漢代の基本的階級関係とは何だと言っていますか。

文法質問

① 「の」の修飾部分はどこからですか。最初の三文字を答えなさい。

② 「それ」は何を指しますか。本文の言葉を使って答えなさい。

③ 「新説」の修飾部分はどこからですか。最初の三文字を答えなさい。

④ 「両者」は何を指しますか。本文の言葉を使って答えなさい。

英訳

Ⓐ しかしまた民の側は、国家権力を媒介として共同体の成員たりえているので、純然たる自由民ではない。このような皇帝権力と人民との支配関係は、個別人身的支配という用語で表現される。皇帝権力は人民のひとりひとりを、何ものをも介在させることなく直接に人身的に支配した、というのである。

さて、個別人身的支配は、六朝以後どうなるのであろうか。この問題について今日まで数多くの論考を発表してきたのは、堀敏一である。堀は、北魏以後の均田体制(1)を意味づけて、国家権力が秦漢以来の個別人身的支配を再編しようとしたもの①だと考える。そして唐の中期以後、両税法・佃戸制など土地を媒介とする収取関係が新たに形成され、民間に階層的な支配体制が確立することによって個別人身的支配の時代は終ると見る②のである。

このように、Ｂ説における古代のメルクマールは、これまでＢ説に指導的な役割を果してきた西嶋・堀両氏の説を総合すれば、国家の小農民に対する個別人身的支配にあったことが確認される。このことに対する立ち入った検討はしばらく措くとして、Ａ説が重点をおく漢から六朝にかけての時代転換③を、Ｂ説ではどのように解するかが、さしあたっての課題となる。

堀の一連の論考によれば、漢代に豪族階級が発生し、郷里社会の小農民との間に密接な関係が結ばれたという（この限りではＡ説と軌を一にする）。豪族は一面大土地所有者であったが、同時に郷里社会の共同体秩序の維持者という性格を有した。六朝期になると、後者の面④が脱落して、地主的収奪が露骨化した。この事態は小農民の没落をうながす結果を生んだので、矛盾緩和のために国家がのり出し、地主支配を抑制し、郷里社会の共同体的諸機能（山沢管理など）を掌握して、小農民に対する直接支配を再建する⑤に至った。Ａこれが均田制、三長制等々のいわゆる均田体制である。そしてこの体制のもとで豪族（貴族）階級は寄生官僚として転身延命することになったというのである。

内容質問

(1) 堀敏一は北魏以後の均田体制をどのように見ていましたか。

(2) Ｂ説における古代のメルクマールは何ですか。本文の言葉を使って答えなさい。

文法質問

① 「もの」の修飾部分はどこからですか。最初の三文字を答えなさい。

② 「見る」の主語は何ですか。本文の言葉を使って答えなさい。

③ 「時代転換」の修飾部分はどこからですか。最初の三文字を答えなさい。

④ 「後者の面」は何を指しますか。本文の言葉を使って答えなさい。

⑤ 「再建する」の主語は何ですか。本文の言葉を使って答えなさい。

英訳

Ⓐ これが均田制、三長制等々のいわゆる均田体制である。そしてこの体制のもとで豪族（貴族）階級は寄生官僚として転身延命することになったというのである。

以上の理解を図式化してみると、個別人身的支配Ⅰ→地主制→個別人身的支配Ⅱ、ということになろうか。地主制の盛行はたしかに個別人身的支配をⅠからⅡへ媒介するものではあったけれども、しかし①その枠組み自体を変えるものではなかった。地主階級たる豪族（貴族）層もまた、結局は国家官僚の枠をのりこえるものではなかった。このような理解からすれば、漢から六朝に至る時代の進展は、個別人身的支配という体制の原理を変革するものではなかったということになる。

国家権力と貴族制

Ⓐ漢から六朝への過程を中心にしてみた場合、A・B両説の理解には以上のようにいちじるしい差異があるが、しかし両説が対象としてとり上げる歴史事象はさほどかけはなれたものでなく、むしろ、同一事象に対する見方の相違が、時代区分上の相違につながっているのである。以下その点について考察し、両説の相違の本質に迫ってみたい。

A説が六朝時代を貴族政治の時代と性格づけるとき、その最大の手がかりとなるのは、いうまでもなく九品官人法である。それではB説では、この制度をどのように理解するのであろうか。②これについては堀による幾つかの論考があるので、③それらを綜合すれば、ほぼつぎのように要約しうる。

Ⓑ九品官人法は、宮崎によって解明されたように、郷品と官品の対応関係にもとづいて運用される、貴族主義的官吏登用法である。郷品は同郷人士の評価によって決定される④等級で、⑤これが登官後の官品と昇進コースを規定する。良い家柄の出身者はそのことによって高い郷品を得、したがって高い官品が保証される。したがって、貴族の官界における地位を保証するものは、皇帝権力にあるのではなくて、その郷里社会における実力である。

内容質問

(1) B説の古代のメルクマールは、漢から六朝にかけてどうなりましたか。

文法質問

① 「その枠組み」は何を指しますか。本文の言葉を使って答えなさい。

② 「これ」は何を指しますか。

③ 「それら」は何を指しますか。本文の言葉を使って答えなさい。

④ 「等級」の修飾部分はどこからですか。最初の三文字を答えなさい。

⑤ 「これ」は何を指しますか。本文の言葉を使って答えなさい。

英訳

Ⓐ 漢から六朝への過程を中心にしてみた場合、A・B両説の理解には以上のように
いちじるしい差異があるが、しかし両説が対象としてとり上げる歴史事象はさほ
どかけはなれたものでなく、むしろ、同一事象に対する見方の相違が、時代区分
上の相違につながっているのである。

Ⓑ 九品官人法は、宮崎によって解明されたように、郷品と官品の対応関係にもとづ
いて運用される、貴族主義的官吏登用法である。

A Practical Guide for Scholarly Reading in Japanese

当時の政権は漢帝国の基礎にあった共同体の崩壊の現実①に直面して、中央集権の強化を計る。九品中正制度は一面でこのような意味②を有した。しかしその一方「地方で実力をにぎっている豪族勢力を顧慮しないわけにはいかない。このような豪族勢力③の意見を官人候補者の選挙に利用しようとしたのが、

5 九品中正制度の一面である」(「九品中正制度の成立をめぐって」『東洋文化研究所紀要』四五、傍点引用者)。

　以上は九品官人法に対する堀の理解であるが、いったいＡ説とどこが異なるのであろうか。そこで試みに、宮崎の九品官人法に関する言説を対置してみよう。

10 「この立法の趣旨Ⓐ (官吏候補者の精選のために厳格な資格審査を行うこと――引用者) は甚だ良かったのであるが、当時は社会に貴族的ムードが横溢していた折なので、この新法は忽ち骨抜きにされ、反って貴族制を擁護する防波堤と化してしまった」(岩波全書版『中国史』上、二二五頁、傍点引用者)。

15 「人材を因縁に左右されずに登用するという当初の目的④は失われながら、地方を中央に結びつけるという効果は収めることが出来たと思われる。併しその結果は、中央地方を通じて混然とした一団の貴族群の成立を見るに至り、その間に自然に全国的な家格の等級が定まることになったのである」(同上、傍点引用者)。

20

内容質問

⑴ P. 120 と P. 122 を読んで、堀の九品官人法の解釈が書いてあるところはどこですか。本文から最初と最後の三文字を答えなさい。

文法質問

① 「現実」の修飾部分はどこからですか。最初の三文字を答えなさい。

② 「このような意味」は何を指しますか。本文の言葉を使って答えなさい。

③ 「このような豪族勢力」は何を指しますか。本文の言葉を使って答えなさい。

④ 「目的」の修飾部分はどこからですか。最初の三文字を答えなさい。

英訳

Ⓐ この立法の趣旨 (…) は甚だ良かったのであるが、当時は社会に貴族的ムードが横溢していた折なので、この新法は忽ち骨抜きにされ、反って貴族制を擁護する防波堤と化してしまった。

堀と宮崎のどちらも国家意志と貴族勢力との関係を主題として述べているが、その内容には微妙なちがいがある。宮崎の方は<u>この両者</u>①のくいちがいを「反って」とか「併しその結果は」の語で表わしているが、堀の方は、国家意思が貴族勢力に対抗し、あるいは<u>これ</u>②を取りこんだ制度として九品官人法を記述している。宮崎の場合、当時の社会全体が貴族主義に染まっているため、国家の政策までもが意図に反して貴族化する<u>傾向</u>③にあったことを述べる。Ⓐ<u>これを敷衍していえば当時の社会の本質は貴族主義にあり、国家権力は</u>④<u>これに比べれば相対的な位置にあって、その規定を受け</u>⑤<u>ざるをえなかった、ということになるであろう。</u>これに反して堀の方はそうではない。貴族勢力の実力を認めつつも、主体はあくまで国家の側にある。九品官人法にかぎらず、当時の私的土地所有の公認を意味するといわれる<u>占田・課田法</u>⑥、あるいは私的従属関係の国家的承認を示すとされる<u>給客制等々</u>⑦もまた、堀は一面でそうした面のあることを認めつつ、他方で国家権力の土地私有制や給客制度への介入・規制を強調している。この論法をより単純化していえば、ひとつの新しい歴史的事態の国家権力による<u>承認</u>②⑧は、すなわち国家権力がそのことによってこの新事態に介入し、支配を深化・拡大することだとするのである。

（中略）

内容質問

(1) 堀は国家権力の主体についてどのように主張していますか。

(2) 「承認」とは何を承認することですか。本文の言葉を使って具体例を答えなさい。

(3) 以下の文はA説（宮崎）かB説（堀）か答えなさい。

❶（　　　）九品官人法は、国家意思が貴族勢力に対抗し、これを取り込んだ制度である。

❷（　　　）当時の社会全体が貴族主義に染まっているため、国家の政策も貴族化する傾向にあった。

❸（　　　）当時の社会の本質は貴族主義にあった。

❹（　　　）国家権力は貴族主義の規定を受けなければならなかった。

❺（　　　）貴族は実力はあったが、主体は国家の側にある。

❻（　　　）国家権力は土地私有制や給客制度を規制していた。

文法質問

① 「この両者」は何を指しますか。本文の言葉を使って答えなさい。

② 「これ」は何を指しますか。本文の言葉を使って答えなさい。

③ 「傾向」の修飾部分はどこからですか。最初の三文字を答えなさい。

④ 「これ」は何を指しますか。本文の言葉を使って答えなさい。

⑤ 「その規定」は何を指しますか。本文の言葉を使って答えなさい。

⑥ 「占田・課田法」の修飾部分はどこからですか。最初の三文字を答えなさい。

⑦ 「給客制等々」の修飾部分はどこからですか。最初の三文字を答えなさい。

⑧ 「承認」の修飾部分はどこからですか。最初の三文字を答えなさい。

英訳

Ⓐ これを敷衍していえば当時の社会の本質は貴族主義にあり、国家権力はこれに比べれば相対的な位置にあって、その規定を受けざるをえなかった、ということになるであろう。

六朝の国家権力を貴族階級から自立した権力とみなし、小農民の対極にある一種の階級と考えるＢ説は、六朝社会をアジア的構成ととらえるところに根ざしていること①が明らかである。ところで、「アジア的」なるものは、右の一節にも述べられているように、「古典的＝ギリシア・ローマ的」古代、すなわちヨーロッパの古代に対置された概念であり、場合によっては、「ゲルマン的」構成を含めたヨーロッパ史の全構成に対して、特異な位置を占めるものとして理解される。端的に言えば、ヨーロッパとの対比によって導き出された概念である。Ｂ説がヨーロッパ史の発展コースを常に念頭において、説を展開してきていること②は、疑いないところである。

一方、Ａ説もまた、湖南以来一種世界史的見地から、中国史の時代区分を試みてきた。しかし、そこ③にはたらいているのは、ヨーロッパ史との類比の意識であって、差異あるものを比較する意識はそれほど強くない。周知のＡように、湖南は中国史の発展を一本の樹にたとえた。それ自身一個の世界史を④形成しているという意味である。この立場からすれば、中国とヨーロッパとは、文明の進歩の上で、大局的には同じ歩みを歩むのである。貴族政治、君主独裁政治等々の概念は、まさにこのような観点②から導き出された文化史的概念に他ならない。

（後略）

内容質問

(1)　B説では六朝の国家権力をどう捉えていますか。

(2)　筆者は、A説において貴族政治、君主独裁政治といった概念がどのような観点から生まれたと述べていますか。

文法質問

①　「こと」の修飾部分はどこからですか。最初の三文字を答えなさい。

②　「こと」の修飾部分はどこからですか。最初の三文字を答えなさい。

③　「そこ」は何を指しますか。

④　「それ自身」は何を指しますか。本文の言葉を使って答えなさい。

英訳

Ⓐ　周知のように、湖南は中国史の発展を一本の樹にたとえた。それ自身一個の世界史を形成しているという意味である。この立場からすれば、中国とヨーロッパとは、文明の進歩の上で、大局的には同じ歩みを歩むのである。貴族政治、君主独裁政治等々の概念は、まさにこのような観点から導き出された文化史的概念に他ならない。

A Practical Guide for Scholarly Reading in Japanese

中国史の時代区分問題をめぐって Chūgokushi no jidaikubun mondai o megutte
── 現時点からの省察 Genjiten kara no shōsatsu──

谷川道雄 TANIGAWA Michio (1987)

Vocabulary

Note: NP＝Name of a person, NB＝Name of a book, PB＝Phonetic borrowing

	本文の語彙	辞書形・漢字	読み方 (現代語表記)	英語
P. 102	～を巡って		～をめぐって	concerning; over
	大方		おおかた	most; nearly all
	周知の		しゅうちの	widely-known
	～をなした	～を為す	～をなす	to constitute ～; to make ～
	至る		いたる	to reach; to result in
	とらえる	捉える	とらえる	to grasp; to perceive
	歴史主義		れきししゅぎ	historicism
	巨視的な		きょしてきな	comprehensive
	事象		じしょう	phenomenon; event
	たがい	互い	たがい	each other
	自らを持して	自らを持す	みずからをじす	to proudly protect one's own stance
	譲らず	譲る	ゆずる	to concede
	形づくった	形づくる	かたちづくる	to form; to shape
P. 104	とは言え		とはいえ	though; although
	恐縮だが		きょうしゅくだが	Pardon me (but)
	東海大学出版会		とうかいだいがくしゅっぱんかい	the name of a publisher
	学生社		がくせいしゃ	the name of a publisher
	刊行中		かんこうちゅう	in the course of publication
	史学雑誌		しがくざっし	the name of a journal
P. 106	一環		いっかん	a part of
	意味づけようとする	意味づける	いみづける	to give meaning (to～)
	自ずから		おのずから	naturally
	たずさわって	携わる	たずさわる	to take part (in～); to engage (in～)
	軌を一にする		きをいつにする	to share the same view
	ともかく		ともかく	setting aside
	ひいては	延いては	ひいては	moreover; furthermore

128

Chapter 2 Section 2 – 中国史の時代区分問題をめぐって TANIGAWA Michio 谷川道雄 (1987) Chūgokushi no jidaikubun mondai o megutte

	本文の語彙	辞書形・漢字	読み方 (現代語表記)	英語
P. 106	からんで	絡む	からむ	to be involved
	食い違い		くいちがい	difference
	発現した	発現する	はつげんする	to appear
P. 108	トータルに		トータルに	holistically
	とらわれない	捉わる	とらわれる	to adhere (to ~); to be caught
	断っておく		ことわっておく	to tell you in advance
	結着をつけよう	結着をつける	けっちゃくをつける	to settle
	あくまで		あくまで	only; just be best of one's ability; to the utmost
	くみして	与する	くみする	to side with; to support
	至難の業		しなんのわざ	an extremely difficult task
	内藤 湖南		ないとう こなん	NP
	明清		みんしん	Ming and Qing Dynasties
	一挙に		いっきょに	at once
	それじたい	それ自体	それじたい	that in itself
	役割を果たした	役割を果たす	やくわりをはたす	to play a role
P. 110	佃戸制		でんこせい	the landlord/tenant system
	小作制		こさくせい	tenant system
	画期		かっき	change of era
	一層		いっそう	even more
P. 112	おおって	覆う	おおう	to cover
	帯びた	帯びる	おびる	to have a trace of
	自ら		みずから	itself
	岡崎 文夫		おかざき ふみお	NP
	きわめる	極める	きわめる	to be extreme; to be the most
	ライト・モチーフ			Leitmotiv; recurring theme
	結びついて	結びつく	むすびつく	to be linked
	この際		このさい	under these circumstances; at this point
P. 114	先鞭をつけた	先鞭をつける	せんべんをつける	to blaze a trail; to take the initiative
	宇都宮 清吉		うつのみや きよよし	NP
	宮崎 市定		みやざき いちさだ	NP

129

A Practical Guide for Scholarly Reading in Japanese

	本文の語彙	辞書形・漢字	読み方 (現代語表記)	英語
P. 114	塢		う	a type of community
	那波 利貞		なば としさだ	NP
	宮川 尚志		みやかわ ひさゆき	NP
	九品官人法		きゅうひんかんじんほう	the Nine-rank system
	且つ		かつ	besides; moreover
	主たる		しゅたる	main; principal
	担い手		にないて	central figure
	なぞらえて	擬える	なぞらえる	to compare; to liken to
	好況		こうきょう	economic prosperity
	不況		ふきょう	recession
P. 116	前田 直典		まえだ なおのり	NP
	加藤 繁		かとう しげる	NP
	均田農民		きんでんのうみん	a farmer under equal-field system
	課役		かえき	distribution of assignments
	徭役		ようえき	statute-labor service
	西嶋 定生		にしじま さだお	NP
	家父長的家内奴隷制		かふちょうてきかないどれいせい	patriarchal domestic slavery system
	仮作制		かさくせい	tenant farming system
	民爵		みんしゃく	a title given to people
P. 118	堀 敏一		ほり としかず	NP
	措く		おく	to put aside
	うながす	促す	うながす	to prompt; to hasten
	のり出し	乗り出す	のりだす	to get involved
	三長制		さんちょうせい	Sanchang system
P. 120	図式化して	図式化する	ずしきかする	to schematize
	枠組み		わくぐみ	framework
	のりこえる	乗り越える	のりこえる	to go beyond
	著しい		いちじるしい	remarkable
	かけはなれた	かけ離れる	かけはなれる	to differ greatly
	性格づける		せいかくづける	to characterize

130

	本文の語彙	辞書形・漢字	読み方 (現代語表記)	英語
P. 120	手がかり		てがかり	clue
	郷品		きょうひん	the qualification for bureaucratic rank
	官品		かんひん	(nine) court ranks
P. 122	紀要		きよう	academic journal
	甚だ		はなはだ	greatly; excessively
	折		おり	time; moment
	忽ち		たちまち	instantly; at once
	骨抜き		ほねぬき	to render ineffective
	反って		かえって	rather; on the contrary
	岩波		いわなみ	岩波書店 the name of a publisher
	因縁		いんねん	fate; destiny
	左右されず	左右する	さゆうする	to influence; to affect
	収める		おさめる	to gain (a success)
	併し		しかし	but
P. 124	敷衍して	敷衍する	ふえんする	to extend
	占田・課田法		せんでん・かでんほう	*Zhantian · Ketian* land ownership system
	給客制(度)		きゅうきゃくせい(ど)	*Geike* labor system
P. 126	対極		たいきょく	polar opposite
	導き出された	導き出す	みちびきだす	to induce
	念頭において	念頭に置く	ねんとうにおく	to bear something in mind
	見地		けんち	a point of view

TANIGAWA Michio

Expressions

1. 今更 too late for/to; now

◆ 本稿のタイトルを見て、いまさら時代区分問題でもあるまいと、大方の読者はお考えであろう。

Upon seeing the title of this essay, most readers will probably think, "The periodization problem? Now?"

1) すでに決まったことだから、いまさら反論してももう遅い。

It's already been decided, so even if you disagree now it's too late.

2) 誰もが知っていることだから、今更説明することもないだろう。

It's something that everyone knows, so there's probably no need to explain it now.

2. (Vpot) よう I/We think it possible to ~   cf. Matsuura

◆ …個々の歴史事象をミクロに観察し記述しようとする傾向へと、歴史学の作風が転換してきた点が挙げられよう。

The point can be raised that the style of writing in the study of history has shifted toward the trend of observing and recounting individual historical phenomena on a micro level.

1) 以上のことから、この説は正しいと結論づけられよう。

Given the above, we can conclude that this theory is correct.

2) あんな素晴らしい景色をどうして忘れられようか。

How could I ever forget such splendid scenery?

3. ～ものの though ~; although ~   cf. Matsuura

◆ 両説は個々の点でたがいに影響しあってきたものの、その原則においては自らを持してゆずらず、…

Although both theories have influenced each other on individual points, they have not made concessions with regard to their fundamental principles.

1) 決心はしたものの、将来が分からず不安であった。

Although I had made my decision, I was anxious at the uncertainty of my future.

2) これは難しくはないと言うものの、誰にでもできることではない。

Although this isn't difficult, it isn't something anyone could do either.

Chapter 2 Section 2 – 中国史の時代区分問題をめぐって TANIGAWA Michio 谷川道雄 (1987) Chūgokushi no jidaikubun mondai o megutte

4. 敢えて dare to ~; force oneself to ~

◆ それにもかかわらず、私があえてここに筆をとったのは、つぎに述べる理由によるのである。

Despite that, I dare to take up my brush here due to the following reasons.

1) 彼は、それが何なのかあえて言わなかったが、私にはよく分かっていた。

He didn't dare to say what it was, but I knew all too well.

2) 失敗を覚悟の上で、敢えてその仕事を引き受けることにした。

Having prepared myself for failure, I daringly accepted the job.

5. X を Y とする / 為す regard X as Y; assume; consider

cf. Kano, Matsuura, Naitō, Ojima, Suzuki, Taki

◆ ここでの中世は、宋代以後を中世とする一方の説を採用している。

The 'medieval' used here follows the theory which regards the medieval period as starting in the Song.

1) この理論を正しいとすると、我々の考えは間違っていないことになる。

If we take this theory to be correct, it would mean that our thinking is not mistaken.

2) 国連は温暖化問題を最重要課題の一つとなしている。

The UN considers global warming to be a problem of the utmost importance.

Note: See Section 5 in Chapter 1.

6. 如何に～とも / ども / ても / でも no matter how ~   cf. Naitō, Taki

◆ ひとがいかに個別的事象に関心を集中させようとも、…その意識は時代区分の意識と決して無縁ではないであろう。

No matter how much one tries to concentrate their interest on individual phenomena, …that consciousness is in no way unrelated to the consciousness of periodization.

1) いかに本物に見えようとも、偽物はやはり偽物だ。

No matter how much it looks like the real thing, a fake is a fake.

2) 人生の道はどんなに険しくとも、笑いながら生きようと思う。

No matter how rough the path of life is, I want to live smiling.

133

A Practical Guide for Scholarly Reading in Japanese

7. ～限り as long as; as far as; to the extent

◆ それを全体史の一環として意味づけようとする意識がはたらいている限り、その意識は時代区分の意識と決して無縁ではないであろう。

As long as there is a consciousness of trying to place its significance within history as a whole, that consciousness is in no way unrelated to the consciousness of periodization.

1) 私が知っている限りでは、過去にこのような研究を行った学者は存在しない。

As far as I know, there has never been a scholar who has conducted this kind of research.

2) できるかどうか分かりませんが、できる限りの努力はします。

I don't know if I can do it or not, but I'll try as much as I can.

8. ～訳だ / である this is why ~; this means ~; it is the case that ~ cf. Kano, Matsuura, Naitō, Ojima, Taki

◆ …それぞれの研究者は決して時代区分と無縁に生きているわけでなく…

Researchers are definitely not living unrelated to periodization…

1) 誰にでも、間違いはあるわけだが、そのあとどう責任をとるかは人それぞれだ。

Of course, everyone makes mistakes, but how you take responsibility afterwards depends on the person.

2) 叔父は学生時代にフランスに留学した。だからフランス語が堪能なわけである。

My uncle studied abroad in France while he was a student. No wonder he is so good at French.

9. 寧ろ rather; rather than otherwise cf. Naitō, Taki

◆ …それぞれの研究者は決して時代区分と無縁に生きているわけでなく、むしろそれを背後に意識しつつ…

Researchers are definitely not living unrelated to periodization, but rather they are conscious of it in the background…

1) 疲労が溜まっているので、明日の日曜日は遊びに行くよりもむしろ家で休みたい。

My exhaustion has built up, so tomorrow, Sunday, instead of going out, I'd rather rest at home.

2) 徳川家康は政治家と言うより寧ろ策士であったと言えようか。

Perhaps it could be said that TOKUGAWA Ieyasu was more of a strategist than a politician.

134

10. 〜つつ while ~

◆ むしろそれを背後に意識しつつ、それぞれの研究にたずさわっているのではなかろうか。

Rather, perhaps they engage in their own research while keeping it in the back of their minds.

1) 大学で助手をしつつ、博士論文を書いた。

I wrote my PhD thesis while working as an assistant at university.

2) 母の無事を祈りつつ、日本に帰国した。

I returned home to Japan while praying for my mother's safety.

11. 〜如し like ~; look like ~   cf. Kano, Naitō, Ojima, Taki

◆ 実情は先に述べたごとくである。

The actual situation is as stated previously.

1) 過ぎたるは及ばざるが如し。

Too much is just like too little.

2) その新人は彗星の如く現れて、その年の全ての賞を独占した。

The newcomer appeared like a comet and monopolized all the awards for that year.

Note: See Section 8.5.7 in Chapter 1.

12. 〜訳には行かない cannot ~; impossible   cf. Naito

◆ これを単に時代名称上での相違と片づけるわけにはゆかない。

We cannot dismiss it as simply a difference in the naming of the periods.

1) 他人のこととはいえ、無関心でいるわけにはいかない。

Even if it is someone else's business, I can't stay unconcerned.

2) 自分が提案した企画なので、途中で諦めるわけにはいかない。

It's a project that I proposed, so I can't give up midway.

A Practical Guide for Scholarly Reading in Japanese

13. 〜恐れがある there is a risk/fear/concern that 〜

◆ このような状況は、個々の研究者をして事象を自由に、トータルに考えることを躊躇させるおそれなしとしないからである。

Because this situation may make individual researchers hesitant to think about phenomena freely and comprehensively.

1) 今週、大きな台風が来る恐れがある。

This week, there is a risk of a large typhoon coming.

2) このまま何もしなかったら、失敗する恐れがあります。

If you keep not doing anything like this, you risk failing.

14. 〜に対するN   N toward 〜; N against 〜 / 〜に対して V/ADJ/ADJ-V   cf. Kano, Naitō, Ojima

◆ そこには戦中の歴史学に対する反省が契機となっており、…

There, reflection on the historiography during the war became the impetus…

1) 彼の芸術に対する情熱は変わることがなかった。

His passion for art never changed.

2) 政府の経済政策に対して国民の不満が高まっている。

The peoples' dissatisfaction toward the government's economic policies is increasing.

15. 且つ also; moreover   cf. Matsuura

◆ 湖南の六朝中世説が与えた影響は広汎であり且つ深刻である。

The influence of Konan's Six Dynasties medieval theory was wide-reaching and profound.

1) この病を克服するための、最も安全、且つ最短な方法は何であろうか。

What is the safest and shortest method to overcome this illness?

2) これは必要かつ十分な条件と言える。

This can be said to be a necessary and sufficient condition.

136

16. 〜得る can ~; possible; able　cf. Naitō

◆ それらを綜合すれば、ほぼつぎのように要約しうる。

Putting them together, they can basically be summarized in the following way.

1) この研究はワクチンの開発に大きな効果をもたらし得るであろう。

This research can surely contribute greatly to the development of a vaccine.

2) 実際に起こりうる様々な問題を考えてみましょう。

Let's think about the various problems which could actually occur.

17. 〜ざるを得ない to have no choice but ~; have to ~

◆ 国家権力はこれに比べれば相対的な位置にあって、その規定を受けざるをえなかった、…

the authority of the state was positioned relative to it and inevitably bound by it.

1) その選手は足を怪我をし、オリンピック出場という夢をあきらめざるを得なかった。

That athlete injured their foot and had no choice but to give up their dream of participating in the Olympics.

2) 副業を会社が許可せざるを得ないのは会社の賃金が安いからだ。

The reason the company has no choice but to allow side jobs is because its salaries are low.

18. 〜に限らず not limited to ~

◆ 九品官人法にかぎらず、…

Not limited to the nine-rank system…

1) 会員に限らず非会員も歓迎いたします。

We welcome not just members but non-members as well.

2) あの選手はボクシングに限らず、格闘技ならなんでも得意だ。

That athlete is skilled at not just boxing but any martial art.

A Practical Guide for Scholarly Reading in Japanese

19. N なるもの = N であるもの so called N; what is called N　　cf. Kano, Naitō, Taki

◆ ところで、「アジア的」なるものは、…「古典的＝ギリシア・ローマ的」古代、すなわちヨーロッパの古代に対置された概念であり、…

By the way, that which is called "Asia-like" is…a concept placed in contrast to "classical", that is, "Greco-Roman" antiquity, in other words, the antiquity of Europe…

1) 自律性なるものは、日々の努力によって初めて身につくのである。

That which is called autonomy is acquired only through daily hard work.

2) 来年退職したら、SNS なるものに挑戦してみたい。

After I retire next year, I want to challenge myself to use that which is called SNS.

20. ～に他 [外] ならない / ならず nothing but ～　　cf. Kano, Suzuki

◆ 貴族政治、君主独裁政治等々の概念は、まさにこのような観点から導き出された文化史的概念に他ならない。

Concepts such as aristocracy or absolute monarchy are none other than cultural historical concepts derived from this viewpoint.

1) 成功とは日々の努力の成果に外ならず。

Success is nothing other than the result of daily hard work.

2) 互いに関係が良好であったのは、共通の敵がいたからに他ならない。

Their relationship was good precisely because they had a common enemy.

138

Chapter 2 Section 3

MATSUURA Tomohisa 松浦友久 (1935–2002). Scholar of Classical Chinese Literature.

Matsuura specializes in the history of Chinese literature, Tang poetry, and Japanese and Chinese comparative poetics. After graduating from the Japanese literature course at Waseda University's Department of Literature, he took up a teaching position at the same department, becoming a professor in 1975.

The theory of rhythm in classical Chinese poetry developed in the essay contained in this textbook was revolutionary, analyzing the beauty of Chinese poetry through rhythm and structure.

Representative works include 『中国詩歌原論―比較詩学の主題に即して』 *Fundamental Theory of Chinese Poetry: Through the Theme of Comparative Poetics* (Taishūkan Shoten, 1986) and 『李白研究―抒情の構造』 *Research on Li Bai: The Structure of the Lyrical* (Sanseidō, 1976).

中国古典詩のリズム
—リズムの根源性と詩型の変遷—

MATSUURA Tomohisa 松浦友久 (1986) Chūgoku kotenshi no rizumu

▊（五）四言詩

歴史的に見て、四言詩は、中国詩の詩型のなかで、最も古くかつ最も基本的なものと考えられる。それは、①現存最古の詩集『詩経(しきょう)』の詩句が明らかに四言を基本としていること、②文言・白話を通じて中国語のリズムの基礎単位が二音節であり、いわゆる"成句・成語"の大部分が、それを二倍にした四字句（四字格）から成立っていること——から見て、まったく疑問の余地がない。つまり、二音節一句の"二言句"が単純に過ぎて、安定した詩句としては成立しがたい以上、①それを重ねた四言句が詩句の基本となることは、②必然の結果と考えられるわけである。それだけに、このリズムは、古代詩以来、一貫して変ることなく保持されてきた。

桃之夭夭　　桃の夭夭たる

灼灼其華　　灼灼たり其の華

之子于帰　　之の子于(ここ)に帰(とつ)ぐ

宜其室家　　其の室家に宜しからん（『詩経』周南「桃夭」）

対酒当歌　　酒に対して当に歌ふべし

人生幾何　　人生　幾何(いくばく)ぞ（魏、曹操「短歌行」）

靄靄停雲　　靄(あい)靄たる停雲よ

濛濛時雨　　濛濛たる時雨よ（晋、陶潜「停雲」）

内容質問

(1) 四言詩が中国詩の中で最も古くて基本のものであるという根拠は何か、２つ答えなさい。

(2) 何が「まったく疑問の余地がない」のですか。

文法質問

① 「それ」は何を指しますか。本文の言葉を使って答えなさい。

② 何が「必然の結果」なのですか。本文の言葉を使って答えなさい。

A Practical Guide for Scholarly Reading in Japanese

八音斯奏　　八音　斯に奏し

三献畢陳　　三献　畢く陳ぶ

宝祚惟永　　宝祚　惟れ永く

暉光日新　　暉光　日に新たなり（初唐、魏徵「寿和」

5 〔享太廟楽章〕）

　　『詩経』の「桃夭」から唐詩の「寿和」まで、時代や作者や題材は異なる
ものの、リズムとしてはまったく共通であることが確認される。

　　四言詩のリズムは、次のようにまとめられよう。一句四字。原則として、
10 一句の第二字・第四字が節奏点（リズムの強調点）となり、従って、その後
に分節線（リズムの切れ目）が入るため、上下に「〇〇〇〇」と二分される。
一首全体の拍節のリズムとしては、「〇〇〇〇、〇〇〇〇、……」という二字
一拍の二拍子が基調となる。リズムの性格としては、句中の節奏点と句末の
節奏点とのあいだに韻律上・構造上の差異がないため、きわめて均質的な、
15 変化の少ないものとなる。

　　むろん、視覚的あるいは内容的な判断から、句末の、詩句と詩句との間に
は、より大きな人為的な休止（あるいは延長）を入れて読むのが普通である
が、それは韻律構造として本来的に内在するものとは異なるため、一首全体
の、リズムとしての均質性は左右されない。

20

142

内容質問

⑴ 『詩経』の「桃夭」と唐詩の「寿和」に共通する点は何ですか。本文の言葉を使って答えなさい。

⑵ 「四言詩」の形式の特徴は何ですか。3つ答えなさい。

⑶ 松浦は四言詩のリズムの性格をどう見ていますか。

文法質問

① 「もの」の修飾部分はどこからですか。最初の三文字を答えなさい。

② 「それ」は何を指しますか。本文の言葉を使って答えなさい。

英訳

Ⓐ むろん、視覚的あるいは内容的な判断から、句末の、詩句と詩句との間には、より大きな人為的な休止（あるいは延長）を入れて読むのが普通であるが、それは韻律構造として本来的に内在するものとは異なるため、一首全体の、リズムとしての均質性は左右されない。

ところで、こうした均質性(1)は、四言詩の表現感覚として、プラスの面では安定感・重厚さ・簡潔性などを生むものであるが、また一面では、平板さ・単調さなどマイナスの要素としても作用することになる。中国語（漢語）の言語構造としては最も安定したものであり①ながら、それゆえに単純明快にすぎて、古代詩歌史以外では中心的な詩型となりえなかった(3)のだと考えてよい。

　魏晋以降の詩歌史でこの詩型が用いられるのは、晋の束晳の「補亡詩、六首」、陸雲の「贈鄭曼季、四首」、鄭豊の「答陸士龍、四首」、や唐の顧況の「上古之什、補亡訓伝、十三章」のように、直接に『詩経』の補遺を志す場合は言うまでもなく、一般にも何ほどか、古代風の内容・詩風・表現感覚等が意図されていること②が多い。初唐の魏徴の「寿和」が、最も正統的・伝統的な宮廷楽府たる「郊廟歌辞」の楽章として、リズム・内容ともに、こうした流れの一環にあることは言うまでもない。

内容質問

(1) 「こうした均質性」のプラス（＝長所）とマイナス（＝短所）は何ですか。

(2) 四言詩の詩型は魏晋以降、どのように使われたか、２つ答えなさい。

(3) 何が「中心的な詩型となりえなかった」のですか。また、その理由は何ですか。

文法質問

① 「最も安定したものであり」の主語は何ですか。

② 「こと」の修飾部分はどこからですか。最初の三文字を答えなさい。

A Practical Guide for Scholarly Reading in Japanese

中国古典詩のリズム Chūgoku kotenshi no rizumu
—リズムの根源性と詩型の変遷 Rizumu no kongensei to shikei no hensen—
（五）四言詩 Shigonshi
松浦友久 MATSUURA Tomohisa (1986)

Vocabulary

Note: NP＝Name of a person, NB＝Name of a book, PB＝Phonetic borrowing

	本文の語彙	辞書形・漢字	読み方 (現代語表記)	英語
P. 140	詩経		しきょう	the Book of Odes (NB)
	〜を通じて		〜をつうじて	through
	いわゆる	所謂	いわゆる	so-called
	それだけに		それだけに	for the very reason
	一貫して		いっかんして	consistently
P. 142	むろん	無論	むろん	needless to say
	左右されない	左右する	さゆうする	to influence; to affect
P. 144	束皙		そく せき	Shu Xi (NP)
	陸雲		りく うん	Lu Yun (NP)
	鄭豊		てい ほう	Zheng Feng (NP)
	顧況		こ きょう	Gu Kuang (NP)
	言うまでもなく		いうまでもなく	not to mention
	魏徴		ぎ ちょう	Wei Zheng (NP)

146

Expressions

1. 且つ also; moreover   cf. Tanigawa

◆ 歴史的に見て、四言詩は、中国詩の詩型のなかで、最も古くかつ最も基本的なものと考えられる。

Viewed historically, the four-character poem can be thought of as the oldest and most fundamental out of the formats of Chinese poetry.

1) この病を克服するための、最も安全、且つ最短な方法は何であろうか。

What is the safest and shortest method to overcome this illness?

2) これは必要かつ十分な条件と言える。

This can be said to be a necessary and sufficient condition.

2. X を Y とする / 為す regard X as Y; assume; consider   cf. Kano, Naitō, Ojima, Suzuki, Taki, Tanigawa

◆ 現存最古の詩集『詩経』の詩句が明らかに四言を基本としている…

The poetic lines in the oldest surviving poetry collection, the *Shijing*, clearly take four-syllables as their foundation…

1) この理論を正しいとすると、我々の考えは間違っていないことになる。

If we take this theory to be correct, it would mean that our thinking is not mistaken.

2) 国連は温暖化問題を最重要課題の一つとなしている。

The UN considers global warming to be a problem of the utmost importance.

Note: See Section 5 in Chapter 1.

3. 〜がたい difficult to 〜

◆ 安定した詩句としては成立しがたい以上、…

Given that it is difficult for it to stand as a stable poetic line…

1) このような偏見に満ちたコメントは耐えがたい。

It is difficult to bear such a comment filled with discrimination.

2) はっきりした証拠がなければ、この記事の妥当性は認めがたい。

It is difficult to acknowledge the appropriateness of this article without clear evidence.

A Practical Guide for Scholarly Reading in Japanese

4. V 以上（は） once; given that; now that; because it is the case　cf. Suzuki

◆ 安定した詩句としては成立しがたい以上、…

Given that it is difficult for it to stand as a stable poetic line…

1) いったん始めた以上は、最後まであきらめないつもりだ。

Now that I've started, I don't intend on giving up until the end.

2) 会議で決まった以上は、会社の方針を変えることはできない。

Since it was decided at a meeting, it is not possible to change the company's policy.

5. 〜訳だ / である　this is why ~; this means ~; it is the case that ~　cf. Kano, Naitō, Ojima, Taki, Tanigawa

◆ 必然の結果と考えられるわけである。

It can therefore be thought of as a necessary result.

1) 誰にでも、間違いはあるわけだが、そのあとどう責任をとるかは人それぞれだ。

Of course, everyone makes mistakes, but how you take responsibility afterwards depends on the person.

2) 叔父は学生時代にフランスに留学した。だからフランス語が堪能なわけである。

My uncle studied abroad in France while he was a student. No wonder he is so good at French.

6. 〜ものの　though ~; although ~　cf. Tanigawa

◆『詩経』の「桃夭」から唐詩の「寿和」まで、時代や作者や題材は異なるものの、…

Although the age, author, and material all differ between Tao Yao of the *Shijing* and Shou He of Tang poetry…

1) 決心はしたものの、将来が分からず不安であった。

Although I had made my decision, I was anxious at the uncertainty of my future.

2) これは難しくはないと言うものの、誰にでもできることでもない。

Although this isn't difficult, it isn't something anyone could do either.

148

Chapter 2 Section 3 – 中国古典詩のリズム MATSUURA Tomohisa 松浦友久 (1986) Chūgoku kotenshi no rizumu

7. (Vpot) よう I/We think it possible to ~   cf. Tanigawa

◆四言詩のリズムは、次のようにまとめられよう。
The rhythm of four-character poems can be summarized as such.

1) 以上のことから、この説は正しいと結論づけられよう。
Given the above, we can conclude that this theory is correct.

2) あんな素晴らしい景色をどうして忘れられようか。
How could I ever forget such splendid scenery?

8. ～ながら while ~; even though ~

◆最も安定したものでありながら、それゆえに単純明快にすぎて、…
While it was the most stable, as a result it was too simple and clear…

1) この本は17世紀に書かれたものでありながら、現代人の生活に通じるものがある。
Even though this book was written in the seventeenth century, there is something which speaks to the lives of people in the modern age.

2) 頭では分かっていながら、実際に言葉で説明するのは難しい。
While [I] understand it in my head, actually explaining it in words is difficult.

149

Chapter 2 Section 4

OJIMA Sukema 小島祐馬 (1881–1966). Scholar of East Asian Intellectual History.

After graduating from the law course at Kyoto Imperial University (presently, Kyoto University), he reentered into the literature course. Following a position at Doshisha University, he started teaching at Kyoto University in 1922. He was one of the founding members of 支那学 (Chinese Studies), the research journal of Chinese studies at Kyoto University, and remained involved in the journal's editing for a long time afterwards.

Characteristic of Ojima's scholarship was his efforts to understand Chinese intellectual history through its connections with the social history behind it, thinking within the framework of social-intellectual historical research. He was the first to establish this viewpoint/method, and his position is carried on in post-war research.

Representative works include 『中国の社会思想』*Chinese Social Thought* (Chikuma Shobō, 1967), 『中国思想史』*History of Chinese Thought* (Sōbunsha, 1968).

封建制度と家族道徳

OJIMA Sukema 小島祐馬 (1943/1988) Hōken seido to kazoku dōtoku

儒家の始祖は言うまでもなく孔子である。孔子の社会思想を一言にして掩うならば、周の封建制度を維持するということに帰着する。しかるに孔子が
5 周の封建制度を是認するのはその形式的方面からするのであって、これを運用する精神までも同時に是認せんとするのではない。従来の封建制度は主として権力服従の関係に立脚するのであるが、孔子はこれを道徳に本づく風化の関係に置こうとするのである。けだし権力服従の関係は権力の推移によって漸次下剋上の世態を馴致するを常とし、かくては社会の秩序は到底いつま
10 でも維持することの出来ないということは、孔子がこれを面のあたり見た所であるからである。しからば孔子が取って以て封建制度の運用に資せんとする道徳とははたして如何なるものであるか。これを知る為めには先ず周の封建制度の特質を検討してみなければならぬ。

周の封建制度の特質はそれが家族制度を骨子としている点に存する。周の
15 封建制度では子弟分封と同姓不婚とがその基調を為して居る。前代の殷の相続法は兄弟相及ぼす制度であったから、王の子弟はみな未来の王であった。しかるに周に至ってはじめて弟に伝えずして子に伝え、嫡長を立つる制度を採った為めに、嫡長以外の嫡子庶子はその父の位を襲うことが出来なくなり、これをそのままに放置することは禍乱を醸す本と考えられた。そこでこれら
20 王の子弟に対しては親族関係の親疏人物の賢愚に応じて、それぞれ領土を与えて諸侯とすることとした。されば周初には武王の兄弟の国十五、同姓の国四十を数えたと言われて居る。

内容質問

(1) 孔子の社会思想は「周の封建制度」の何を是認しましたか。

(2) 封建制度における権力服従の関係が社会の秩序を維持できないのはなぜですか。

(3) 殷の相続法は、周に至ってどのように変わりましたか。

(4) 「父の位を襲う」とはどういう意味ですか。

文法質問

① 「これ」は何を指しますか。本文の言葉を使って答えなさい。

② 「これ」は何を指しますか。本文の言葉を使って答えなさい。

③ 「道徳」の修飾部分はどこからですか。最初の三文字を答えなさい。

④ 「その基調」とは何の基調ですか。本文の言葉を使って答えなさい。

⑤ 「こと」の修飾部分はどこからですか。最初の三文字を答えなさい。

ところがこの子弟を分封することから、王と諸侯との間に君臣の分というものがはじめて発生することとなったのである。想うに殷以前に在っては、王と他の領主との関係は後世の盟主と諸侯との関係の如き**もの**①で、未だその間に君臣の分というものは定まっていなかったようである。周に至って王の一族を分封した爲めに王は従来の如く単に諸領主の盟主であるばかりでなく、王は諸領主の父であり兄であるという関係を生じ、ここに王と諸侯との間に血族関係に本づく君臣関係が生じ、Ⓐ同時に同姓の諸侯相互の間も家族制度を以て律せらるることとなった。しかるに周の諸侯の中にはもちろん多数の異姓のものがあった。これら異姓の諸侯に対しては同姓の諸侯と同じく家族制度に本づく**服従関係**②を強いることが出来ないわけであるが、**この難関**③を疏通したものがすなわち同姓不婚の制度である。同姓不婚の制度は原始社会に存する習俗に本づくものであって、殷代にはすでに六世以後は同姓の通婚を許して居り、百世の後までも通婚を禁ずるは周に始まると言われて居る。けだし周民族の文化が殷のそれに後れていただけこの制度がなお比較的厳格に維持されていて、**それ**④が都合よく諸侯統制の上に利用せられたものであろう。すなわちこの制度によって周の王室と異姓の諸侯との間は婚姻によって結合され、ひいて同姓異姓の諸侯相互の間にも婚姻関係が設定され、これを血族関係に本づく服従関係に**準ぜしめた**⑤ものと思われる。王国維『殷周制度論』参照。

Chapter 2 Section 4 – 封建制度と家族道徳 OJIMA Sukema 小島祐馬 (1943/1988) Hōken seido to kazoku dōtoku

内容質問

(1) 同姓不婚とは何ですか。

(2) 同姓不婚の制度によって、王と異姓（もともと王の親戚ではない諸侯）の関係がどう変わりましたか。

文法質問

① 「もの」の修飾部分はどこからですか。最初の三文字を答えなさい。

② 「服従関係」の修飾部分はどこからですか。最初の三文字を答えなさい。

③ 「この難関」は何を指しますか。

④ 「それ」は何を指しますか。

⑤ 「準ぜしめた」の意味は次のどれですか。
　❶ 「準ずる」ことをさせた　　　　　　　❷ 「準ずる」ことをした
　❸ 「準ずる」ことをされた　　　　　　　❹ 「準ずる」ことをさせられた

英訳

Ⓐ 同時に同姓の諸侯相互の間も家族制度を以て律せらるることとなった。

155

この原始的な同姓不婚の習俗が後には漸次卿大夫士に及ぼされ、ついには庶人階級にまで拡められ、文化の発展とは関係なく今日まで長く中国の社会を支配して来たという①ことについては、周代の人為的強制が与って力あるものと見なければならぬ。

以上述ぶる所に由って観れば、周の封建制度の拠って立つ精神的基礎は、その家族道徳に存すると謂っても②過言ではないであろう。Ⓐ周の封建制度を道徳的に維持せんが爲めには、その家族道徳を鞏固なものにしなければならぬ。孔子はすなわちこの点に着眼したものである。

Chapter 2 Section 4 – 封建制度と家族道徳 OJIMA Sukema 小島祐馬 (1943/1988) Hōken seido to kazoku dōtoku

内容質問

⑴　同姓不婚の習俗はその後どのように受け継がれますか。

⑵　筆者は、周の封建制度の精神的基礎はどこにあると言っていますか。本文の言葉を使って答えなさい。

文法質問

①　「こと」の修飾部分はどこからですか。最初の三文字を答えなさい。

②　筆者によると、何が「過言ではない」のですか。

英訳

Ⓐ　周の封建制度を道徳的に維持せんが爲めには、その家族道徳を鞏固なものにしなければならぬ。

157

A Practical Guide for Scholarly Reading in Japanese

封建制度と家族道徳 Hōken seido to kazoku dōtoku

小島祐馬 OJIMA Sukema (1943/1988)

Vocabulary

Note: NP=Name of a person, NB=Name of a book, PB=Phonetic borrowing

	本文の語彙	辞書形・漢字	読み方 (現代語表記)	英語
P. 152	儒家		じゅか	Confucianism
	始祖		しそ	the founder
	言うまでもなく		いうまでもなく	needless to say
	掩う		おおう	to summarize
	帰着する		きちゃくする	to come down to
	しかるに	然るに	しかるに	however
	運用する		うんようする	to utilize
	立脚する		りっきゃくする	to be rooted in; to be based on
	本づく		もとづく	to be based on
	風化		ふうか	the inspiration of moral conduct in others
	漸次		ぜんじ	gradually
	下剋上		げこくじょう	inferiors overthrowing their superiors
	世態		せたい	the situation of the world/society
	馴致する		じゅんちする	to normalize; to cause one to get used to something
	かくては	斯くては	かくては	at this rate; in this way
	到底〜ない		とうてい〜ない	could never
	面のあたり		まのあたり	directly; before one's eyes
	しからば	然らば	しからば	in that case
	資せん	資す	しす	to contribute
	はたして	果たして	はたして	(what) on earth
	骨子		こっし	backbone
	分封		ぶんぽう	dividing territories
	不婚		ふこん	not marrying
	基調		きちょう	keynote
	〜を為して	〜を為す	〜をなす	to constitute 〜; to make 〜
	相続法		そうぞくほう	the law of succession
	嫡長		ちゃくちょう	the eldest son; heir

158

Chapter 2 Section 4 – 封建制度と家族道徳 OJIMA Sukema 小島祐馬 (1943/1988) Hōken seido to kazoku dōtoku

	本文の語彙	辞書形・漢字	読み方 (現代語表記)	英語
P. 152	嫡子		ちゃくし	legitimate child
	庶子		しょし	illegitimate child
	襲う		おそう	to inherit; to succeed to
	放置する		ほうちする	to neglect
	醸す		かもす	to cause
	本		もと	the origin; the cause
	親疏		しんそ	close and distant
	賢愚		けんぐ	the wise and the foolish
	～に応じて		～におうじて	depending on ～
	されば	然れば	されば	therefore
P. 154	盟主		めいしゅ	alliance leader
	律せらるる	律す(る)	りっす(る)	to govern; to regulate
	難関		なんかん	obstacle
	疏通した	疏通する	そつうする	to overcome
	すなわち	即ち	すなわち	that is to say; namely
	通婚		つうこん	marriage (between people with the same surname or within the same family)
	後れて	後れる	おくれる	to fall behind
	だけ(に)		だけ(に)	because
	厳格に		げんかくに	strictly
	ひいて	延いて	ひいて	in addition
	設定され	設定する	せっていする	to establish
	準ぜしめた	準ず(る)	じゅんず(る)	to follow
P. 156	卿 / 大夫 / 士		けい / たいふ / し	government ranks
	庶人		しょじん	commoner
	支配して	支配する	しはいする	to rule
	人為的		じんいてき	artificial; factitious
	与って	与る	あずかる	to be concerned (in a matter)
	過言ではない		かごんではない	no exaggeration
	鞏固		きょうこ	firm; strong
	着眼した	着眼する	ちゃくがんする	to bring one's attention to

159

A Practical Guide for Scholarly Reading in Japanese

OJIMA Sukema

Expressions

1. けだし / 蓋し in my opinion; probably; indeed cf. Suzuki

◆ けだし権力服従の関係は権力の推移によって漸次下剋上の世態を馴致するを常とし、…

Certainly, relationships of submission to authority often lead to the gradual normalization of the condition of those below overthrowing those above along with shifts in authority.

1) 真理というものは、けだし、永遠に古くして、かつ永遠に新しいものではなかろうか。

Perhaps that which is called truth is eternally old and yet eternally new.

2)「一期一会」、けだしこれ名言と言えよう。

"One lifetime, one meeting." Truly, this can be called a great saying.

2. かくては / 斯くては at this rate; in this way

◆ かくては社会の秩序は到底いつまでも維持することの出来ないということは、…

The fact that order in society can never be preserved in this way…

1) 我が国では少子高齢化社会が進んでおり、かくては、年金を負担する側と受給者側のバランスが崩壊するであろう。

In our country, the low birthrate and aging in society is progressing, and, at this rate, the balance between those who contribute to pensions and those who receive them will collapse.

2) 戦により寺の建立が頓挫した。斯くて一年が過ぎた。

The temple's construction came to an abrupt stop due to the war. In this way, a year passed.

3. X を Y とする / 為す regard X as Y; assume; consider cf. Kano, Matsuura, Naitō, Suzuki, Taki, Tanigawa

◆ 周の封建制度の特質はそれが家族制度を骨子としている点に存する。

The special characteristic of feudalism in the Zhou was that it took the family system as its backbone.

1) この理論を正しいとすると、我々の考えは間違っていないことになる。

If we take this theory to be correct, it would mean that our thinking is not mistaken.

2) 国連は温暖化問題を最重要課題の一つとなしている。

The UN considers global warming to be a problem of the utmost importance.

Note: See Section 5 in Chapter 1.

160

Chapter 2 Section 4 – 封建制度と家族道徳 OJIMA Sukema 小島祐馬 (1943/1988) Hōken seido to kazoku dōtoku

4. 〜て始（初）めて only after 〜 　cf. Taki

◆ しかるに周に至ってはじめて弟に伝えずして子に伝え、…

However, with the Zhou, for the first time, [the throne] was passed on to the child without passing it to the younger brothers…

1) 病気になってはじめて、健康のありがたみがわかる。

It is not until you get sick that you realize the value of good health.

2) 苦労して初めて人の気持ちがわかるようになった。

After going through hardship, I understood others' feelings for the first time.

5. 〜ずして without 〜ing 　cf. Kano, Naitō, Suzuki

◆ しかるに周に至ってはじめて弟に伝えずして子に伝え、…

However, with the Zhou, for the first time, [the throne] was passed on to the child without passing it to the younger brothers…

1) 風が止むのを待たずして、出発することは危険であろう。

Surely it is dangerous to depart without waiting for the wind to stop.

2) 論語を読まずして、中国の思想は理解できない。

One cannot understand Chinese thought without reading the *Lunyu*.

Note: See Section 8.6.4 in Chapter 1.

6. 〜に対して V/ADJ/ADJ-V/ 〜に対する N 　N toward 〜; N against 〜 　cf. Kano, Naitō, Tanigawa

◆ そこでこれら王の子弟に対しては…

Therefore, to these children and younger brothers of the king…

1) 政府の経済政策に対して国民の不満が高まっている。

The peoples' dissatisfaction toward the government's economic policies is increasing.

2) 彼の芸術に対する情熱は変わることがなかった。

His passion for art never changed.

A Practical Guide for Scholarly Reading in Japanese

7. ～事と / になった it has turned out ~; it has been decided ~   cf. Kano, Naitō

◆ 王と諸侯との間に君臣の分というものがはじめて発生することとなったのである。

Something which may be called the status of the lord and retainer emerged between the king and the various dukes for the first time.

1) 長い間入院していた父が、明日ようやく退院できることになった。

It has been decided that my father, who has been hospitalized for a long time, can finally be discharged tomorrow.

2) 次のオリンピックは我が国で開催されることとなった。

It has been decided that the next Olympics will be held in our country.

8. ～如し like ~; look like ~   cf. Kano, Naitō, Taki, Tanigawa

◆ 王と他の領主との関係は後世の盟主と諸侯との関係の如きもので、…

The relationship between the king and other lords was like that between the alliance leader and the various dukes in later times…

1) 過ぎたるは及ばざるが如し。

Too much is just like too little.

2) その新人は彗星の如く現れて、その年の全ての賞を独占した。

The newcomer appeared like a comet and monopolized all the awards for that year.

Note: See Section 8.5.7 in Chapter 1.

9. ～ばかりで（は）なく not only ~; not limited to ~

◆ 王は従来の如く単に諸領主の盟主であるばかりでなく、…

The king was not simply the alliance leader of the various lords as before…

1) 最新のAIは技術的に高度であるばかりではなく、芸術的なピアノ演奏も出来るらしい。

The latest AI is not only technologically advanced but can also apparently play the piano artistically.

2) 机上の空論で終わらぬよう、頭の中で考えるばかりではなく、実行に移すべきだ。

So that this does not end up as an empty theory on paper, you should not only think about it in your head but also put it into practice.

162

Chapter 2 Section 4 – 封建制度と家族道徳 OJIMA Sukema 小島祐馬 (1943/1988) Hōken seido to kazoku dōtoku

10. 〜訳だ / である this is why ~; this means ~; it is the case that ~
cf. Kano, Matsuura, Naitō, Taki, Tanigawa

◆ これら異姓の諸侯に対しては（王は）服従関係を強いることが出来ないわけであるが、…

Of course, the king could not force a relationship of submission onto the various dukes of different surnames…

1) 誰にでも、間違いはあるわけだが、そのあとどう責任をとるかは人それぞれだ。

Of course, everyone makes mistakes, but how you take responsibility afterwards depends on the person.

2) 叔父は学生時代にフランスに留学した。だからフランス語が堪能なわけである。

My uncle studied abroad in France while he was a student. No wonder he is so good at French.

11. 〜と謂（言）っても過言ではない it is no exaggeration to say...

◆ 精神的基礎は、その家族道徳に存すると謂っても過言ではないであろう。

It would not be an exaggeration to say that the spiritual foundation lies in familial morals.

1) 中学の頃、彼は天才と言っても過言ではないぐらい優秀であった。

In middle school, he was so exceptional that it wouldn't have been an exaggeration to call him a genius.

2) 医学の歴史は感染症の歴史に始まったと言っても過言ではない。

It would not be an exaggeration to say that the history of medicine started with the history of infectious diseases.

Chapter 2 Section 5

NAITŌ Konan 内藤湖南 (1866–1934). Representative pre-war scholar of East Asia.

After graduating from Akita Normal School, Naitō traveled to Taiwan as a journalist, eventually came to be in charge of editorials at Osaka Asahi Shinbunsha, and, as the leading figure in media discourse on Chinese issues, even advised the Ministry of Foreign Affairs on policies directed at China. In 1907, he took up a teaching position in history at Kyoto Imperial University (presently, Kyoto University), becoming a professor in 1942. His research included Chinese history from the ancient to early modern period, periodization, and even Japanese history.

The so-called 唐宋変革論 (とうそうへんかくろん) "Tang-Song Transition Theory" which places a large divide between the Tang and Song in the periodization of Chinese history found in the essay contained in this textbook is Naitō's representative theory and exerted much influence on later scholarship of East Asian history.

Naitō's theory was further developed after his death by the next generation of scholars such as MIYAZAKI Ichisada, who designated the Tang and before as medieval and the Song and after as early modern. This started the periodization debate with the Historical Science Society of Japan faction, which advocated for designating the Song and after as medieval.

Representative works include 『支那史学史』(しなしがくし) *History of the Historical Study of China*, 2 volumes (Tōyō Bunko, Heibonsha, 1993) and 『清朝史通論』(しんちょうしつうろん) *Outline of the History of the Qing Dynasty* (Tōyō Bunko, Heibonsha, 1992).

概括的唐宋時代觀

NAITŌ Konan 内藤湖南 (1922) Gaikatsuteki Tō-Sō jidai kan

唐宋時代といふことは普通に用ふる語なるが、歴史特に文化史的に考察すると、實は意味をなさぬ語である。①それは唐代は中世の終末に屬し、而して宋代は近世の發端となりて、其間に唐末より五代に至る過渡期を含むを以て、唐と宋とは文化の性質上著しく異りたる點がある。但し從來の歴史家は多く朝代によりて時代を區劃したから、唐宋とか元明清とか一の成語になつて居るが、學術的には(1)かゝる區劃法を(2)改むる必要がある。但し今は便宜上、普通の歴史區劃に從ひ唐宋時代の名を用ひて、支那の中世より近世に移る間の變化の②狀態を總括して說いて見ようと思ふ。

③中世と近世との文化の狀態は、如何なる點に於て異るかといふに、政治上よりいへば貴族政治が廢頹して君主獨裁政治が起りたる③事で、貴族政治は六朝から唐の中世までを最も盛なる時代とした。勿論此貴族政治は、上古の氏族政治とは全く別物で、周代の封建制度とも關係がなく、一種特別のものである。A此時代の支那の貴族は、制度として天子から領土人民を與へられたといふのではなく、其家柄が自然に地方の名望家として永續したる關係から生じたるもので、所謂郡望なるものゝ本體がこれである。それ等の家柄は皆系譜を重んじ、其ために當時系譜學が盛んになつた位である。現に存在する諸書の中でも、唐書の宰相世系表は即ち其有樣を示したもの、又、李延壽の南北史の中には、朝代に拘らず各家の人を祖先から子孫まで續けて纏まれる傳を書いたから、人のために家傳を作つた體裁になつたといふ非難を受けたが、④これは南北朝時代の實際狀態が無意識の裡に歴史の上に現れたのである。

内容質問

⑴ 「かゝる區劃法」はどのような区画法ですか。

⑵ 湖南が、⑴の歴史区画法を「改むる必要がある」と言っているのはなぜですか。

⑶ 湖南は、中世と近世の文化の状態は「如何なる點に於て異る」と言っていますか。

文法質問

① 「それ」は何を指しますか。

② 「狀態」の修飾部分はどこからですか。最初の三文字を答えなさい。

③ 「事」の修飾部分はどこからですか。最初の三文字を答えなさい。

④ 「これ」は何を指しますか。

英訳

Ⓐ 此時代の支那の貴族は、制度として天子から領土人民を與へられたといふのではなく、其家柄が自然に地方の名望家として永續したる關係から生じたるもので、所謂郡望なるものゝ本體がこれである。

167

かくの如き名族は、當時の政治上の位置から殆ど超越して居る。即ち當時の政治は貴族全體の專有ともいふべきものであつて、貴族でなければ高い官職に就く事が出來なかつたが、しかし第一流の貴族は必ず天子宰相になるとも限らない。ことに天子の位置は尤も特別のものにて、これは實力あるものゝ手に歸したるが、天子になつても其家柄は第一流の貴族となるとは限らない。唐太宗が天子になれるとき、貴族の系譜を調べさせたが、第一流の家柄は北方では博陵の崔氏、范陽の盧氏などにて、太宗の家は隴西の李氏で三流に位するといふことなりしも、此家柄番附は、天子の威力でもこれを變更する事が出來なかつた。南朝に於ても王氏、謝氏などが天子の家柄よりも遙に重んぜられた。是等は皆同階級の貴族の間で結婚をなし、それ等の團體が社會の中心を形成して、最もよき官職は皆此仲間の占むる所となつた。

この貴族政治は唐末より五代までの過渡期に廢頹して、これに代れるものが君主獨裁政治である。貴族廢頹の結果、君主の位置と人民とが近接し來りて、高い官職につくのにも家柄としての特權がなくなり、全く天子の權力によりて任命せらるゝ事となつた。この制度は宋以後漸次發達して、明清時代は獨裁政治の完全なる形式をつくることゝなり、國家に於ける凡ての權力の根本は天子一人これを有して、他の如何なる大官も全權を有する事なく、君主は決して如何なる官吏にも其職務の全權を委任せず、從て官吏は其職務について完全なる責任を負ふ事なくして、君主一人がこれを負擔する事となつた。

内容質問

(1) この時代の貴族政治において、高い官職に就くのはどのような人でしたか。

(2) 君主独裁政治においては、何が変わりましたか。当てはまるものをすべて選びなさい。

❶ 君主一人が、国家の権力の根本を有することとなった。
❷ 家柄としての特権がなくなったが、高い官職に就くことができた。
❸ 貴族が廃頽して、君主と人民が近接し、人民が君主を選ぶことになった。
❹ 高い官職は、第一流の貴族たちに占領されていた。
❺ 君主だけが、高官たちを任命できることになった。

文法質問

① 「これ」は何を指しますか。

② 「これ」は何を指しますか。

英訳

Ⓐ ことに天子の位置は尤も特別のものにて、これは實力あるものゝ手に歸したるが、天子になつても其家柄は第一流の貴族となるとは限らない。

A Practical Guide for Scholarly Reading in Japanese

　この二種の政治状態を比較すると、貴族政治時代に於ける君主の位置は、時として實力あるものが階級を超越して占むる事ありても、既に君主となれば貴族階級中の一の機關たる事を免るゝ事が出來ない。即ち君主は貴族階級の共有物で、その政治は貴族の特權を認めた上に實行し得るのであつて、一人で絕對の權力を有することは出來ない。孟子は嘗て卿に異姓の卿と、貴戚の卿とあつて、後者は君主に不都合あればこれを諫め、聽かざればこれを取り換へるといへる事があるが、かゝる事は上代のみならず、中世の貴族政治時代にも屢々實行された。君主は一族即ち外戚從僕までも含める一家の專有物で、從てこれ等一家の意に稱はないと廢立が行はれ、或は弑逆が行はれた。六朝より唐に至るまで、弑逆廢立の多いのは、かゝる事情によるので、この一家の事情は多數の庶民とは殆んど無關係であつた。庶民は國家の要素として何等の重きをなさず、政治とは沒交涉である。

　かくの如く君主は單に貴族の代表的位置に立つて居つたのは中世の狀態なるが、近世に入りて其貴族が沒落すると、君主は直接に臣民全體に對する事となり、臣民全體の公の所有物で、貴族團體の私有物でなくなつた。かくして臣民全體が政治に關係する事となれば、君主は臣民全體の代表となるべき筈のやうであるが、支那にはかゝる場合なかりしために、君主は臣民全體の代表者にあらずして、夫自身が絕對權力の主體となつた。しかし兎も角、君主の位置は貴族時代よりは甚だ安全となり、從て廢立も容易に行はれず、弑逆も殆んどなくなつた事は宋以後の歷史は其然るを證明する。

170

内容質問

⑴ 孟子の引用はどこからどこまでですか。最初と最後の５字を記しなさい。

文法質問

① 「これ」は何を指しますか。本文の言葉を使って答えなさい。

② 「かゝる事」とは何を指しますか。

③ 「かゝる場合」とは何を指しますか。

④ 「其然る」の「其」は何を指しますか。

A Practical Guide for Scholarly Reading in Japanese

尤も元代のみは頗る異例がある。^①これは蒙古文化の程度によるので、蒙古の文化は支那の同時代に比較すると甚しく遅れて、却て支那の上古時代と同程度であるのに、支那を征服せるがために、突然に近世的の國家組織の上に君臨したのであるから、其帝室には依然として貴族政治の形骸が殘つて居り、

5 民政の方のみが近世的色彩になつたから、⁽¹⁾一種の矛盾した状態をあらはしたのである。

貴族政治の時代には、貴族が權力を握る習慣であるから、隋の文帝・唐の太宗の如き英主が出で、制度の上に於ては貴族の權力を認めぬ事にしても、實際の政治には尚其形式が殘つて、政治は貴族との協議體となつた。勿論こ

10 の協議體は代議政治ではない。

唐代に於ける政治上の重要機關は三つあつた。曰く尚書省、曰く中書省、曰く門下省である。その中で中書省は天子の祕書官で、詔勅命令の案を立て、臣下の上奏に對して批答を與へることになつて居るが、この詔勅が確定するまでには門下省の同意を必要とする。門下省は封駁の權を有して、若し中書

15 省の案文が不當と認むるときには、^②これを駁撃し、これを封還することも出來る。そこで中書と門下とが政事堂で協議して決定する事となる。尚書省はこの決定を受取つて執行する職務である。中書省は天子を代表し、門下省は官吏の輿論、即ち貴族の輿論を代表する形式になつて居るのではあるが、勿論、中書・門下・尚書三省ともに大官は皆貴族の出身であるので、貴族は天

20 子の命令に絕對に服從したのではない。夫故に⁽²⁾天子が臣下の上奏に對する批答なども、極めて友誼的で、決して命令的でない。^A然るに明清時代になりては、批答は全く從僕などに對すると同樣、ぞんざいな言葉遣ひで命令的となり、封駁の權は宋以後益々衰へ、明清に在りては殆んどなくなつた。

172

内容質問

(1) 「一種の矛盾した狀態をあらはした」のはいつの時代ですか。それはなぜですか。

(2) 「天子が臣下の上奏に對する批答なども、極めて友誼的で、決して命令的でない」のはいつの時代ですか。それはなぜですか。

文法質問

① 「これ」は何を指しますか。

② 「これ」は何を指しますか。

英訳

Ⓐ 然るに明清時代になりては、批答は全く從僕などに對すると同様、ぞんざいな言葉遣ひで命令的となり、封駁の權は宋以後益々衰へ、明清に在りては殆んどなくなつた。

A Practical Guide for Scholarly Reading in Japanese

(1)
かくの如き變化の結果、宰相の位置は天子を輔佐するものでなくして、殆ど祕書官同樣となりたるが、尚宋代にては唐代の遺風も存在して、宰相は相當の權力を有したるも、明以後には全く宰相の官を置かぬ事になり、事實宰相の仕事をとれるものは殿閣大學士であつて、これは官職の性質としては天子の祕書役、代筆の役で、天子を輔佐し、其責任を分ち、若くは責任を全く負擔する古代の宰相の俤はなくなり、君權のみが無限に發達した。唐の時の宰相は、皆貴族階級の中より出で、一度其位置に到ると、天子と雖も其權力を自由に動かす事が出來ない習慣であつたが、明以後は如何に強大なる權力を有する宰相でも、天子の機嫌を損ねると、忽ち廢黜せられ、一個の平民とせられ、囚人と墜さるゝ。宋代は恰も唐と明淸との間に立つので、明淸の如く宰相に權力がないといふ譯ではないが、天子の權力を笠に被て居る間は全盛を極めても、天子の背景を失ふと忽ち一匹夫となる。宋の寇準・丁謂、南宋の賈似道などの境遇の變化を見ても分るのである。地方官なども、唐代には、中央の權力と關係して、各地方に於て、殆ど君主同樣の權力を有するもの多き習慣なりしが、宋以後は、如何なるよき位置の地方官も、君主一片の命令で容易に交迭せらるゝ事となつた。宦官は天子の從僕であるが、唐代の宦官は天子の眷族の有力なる部分となつて、定策國老門生天子といふ諺さへ出來たが、後に明の時にも宦官が跋扈せるも、天子の恩寵あるときにのみ權力があつて、恩寵が衰へると其勢力は全くなくなる。唐と明との宦官にかくの如き相違あるは、卽ち貴族政治と君主獨裁政治との相違ある結果である。

174

内容質問

(1) 「かくの如き變化」とは、どのような変化ですか。

(2) 天子の権力は、唐代、宋代、明清で、どのように変化しますか。弱い方から順番に述べなさい。

(3) 「定策國老門生天子」という諺は何を表していますか。正しいものを選びなさい。
- ❶ 宦官が権力を失って、天子の生徒になること
- ❷ 宦官の権力が強くなって、天子は宦官に従うようになったこと
- ❸ 宦官が天子の家族から選ばれるようになること

文法質問

① 「俤」の修飾部分はどこからですか。最初の三文字を答えなさい。

② 「習慣」の修飾部分はどこからですか。最初の三文字を答えなさい。

③ 「もの」の修飾部分はどこからですか。最初の三文字を答えなさい。

④ 「其勢力」は何を指しますか。

それと同時に人民の地位も著しく變化して來た。元來法治國とは違ひ、人民の權力を明らかに認める事はないけれども、人民の地位と財産上の私權とは、貴族政治時代と①大に趣を異にするやうになつた。貴族時代には人民は貴族全體の奴隷の如く視られしが、隋唐の代となり、人民を貴族の手から解放して國家の直轄とし、殊に農民を國家の小作人の如く取扱ふ制度が作られたが、事實は政治の權力は貴族にあつたから、君主を擁したる貴族團體の小作人といふ狀態であつた。土地の分配制度なども、②かくの如き意義と密接の關係があり、殊に租税の性質は其意義を尤もよく現して居る。即ち唐代の租・庸・調の制度は、人民は政府に對して地代を納め、力役に服し、工作品を提供する意味のものであつた。唐の中世から③此制度自然に壞れて兩税制度となり、人民の居住が制度上自由に解放さるゝことゝなり、地租などの收納も錢で代納することゝなつたので、人民は土地に拘束せらるゝ奴隷小作人たる位置から、自然に解放さるゝ④端緒を開きしが、(1)宋代に至り、王安石の新法によりて、人民の土地所有の⑤意味が益々確實になつて來た。青苗錢の如き低利資金融通法も、人民が土地の收穫を自由に處分する事を認める意味とも解さるゝ。又從來の差役を改めて雇役とし、隨分反對者の攻擊を受けたが、此雇役制度は尤も當時の事情に適せるを以て、後に司馬光が王安石の新法を改めた時に、新法反對論者の中にも、蘇東坡始め、差役を復舊することはこれを否なりとした人が多い。支那は人民の參政權を認むるといふことは全くなかりしも、貴族の階級を消滅せしめて、君主と人民と直接に相對するやうになつた⑥のは、即ち近世的政治の狀態となつたのである。

内容質問

⑴ 宋代に至って、君主と人民の関係はどのようになり、政治の形はどのように変わりましたか。

文法質問

① 「大に趣を異にするやうになつた」の主語は何ですか。

② 「かくの如き意義」とは何を指しますか。

③ 「此制度」とは何ですか。

④ 「端緒」の修飾部分はどこからですか。最初の三文字を答えなさい。

⑤ 「意味」の修飾部分はどこからですか。最初の三文字を答えなさい。

⑥ 「の」の修飾部分はどこからですか。最初の三文字を答えなさい。

又官吏即ち君主と人民との中間の階級も選擧となつた。勿論この選擧とは、今の代議政治の如く代議的ではなくして、一種の官吏登用の形式を指すものなるが、即ち選擧の方法が貴族的階級からの登用を一變して、試驗登用、即ち科擧となつたのである。六朝時代には天下の官吏を九品中正の方法<ruby>九品中正<rt>きゅうひんちゅうせい</rt></ruby>で選擧し、全く貴の權力で左右したのであつて、當時の諺に上品無寒門、下品無勢族といふ事があつたが、隋唐以來此弊を破るために科擧を行ふことゝなつた。然し唐代の<u>科擧は其方法が<ruby>矢張<rt>やはり</rt></ruby>依然として貴族的なりしが、これも宋の王安石時代から一變した</u>。即ち唐代より宋の初期の科擧は帖括と詩賦とを主とした。經書を暗誦する力を試驗するのが帖括で、文學上の創作力を試むるのが詩賦である。<ruby>夫れ<rt>そ</rt></ruby><ruby>故<rt>ゆえ</rt></ruby>、其試驗は學科の試驗といふよりは、<ruby>寧ろ<rt>むし</rt></ruby>人格試驗と文章草案の力とを試驗するといふ<u>方法</u>①であつた。<ruby>處<rt>ところ</rt></ruby>が王安石の制度では帖括に代ふるに<ruby>經義<rt>けいぎ</rt></ruby>を以てし、詩賦に代ふるに策論を以てした。經義は經書の中の義理に關して意見を書かせ、策論は政治上の意見を書かせた。勿論②<u>これ</u>も後には、經義は單に一時の思ひ付きを以て試驗官を驚かす文章の<u>遊戯</u>③と變じ、策論も單に粗末な歴史上の事蹟を概説するに過ぎないものとなつて、實際の政務とは何等の關係もなく<u>なつた</u>④が、兎も角これを變ずるだけは、從來の人格主義から實務主義に<ruby>改むる<rt>あらた</rt></ruby>のが目的である。試驗に應ずるものも、唐代では一ヶ年に五十人位より及第しなかつたが、明以後、科擧の及第者は非常に増加して、<ruby>或時<rt>あるとき</rt></ruby>は三年に一度であるけれども、數百人を超え、ことに應試者は何時でも一萬以上を<ruby>數ふる<rt>かぞ</rt></ruby>事となつた。即ち君主獨裁時代に於て、官吏の地位は一般庶民に分配さるゝことに於て、機會均等を許さるゝ事となつたのである。

内容質問

⑴ 「科擧は其方法が矢張依然として貴族的なりしが、これも宋の王安石時代から一變した」とありますが、どのように変わりましたか。正しい文を全て選びなさい。

❶ 帖括を経義に変え、詩賦を策論に変えて、人格主義から実務主義に改めようとした。

❷ 科挙の試験で政治上の意見を書かせることがなくなった。

❸ 合格者数が急増した。

❹ 一般庶民は官吏となることができなくなった。

文法質問

① 「方法」の修飾部分はどこからですか。最初の三文字を答えなさい。

② 「これ」は何を指しますか。本文の言葉を使って答えなさい。

③ 「遊戯」の修飾部分はどこからですか。最初の三文字を答えなさい。

④ 「なつた」の主語は何ですか。本文の言葉を使って答えなさい。

A Practical Guide for Scholarly Reading in Japanese

政治の實際の状態に於ても變化を來して、殊に黨派の如きは其性質を一變した。唐の時にも、宋の時にも、朋黨が喧かりしが、唐の朋黨は單に權力の爭ひを專らとする貴族中心のものにして、宋代になりては、著しく政治上の主義が朋黨の上に表はれた。①これは政權が貴族の手を離れてから、婚姻や親戚關係から來る黨派が漸次衰へて、政治上の意見が黨派を作る主要なる②目的となつたのである。勿論(1)この黨派の弊害は、政治上の主義から來たものでも、漸次貴族時代と類似したものとなつて、明代にては、師弟の關係、出身地方の關係などが重にこれを支配して、所謂君子によりて作られた黨派も其弊害も、小人の黨派と差別がなくなり、明は遂に東林黨のために滅亡したといはるゝに至り、清朝にては甚だしく臣下の黨派を嫌ひ、其ために君主の權力を益々絶對ならしめた。

經濟上に於ても(2)著しき變化を來した。唐代では有名な開元通寶の鑄造を行ひ、貨幣の鑄造は引續き行はれしも、其流通高は割に少ない。貨幣の流通が盛んになりしは宋代になつてからである。唐代は實物經濟といふ譯ではないけれども、多く物の價値を表はす貨幣の利用を、絹布によりて行つた。然るに宋代にありては、絹布、綿などの代りに銅錢を使用する事となり、更に發達すると紙幣さへ盛んに用ひられた。紙幣は唐代からして已に飛錢といつて、これを用ひたといふ事であるが、宋代に至りては③其利用が非常に盛んで、これを交子、會子等と稱し、南宋時代は紙幣の發行高は非常の額に上り、④其ために物價の變動も甚しかつた。

180

内容質問

(1) 「この黨派の弊害」とは何ですか。

(2) 経済の「著しき變化」において、正しいものを全て選びなさい。
- ❶ 唐代に「開元通宝」の鋳造が行われ、貨幣の流通が著しく増えた。
- ❷ 宋代にも銅銭があったが、絹布、綿なども貨幣のかわりに用いられた。
- ❸ 紙幣は宋代から初めて用いられるようになった。
- ❹ 宋代には紙幣を多く発行したため、物価の変動が激しくなった。
- ❺ 元の時代には紙幣と銅銭の両方が作られた。
- ❻ 貨幣経済が盛んになったのは宋代からである。
- ❼ 銀は貨幣として使われなかった。
- ❽ 銭の数え方は時代によって変化した。

文法質問

① 「これ」は何を指しますか。

② 「目的」の修飾部分はどこからですか。最初の三文字を答えなさい。

③ 「其利用」とは何を指しますか。

④ 「其ため」とは何を指しますか。

兎も角充分に利用され、次の元代に於ては殆ど、銅錢鑄造の事なくして、單に紙幣のみを流通せしむることゝなつた。明以後不換紙幣政策が極端に行はれたので、遂に敗滅せるが、要するに宋代に入りて貨幣經濟が非常に盛んになつた①といふ事が出來る。銀も此頃よりして漸次貨幣として重要の位置を占むる事となり、北宋時代などは僅かの流通にとゞまりしも、南宋に至りては餘程盛んになりしものらしく、[A]元の伯顏が南宋を滅ぼして北京に歸る時に、南宋の庫から收得した銀を、北京に運ぶために一定の形に鑄造した②のが、今日の元寶銀の始めだといはれて居るから、宋末には餘程流通をしたものと見える。明淸に至り益々(1)此傾向盛大となり、終に全く銀が紙幣の位置を奪ふに至つた。兎も角、唐宋の代り目が、實物經濟の終期と貨幣經濟の始期と交代する時期に當るので、其間に貨幣の名稱なども自然に變化を來した。昔は錢も兩とか銖とかで稱へられたが、これは勿論重量の名稱にて、昔は一兩が二十四銖と算せられた。宋以後一兩を十錢と計算することゝなり、即ち一錢が二銖四絫に當る。元來開元通寶一文が重量二銖四絫で、十文が一兩となるのであるから、宋代よりは重量の名稱を廢して錢の箇數であらはすことゝなり、これによりても錢の使用の當時如何に盛大なりしかを知るに足るのである。日本で重量の名稱を一匁（一文目）といふ如きは、支那の錢の名稱を逆に使用したものである。

③學術文藝の性質も著しく變化して來た。假に之を經學文學で說いて見れば、經學の性質は唐代に於て已に變化の兆候をあらはした。唐の初期までは、漢魏六朝の風を傳へて、經學は家法若くは師法を重んじた。昔から傳へ來つた說を以てこれを敷衍する事は許されたが、師說を變じて新說を立てる事は一般に許されなかつた。勿論其間には、種々の拔道を考へて、幾度も舊說を變じたるも、公然と③かくの如き試みをする事は出來ない事であつた。

内容質問

(1) 「此傾向」とは、どのような傾向ですか。

(2) 銭の数え方は宋代からどのようになりましたか。

(3) 「學術文藝の性質も著しく變化して來た」とありますが、経学では何が変わりましたか。

文法質問

① 「と」の修飾部分はどこからですか。最初の三文字を答えなさい。

② 「の」の修飾部分はどこからですか。最初の三文字を答えなさい。

③ 「かくの如き試み」とは何ですか。

英訳

Ⓐ 元の伯顔が南宋を滅ぼして北京に歸る時に、南宋の庫から收得した銀を、北京に運ぶために一定の形に鑄造したのが、今日の元寶銀の始めだといはれて居るから、宋末には餘程流通をしたものと見える。

其結果、當時の著述は義疏を以て主とした。義疏とは經書の注に對して細かい解說をしたので、これが原則としては疏不破注といふ事になつて居る。然るに唐の中頃から古來の注疏に疑を挾み、一己の意見を立てる<u>事</u>①が行はれた。其尤も早いのは春秋に關する新說である。其後宋代になると此傾向が極端に發達して、學者は千古不傳の遺義を遺經から發見したと稱し、凡て自己の見解で新解釋を施すのが一般の風となつた。文學の中でも、文は六朝以來唐まで四六文が流行したが、唐の中頃から韓柳諸家が起り、所謂古文體を復興し、凡ての文が散文體になつて來た、即ち形式的の文が自由な表現法の文に變つて來た。詩の方では六朝までは五言の詩で、選體即ち文選風のものが盛んであつたが、盛唐の頃から其風一變し、李杜以下の大家が出て、益々從來の形式を破る事につとめた。唐末からは又詩の外に、詩餘即ち詞が發達して來て、五言・七言の形式を破り、頗る自由な形式に變化し、音樂的に特に完全に<u>發達して來た</u>②。其結果、宋から元代にかけて曲の發達を來し、從來の短い形式の敍情的のものから、複雜な形式の劇となつて來た。其詞なども典故ある古語を主とせずして、俗語を以て自由に表現するやうに變つた。これがために<u>一時は貴族的の文學が一變して、庶民的のものにならんとした</u>(1)。

　又、藝術の方では、六朝・唐代までは壁畫が盛に行はれ、主として彩色を主としたが、盛唐の頃から白描水墨の新派が盛んになつたけれども、唐代を通じては新派が舊派を壓倒する譯には行かなかつた。然るに五代から宋にかけて、壁畫が漸次屏障畫と變じて、金碧の山水は衰へ、墨繪が益々發達した。

内容質問

(1) 「一時は貴族的の文學が一變して、庶民的のものにならんとした」のはなぜですか。

文法質問

① 「事」の修飾部分はどこからですか。最初の三文字を答えなさい。

② 「發達して來た」の主語は何ですか。本文の言葉を使って答えなさい。

A Practical Guide for Scholarly Reading in Japanese

A 五代を中心として、以前の畫は、大體は傳統的の風格を重んじ、畫は事件の説明として意味あるものにすぎざりしが、新らしき水墨畫は、自己の意志を表現する自由な方法をとり、從來貴族の道具として、宏壯なる建築物の装飾として用ゐられたものが、卷軸が盛んに行はれる事となり、庶民的といふ譯

5 ではないが、平民より出身した官吏が、流寓する中にも、これを携帯して樂しむ事が出來る種類のものに變化した。

音樂も唐代は舞樂が主で、即ち音を主として、それに舞の動作を附屬さしたもので、樂律も形式的であり、動作に物眞似などの意味は少くして、ことに貴族的な儀式に相應せるものなりしが、宋以後、雜劇の流行につれて、物

10 眞似の如き卑近の藝術が盛んになり、其動作も比較的複雜になつて、品位に於ては古代の音樂より下れるも、單純に低級な平民の趣味にあふ樣に變化した。其尤も著しき發達を表はしたのは南宋時代である。

以上の如く、唐と宋との時代に於て、あらゆる文化的生活が變化を來したので、此他にも微細に個人的生活を観察すると、其何れもの點に、此時代に

15 於ける變化の表れたことを認むるが、今はかくの如き微細の點を述べる事は避ける。

要するに支那に於ける中世・近世の一大轉換の時期が、唐宋の間にある事は、歴史を讀むものゝ尤も注意すべき所である。

186

内容質問

⑴ 「唐と宋の時代に於て、あらゆる文化的生活が變化を來したので」とありますが、どのような分野ですか。本文の言葉を使って、具体的に３つ述べなさい。

文法質問

① 「もの」の修飾部分はどこからですか。最初の三文字を答えなさい。

② 「もの」の修飾部分はどこからですか。最初の三文字を答えなさい。

③ 「變化した」の主語は何ですか。本文の言葉を使って答えなさい。

④ 「所」の修飾部分はどこからですか。最初の三文字を答えなさい。

英訳

Ⓐ 五代を中心として、以前の畫は、大體は傳統的の風格を重んじ、畫は事件の説明として意味あるものにすぎざりしが、新らしき水墨畫は、自己の意志を表現する自由な方法をとり、從來貴族の道具として、宏壯なる建築物の装飾として用ゐられたものが、巻軸が盛んに行はれる事となり、庶民的といふ譯ではないが、平民より出身した官吏が、流寓する中にも、これを携帯して樂しむ事が出來る種類のものに變化した。

A Practical Guide for Scholarly Reading in Japanese

概括的唐宋時代觀 Gaikatsuteki Tō-Sō jidai kan
内藤湖南 NAITŌ Konan (1922)

Vocabulary

Note: NP＝Name of a person, NB＝Name of a book, PB＝Phonetic borrowing

	本文の語彙	辞書形・漢字	読み方 (現代語表記)	英語
P. 166	〜をなさぬ	〜を爲す	〜をなす	to constitute ~; to make ~
	而して		しかして	and then (＝ そうして)
	發端		ほったん	the beginning
	廢頽して	廢頽する	はいたいする	to become corrupt
	郡望		ぐんぼう	prefectural gentry; people of good social position
	系譜		けいふ	lineage; genealogy
	纏まれる	纏まる	まとまる	to be arranged/organized
P. 168	尤も		もっとも	most, above all
	〜の手に歸したる	〜の手に歸する	〜のてにきする	to fall into someone's hands
	番附		ばんづけ	a ranking list
	威力		いりょく	power; authority
	委任せず	委任する	いにんする	to entrust
P. 170	免る〻	免る	まぬかる	to escape (＝ まぬがれる)
	卿		けい / きょう	state ministers
	貴戚		きせき	ruler's (maternal) relative
	諫め	諫める	いさめる	to remonstrate; to advise ~ not to do
	屢々		しばしば	often
	外戚		がいせき	a maternal relative
	從僕		じゅうぼく	a servant
	意に稱はない		いにかなわない	not satisfy
	廢立		はいりつ	dethronement
	弑逆		しいぎゃく / しぎゃく	murder of one's own lord or father
P. 172	頗る		すこぶる	considerably
	異例		いれい	exception; exceptional case
	君臨した	君臨する	くんりんする	to reign
	形骸		けいがい	skeleton; shell
	英主		えいしゅ	great ruler

Chapter 2 Section 5 – 概括的唐宋時代觀 NAITŌ Konan 内藤湖南 (1922) Gaikatsuteki Tō-Sō jidai kan

	本文の語彙	辞書形・漢字	読み方 (現代語表記)	英語
P. 172	協議體		きょうぎたい	council
	代議政治		だいぎせいじ	representative government
	尚書省		しょうしょしょう	the Department of State Affairs
	中書省		ちゅうしょしょう	the Palace Secretariat
	門下省		もんかしょう	the Chancellery
	詔勅		しょうちょく	Imperial rescript
	上奏		じょうそう	report to the throne
	批答を與へる		ひとうをあたえる	to give an official written reply
	封駁		ふうばく	to repel the imperial rescript/edict
	不當		ふとう	unjust; inappropriate
	駁撃し	駁撃する	ばくげきする	to argue against
	封還する		ふうかんする	to return (a proposal)
	協議して	協議する	きょうぎする	to discuss
	執行する		しっこうする	to execute
	ぞんざいな		ぞんざいな	rude; rough
	益々	益々	ますます	more and more; increasingly
P. 174	遺風		いふう	old traditions and customs
	とる	執る	とる	conduct; serve
	大學士		だいがくし	grand secretary (Lit. grand scholar)
	代筆		だいひつ	writing (e.g. a letter) for somebody
	若くは		もしくは	or
	俤		おもかげ(国字)	image
	君權		くんけん	sovereign rights
	機嫌を損ねる		きげんをそこねる	to displease; to offend
	廢黜せられ	廢黜する	はいちゅつする	to dismiss
	囚人		しゅうじん	a prisoner; a convict
	笠に被て	笠に被る	かさにきる	to take advantage of ~ (e.g. authority)
	匹夫		ひっぷ	an ordinary man
	寇 準		こう じゅん	Kou Zhun (NP)
	丁 謂		てい い	Ding Wei (NP)
	賈 似道		か じどう	Jia Sidao (NP)

	本文の語彙	辞書形・漢字	読み方 (現代語表記)	英語
P. 174	交迭せらる〻	交迭する	こうてつする	to replace; to remove from one's position
	宦官		かんがん	eunuch
	眷族		けんぞく	follower
	恩寵		おんちょう	(Emperor's) grace
P. 176	法治國		ほうちこく	country governed by law
	私權		しけん	private right
	趣を異にする		おもむきをことにする	be different
	直轄		ちょっかつ	direct control
	租庸調		そようちょう	tax system
	地代		じだい	land rent
	力役		りきやく	physical labor duty imposed by the state
	工作品		こうさくひん	handicraft
	地租		ちそ	land tax
	収納		しゅうのう	receiving money; storing something
	拘束せらる〻	拘束する	こうそくする	to bind; to imprison
	端緒		たんしょ	the first step; clue
	王 安石		おう あんせき	Wang Anshi (NP)
	新法		しんぽう	the New Policies (initiated by Wang Anshi)
	青苗錢 (aka. 青苗法)		せいびょうせん (aka. せいびょうほう)	the Green Sprouts Program; government loan
	低利資金融通法		ていりしきんゆうずうほう	a program that provides a loan at a low interest rate
	差役		さえき	corvée labor; unpaid labor
	雇役		こえき	paid employment
	司馬 光		しば こう	Sima Guang (NP)
	蘇 東坡		そ とうば	Su Dongpo (NP)
	復舊する		ふっきゅうする	to restore
P. 178	官吏登用		かんりとうよう	the appointment of a government official
	帖括		じょうかつ	a subject of the imperial exam

Chapter 2 Section 5 – 概括的唐宋時代觀 NAITŌ Konan 内藤湖南 (1922) Gaikatsuteki Tō-Sō jidai kan

	本文の語彙	辞書形・漢字	読み方 (現代語表記)	英語
P. 178	經書		けいしょ	classic Confucian writings
	暗誦する		あんしょうする	to recite
	經義		けいぎ	the interpretation of the Confucian Classics (経書)
	策論		さくろん	Policy Essays; questions about politics
	事蹟		じせき	evidence
	概說する		がいせつする	to give an outline
	〜より…ない			no more than ~; not…other than ~
	及第しなかつた	及第する	きゅうだいする	to pass (an exam)
	應試者		おうししゃ	exam applicant
P. 180	黨派		とうは	political party; faction
	朋黨		ほうとう	the name of a political party
	專ら		もっぱら	exclusively
	東林黨		とうりんとう	the name of a political party
	開元通寶		かいげんつうほう	the currency of the Tang Dynasty
	流通高		りゅうつうだか	amount of circulation
	飛錢		ひせん	flying cash; a paper currency of the Tang Dynasty
P. 182	元寶銀		げんぽうぎん	silver ingot currency; sycee (Cantonese)
	兩		りょう	a unit of weight
	銖		しゅ	a unit of weight
	絫		るい	a unit of weight
	錢		せん	a unit of weight
	文		もん	a unit of weight
	勾		もんめ	a unit of weight
	經學		けいがく	the study of the Confucian classics
	家法		かほう	domestic discipline
	師法		しほう	knowledge handed down by one's master
	拔道		ぬけみち	loophole
	公然と		こうぜんと	openly; publicly

191

A Practical Guide for Scholarly Reading in Japanese

	本文の語彙	辞書形・漢字	読み方 (現代語表記)	英語
P. 184	義疏		ぎそ	commentaries on classics
	疏不破注		そふはちゅう	new commentaries should not refute the original annotations
	注疏		ちゅうそ	commentary and sub-commentary
	一己		いっこ	oneself
	千古不傳		せんこふでん	something nobody has passed on for the past 1000 years
	四六文		しろくぶん	a type of couplet used in classical Chinese
	韓柳		かんりゅう	韓愈 and 柳宗元
	韓愈		かん ゆ	Han Yu (NP)
	柳宗元		りゅう そうげん	Liu Zongyuan (NP)
	文選		もんぜん	Wen Xuan (NB)
	李杜		りと	李白 and 杜甫
	李白		り はく	Li Bai (NP)
	杜甫		と ほ	Du Fu (NP)
	詞		し	a type of lyric poetry
	敍情的		じょじょうてき	lyrical
	典故		てんこ	literary quotation
	白描水墨		はくびょうすいぼく	bai miao style ink wash painting
	壓倒する		あっとうする	to overwhelm
	屛障畫		へいしょうが	pictures on (room) partitions
	金碧の山水		きんぺきのさんすい	a type of Chinese-style landscape painting
	墨繪		すみえ	black-and-white painting
P. 186	水墨畫		すいぼくが	a type of black-and-white painting
	宏壯		こうそう	magnificent; splendid
	流寓する		りゅうぐうする	to roam around
	物眞似 (PB)		ものまね	mimicry
	相應せる	相應する	そうおうする	suitable; appropriate
	雜劇		ざつげき	a form of Chinese opera
	卑近		ひきん	familiar (to the general public)
	品位		ひんい	quality; aesthetic taste

192

Expressions

1. 斯かる such; like this cf. Suzuki

◆ 學術的にはかゝる區劃法を改むる必要がある。
Academically, there is a need to reform such a method of division.

1) かかる行為は許されない。
Such an action will not be forgiven.

2) かかる慣習は中国に限らず、日本でも行われていたのである。
Such a custom was practiced not just in China but in Japan as well.

2. ～点に於て in terms of ~; in regard to ~ cf. Taki

◆ 中世と近世との文化の状態は、如何なる點に於て異るかといふに、…
When asking in what aspects the condition of culture differed between the medieval and early modern periods…

1) 両者はあらゆる点において意見が一致している。
Their opinions coincide in every aspect.

2) 品質の点においては、この商品に勝るものはない。
In terms of quality, there is nothing better than this product.

3. X を Y とする / 為す regard X as Y; assume; consider cf. Kano, Matsuura, Ojima, Suzuki, Taki, Tanigawa

◆ 貴族政治は六朝から唐の中世までを最も盛なる時代とした。
Aristocratic rule had its most flourishing period from the Six Dynasties to the middle of the Tang.

1) この理論を正しいとすると、我々の考えは間違っていないことになる。
If we take this theory to be correct, it would mean that our thinking is not mistaken.

2) 国連は温暖化問題を最重要課題の一つとなしている。
The UN considers global warming to be a problem of the utmost importance.

Note: See Section 5 in Chapter 1.

A Practical Guide for Scholarly Reading in Japanese

4. N なるもの＝N であるもの so called N; what is called N cf. Kano, Taki, Tanigawa

◆ 所謂郡望なるもの丶本體がこれである。

This is the essence of so-called district dignitaries.

1) 自律性なるものは、日々の努力によって初めて身につくのである。

That which is called autonomy is acquired only through daily hard work.

2) 来年退職したら、SNS なるものに挑戦してみたい。

After I retire next year, I want to challenge myself to use that which is called SNS.

5. ～得る can ~; possible; able cf. Tanigawa

◆ その政治は貴族の特權を認めた上に實行し得るのであつて…

His politics could be practiced only after having recognized the special privileges of the aristocrats.

1) この研究はワクチンの開発に大きな効果をもたらし得るであろう。

This research can surely contribute greatly to the development of a vaccine.

2) 実際に起こりうる様々な問題を考えてみましょう。

Let's think about the various problems which could actually occur.

6. ～に対する N　N toward ~; N against ~ / ～に対して V/ADJ/ADJ-V cf. Kano, Ojima, Tanigawa

◆ 君主は直接に臣民全體に對する事となり、…

It became so that the emperor directly faced his subjects as a whole…

1) 彼の芸術に対する情熱は変わることがなかった。

His passion for art never changed.

2) 政府の経済政策に対して国民の不満が高まっている。

The peoples' dissatisfaction toward the government's economic policies is increasing.

Chapter 2 Section 5 – 概括的唐宋時代觀 NAITŌ Konan 内藤湖南 (1922) Gaikatsuteki Tō-Sō jidai kan

7. ～ずして without ~ing   cf. Kano, Ojima, Suzuki

◆ 君主は臣民全體の代表者にあらずして、夫自身が絶對權力の主體となつた。

The monarch was not a representative of all his subjects but rather himself became the agent of absolute authority.

1) 風が止むのを待たずして、出発することは危険であろう。

Surely it is dangerous to depart without waiting for the wind to stop.

2) 論語を読まずして、中国の思想は理解できない。

One cannot understand Chinese thought without reading the *Lunyu*.

Note: See Section 8.6.4 in Chapter 1.

8. ～如し like ~; look like ~   cf. Kano, Ojima, Taki, Tanigawa

◆ 隋の文帝・唐の太宗の如き英主が出で、…

A great ruler like Emperor Wen of Sui or Taizong of Tang appears…

1) 過ぎたるは及ばざるが如し。

Too much is just like too little.

2) その新人は彗星の如く現れて、その年の全ての賞を独占した。

The newcomer appeared like a comet and monopolized all the awards for that year.

Note: See Section 8.5.7 in Chapter 1.

9. ～にせよ / ～にしても even supporting ~; even though ~   cf. Kano, Taki

◆ 制度の上に於ては貴族の權力を認めぬ事にしても、…政治は貴族との協議體となつた。

Even if they did not institutionally recognize the authority of the aristocrats…politics became a joint effort with the aristocrats.

1) 何を始めるにせよ、慎重に準備することが肝心だ。

Whatever you are starting, it is important to prepare carefully.

2) たとえ冗談にしても他人を傷つけるようなことを言ってはいけない。

Even if it is a joke, you must not say things which could hurt others.

A Practical Guide for Scholarly Reading in Japanese

10. 〜と（は）雖も even ~; even though ~　cf. Taki

◆ 天子と雖も其権力を自由に動かす事が出來ない習慣であつたが、…

It was customary that even the emperor could not freely exercise his authority…

1) その推論は当らずと雖も遠からずであろう。

That conjecture, although not exactly correct, is perhaps not too far off.

2) 如何に天才と雖も、一人の手でこれを造り上げることは不可能に近い。

No matter how genius one may be, it would be close to impossible for just one person to create this.

11. 如何に〜とも / ども / ても / でも no matter how ~　cf. Taki, Tanigawa

◆ 如何に強大なる権力を有する宰相でも、天子の機嫌を損ねると、…囚人と墜

さる〟。

No matter how great the authority a prime minister held, if he were to displease the emperor, … he would be made a prisoner.

1) いかに本物に見えようとも、偽物はやはり偽物だ。

No matter how much it looks like the real thing, a fake is a fake.

2) 人生の道はどんなに険しくとも、笑いながら生きようと思う。

No matter how rough the path of life is, I want to live smiling.

12. （時）恰も just then

◆ 宋代は恰も唐と明清との間に立つので…

The Song Dynasty stands just between the Tang and the Ming/Qing, so…

1) その小説の舞台は時恰も関東大震災の年だった。

The novel's setting is exactly the year of the Great Kantō Earthquake.

2) 二人が出会ったのは時恰も春たけなわのころであった。

The two met when spring was just at its peak.

196

Chapter 2 Section 5 – 概括的唐宋時代觀 NAITŌ Konan 内藤湖南 (1922) Gaikatsuteki Tō-Sō jidai kan

13. 〜訳だ / である this is why ~; this means ~; it is the case that ~
cf. Kano, Matsuura, Ojima, Taki, Tanigawa

◆ 明清の如く宰相に權力がないといふ譯ではないが、…

It was not the case that the prime minister had no authority as in the Ming and Qing, but…

1) 誰にでも、間違いはあるわけだが、そのあとどう責任をとるかは人それぞれだ。

Of course, everyone makes mistakes, but how you take responsibility afterwards depends on the person.

2) 叔父は学生時代にフランスに留学した。だからフランス語が堪能なわけである。

My uncle studied abroad in France while he was a student. No wonder he is so good at French.

14. 〜事と / になった it has turned out ~; it has been decided ~   cf. Kano, Ojima

◆ 如何なるよき位置の地方官も、君主一片の命令で容易に交迭せらる〻事となつた。

It became so that any provincial official, no matter how good his position, could be easily switched out by a single order from the emperor.

1) 長い間入院していた父が、明日ようやく退院できることになった。

It has been decided that my father, who has been hospitalized for a long time, can finally be discharged tomorrow.

2) 次のオリンピックは我が国で開催されることとなった。

It has been decided that the next Olympics will be held in our country.

15. 寧ろ rather; rather than otherwise   cf. Taki, Tanigawa

◆ 其試験は學科の試験といふよりは、寧ろ人格試験と文章草案の力とを試験するといふ方法であつた。

The exam was not so much an academic test as it was a method of testing personality and composition ability.

1) 疲労が溜まっているので、明日の日曜日は遊びに行くよりもむしろ家で休みたい。

My exhaustion has built up, so tomorrow, Sunday, instead of going out, I'd rather rest at home.

2) 徳川家康は政治家と言うより寧ろ策士であったと言えようか。

Perhaps it could be said that TOKUGAWA Ieyasu was more of a strategist than a politician.

197

A Practical Guide for Scholarly Reading in Japanese

16. 〜に過ぎない only ~; no more than ~; nothing but ~

◆ 策論も單に粗末な歴史上の事蹟を概説するに過ぎないものとなつて、…

The celun (policy treatise), too, became no more than simply a rough explanation of historical events…

1) これは私の個人的な感想にすぎない。

These are no more than my personal impressions.

2) ニュースで報道されていることは氷山の一角に過ぎないのだ。

What's being reported on the news is no more than the tip of the iceberg.

17. 〜訳には行かない cannot ~; impossible   cf. Tanigawa

◆ 唐代を通じては新派が舊派を壓倒する譯には行かなかつた。

Throughout the Tang, the new faction could never have overwhelmed the old faction.

1) 他人のこととはいえ、無関心でいるわけにはいかない。

Even if it is someone else's business, I can't stay unconcerned.

2) 自分が提案した企画なので、途中で諦めるわけにはいかない。

It's a project that I proposed, so I can't give up midway.

198

Chapter 2 Section 6

SUZUKI Torao 鈴木虎雄 (1878–1963). Scholar of classical Chinese literature.

He was one of the first to create the specialized field of research of Chinese literature, breaking from the tradition of all-encompassing Sinology. He translated and wrote on many classical Chinese poems and composed many himself.

After graduating from the Chinese literature course at Tokyo Imperial University (presently, Tokyo University), in 1908 Suzuki became an assistant professor at the newly established Faculty of Letters of Kyoto Imperial University (presently, Kyoto University). He became a professor in 1919.

The roughly 14,000 books, primarily Chinese, he collected in his lifetime are stored at the library of Kyoto University's literature department. A catalog has been published.

The essay contained in this textbook is from 『支那詩論史』 *History of Chinese Poetics* (Kōbundō Shodō, 1925), a history of criticism which collects poetry criticism throughout the ages and Suzuki's representative work.

Other representative works include 『支那文学研究』 *Chinese Literature* (Kōbundō Shodō, 1925).

格調・神韻・性靈の三詩說を論ず

SUZUKI Torao 鈴木虎雄 (1940) Kakuchō, shin'in, seirei no sanshisetsu o ronzu

緒　　　言

支那の詩の歴史に於て　　格調　神韻　性靈　　と稱する詩說、詩派を見るは明の弘治、正德の頃より清の康熙、乾隆、嘉慶に亘りてのことなり。固より珍らしき問題に非ず。然れども此等の詩說、詩派は獨り支那本土に於て流行せしのみならず、順次に本邦にも傳來し今日に至るも猶ほ消長の跡を絕たず、或は將來亦た然るべし。蓋し三者は支那にて起れる諸の詩派中にありては重要なる地位を占むるが故に其の發生以來今日に至るまで之に關する議論多し。獨り憾らくは問題のふるきに比しては其の各の主張未だ明白ならざるものあり。余輩蒙昧自ら揣らず此に三派の各の言ふ所に聽きて聊か其の眞相を明にすんことを期す。恐るゝ所は由來說明的態度を取ること少き支那の詩說に向ひて、立說者の原意を得ずして余輩の獨斷的解釋に流れしもの多からんことを。

本論に於ては左の六章を分つ。

第一章　　用語の意義及び三說關係の大要、

第二章　　三說發生以前の詩說梗概、

第三章　　格調の說を論ず、

第四章　　神韻の說を論ず、

第五章　　性靈の說を論ず、

第六章　　結論、

以下順次に之を述べん。

内容質問

(1) 中国の詩の歴史で大切な３つの詩説とは何ですか。本文の言葉を使って答えなさい。

(2) 筆者はなぜそれらの３つの詩説を論じますか。

文法質問

① 「其」は何を指しますか。本文の言葉を使って答えなさい。

② 「之」は何を指しますか。本文の言葉を使って答えなさい。

③ 「未だ明白ならざるものあり」は何について言っていますか。

英訳

[A] 然れども此等の詩説、詩派は獨り支那本土に於て流行せしのみならず、順次に本邦にも傳來し今日に至るも猶ほ消長の跡を絶たず、或は將來亦た然るべし。蓋し三者は支那にて起れる諸の詩派中にありては重要なる地位を占むるが故に其の發生以來今日に至るまで之に關する議論多し。

[B] 恐るゝ所は由來説明的態度を取ること少き支那の詩説に向ひて、立説者の原意を得ずして余輩の獨斷的解釋に流れしもの多からんことを。

第一章　用語の意義及び三説關係の大要

　格調、神韻、性靈等の語は支那に於て普通の語として用ゐらるゝ、ものなり。之を詩派に名くるに及びて普通語と全然異なるには非れども少しく特別の意義を有するに至る。此の特別の意義にして明かならんか、則ち三詩派の意義を明にすることゝなるなり。今先づ其の普通語としての意義と、特別の意義に於ける大體の說明を試み次に各章に入りて各其の主張者の說をきかんとす。

　格調とは之を連稱するも本來は格と調との二つなり。格とは普通の用語として骨格、體格などいへる格、最も其義を得たり。乃ち骨格は一本一本の骨が或る工合ひに組立てられて一定の形體を爲すものをいふ。骨格とは其の組立てらるゝ點より名づけ、體格とは其の出來あがりたる上の形體につきて言ふに似たり。詩に於て（文につきても言ひうべし）若干の文字を集めて一句をつくる以上は其の文字の組立て如何によりて此に句格を生ず。又た此の句を若干組立てゝ一篇をつくる以上は其の一篇の格を生ず。此く出來あがりたる詩篇は一箇人により、又た其の箇人は同一人にても或る時期によりて其の格、一樣ならざることあり。

内容質問

(1) 「格」の普通語と特別語の（詩における）意味は何ですか。

(2) この章の目的は何ですか。

文法質問

① 「もの」の修飾部分はどこからですか。最初の三文字を答えなさい。

② 「もの」の修飾部分はどこからですか。最初の三文字を答えなさい。

英訳

Ⓐ 之を詩派に名くるに及びて普通語と全然異なるには非れども少しく特別の意義を有するに至る。

-

Ⓑ 乃ち骨格は一本一本の骨が或る工合ひに組立てられて一定の形體を爲すものをいふ。

⒜各箇人の詩格は多少の相異ありとするも之を一定の時代に限りて見るときは
其時代に共通せる詩格を有することあり。かゝる意義に於ての格は時として
「體」といふ語と差別なく用ゐらる。例へば此に漢魏の格（或は體）、齋梁の
格（體）と言はゞ漢魏齋梁なる時代の組立て方に基きたる詩篇を意味し、盛
5　唐、晩唐の格と言はゞ亦た唐代の或る時期に於て何等か共通の組立て方あり
と見做し、それに基きたる詩篇を意味す。陶淵明の體（或は格）、李白、杜甫、
白居易の體（格）といへば箇人につきていへるものに外ならず。
　　　格は「組立ての樣式」なりといふも可なり。之を外面より見れば字音によ
り、内面より見れば詩意（其詩をなす所の作者の趣旨）によりて成る。故に格と意とは密接なる
10　關係あり。後世、聲音の規則一定してよりは其の規則に從ふ詩、之を「律詩」
といふ。⒝律詩に對して聲音の規則に從はざる詩を時として「格詩」といふこ
とあり。（「白氏文集」に格詩あり、此にいふ意味の格詩なり、其中には古體・
歌行・樂府を含めり、我が弘法大師の「文筆眼心抄」に格とは意を主として
名け律とは聲を主として名くる稱號なりといへるは最も明瞭なる説明なり。
15　清の王漁洋は格詩を律詩と誤解して趙執信のために「談龍録」の中にて笑は
れたり）⒞律詩に對する格詩は近體詩に對する古體詩といふに同じ。かゝる意
味に於ける格は頗る廣き意義を有す。

内容質問

(1) 律詩は格詩とどう違いますか。

(2) 趙執信が清の王漁洋を笑ったのはなぜですか。

文法質問

① 「之」は何を指しますか。本文の言葉を使って答えなさい。

② 「詩篇」の修飾部分はどこからですか。最初の三文字を答えなさい。

③ 「それ」は何を指しますか。

④ 「詩」の修飾部分はどこからですか。最初の三文字を答えなさい。

英訳

Ⓐ 各箇人の詩格は多少の相異ありとするも之を一定の時代に限りて見るときは其時代に共通せる詩格を有することあり。

Ⓑ 律詩に對して聲音の規則に從はざる詩を時として「格詩」といふことあり。

Ⓒ 律詩に對する格詩は近體詩に對する古體詩といふに同じ。

調は音調なり。文字より句が出來るときは一句の音調あるべく、句より篇が出來る上は一篇の音調あるべし。格と調とは本來二事なれども一定の詩格には必ず一定の音調を伴隨し二者離る可らざる關係あり。漢魏の格に依れる詩には自から漢魏の調あるべく、唐宋の格に依れる詩には自から唐宋の調あるべきこと論を待たず。宛かも萬葉集の歌格を用うれば萬葉調を生じ、古今集の歌格に從へば古今調を生ずると同じ。其の不可離の關係あるによりて格と調とは連稱せられて此に『格調』として用ゐらる。是格調の普通の意義なり。

文法質問

① 「こと」の修飾部分はどこからですか。最初の三文字を答えなさい。

② 「其」は何を指しますか。本文の言葉を使って答えなさい。

英訳

Ⓐ 格と調とは本來二事なれども一定の詩格には必ず一定の音調を伴隨し二者離る可らざる關係あり。

Ⓑ 其の不可離の關係にあるによりて格と調とは連稱せられて此に『格調』として用ゐらる。是格調の普通の意義なり。

A Practical Guide for Scholarly Reading in Japanese

格調・神韻・性靈の三詩說を論ず Kakuchō, shin'in, seirei no sanshisetsu o ronzu—緒言 Chogen
鈴木虎雄 SUZUKI Torao (1940)

Vocabulary

Note: NP=Name of a person, NB=Name of a book, PB=Phonetic borrowing

	本文の語彙	辞書形・漢字	読み方（現代語表記）	英語
P. 200	亘りて	亘る	わたる	to range
	固より		もとより	from the outset; originally
	然れども		しかれども / されども	however
	本邦		ほんぽう	this country; our country (Japan)
	消長		しょうちょう	decline and rise
	亦た		また	also; as well
	憾らくは		うらむらくは	regrettably; unfortunately
	余輩		よはい	I
	蒙昧		もうまい	ignorant
	揣らず	揣る	はかる	to guess; to estimate
	聊か		いささか	a little
	梗概		こうがい	summary; outline
P. 202	名くる		なづくる	to name
	全然		ぜんぜん	totally (Cf. P. 87)
	則ち		すなわち	that is; namely
	連稱する		れんしょうする	to combine (words, etc.)
	乃ち		すなわち	in fact; indeed
	工合ひ		ぐあい	appearance; form
	～を爲す		～をなす	to constitute ～; to make ～
	又た		また	moreover
	此く		かく	like this
	箇人		こじん	each person
P. 204	差別なく		さべつなく	without distinction
	陶淵明		とう えんめい	Tao Yuanming (NP)
	李白		り はく	Li Bai (NP)
	杜甫		と ほ	Du Fu (NP)
	白居易		はく きょい	Bai Juyi (NP)

Chapter 2 Section 6 – 格調・神韻・性靈の三詩說を論ず SUZUKI Torao 鈴木虎雄 (1940) Kakuchō, shin'in, seirei no sanshisetsu o ronzu

	本文の語彙	辞書形・漢字	読み方（現代語表記）	英語
P. 204	律詩		りっし	*lüshi*: one type of Modern Style Poetry（近体詩）which consists of 8 line stanzas
	格詩		かくし	*geshi*: the type of Chinese poems which does not follow the phonetic rules
	白氏文集		はくしもんじゅう／はくしぶんしゅう	NB
	弘法大師		こうぼうだいし	NP (aka. 空海) (774–835)
	近體詩		きんたいし	modern style poetry
	古體詩		こたいし	ancient style poetry
	頗る		すこぶる	very
P. 206	依れる		よれる	depending on
	自から		おのずから	naturally

209

Expressions

1. 固より in the first place; to begin with; originally

◆ 固より珍らしき問題に非ず。

It is not an unusual problem to begin with.

1) もとより死は覚悟の上だ。

I was prepared to die to begin with.

2) 責任は、もとより自分にある。

The responsibility was mine to begin with.

2. ～に非ず (It) is not ~   cf. Kano

◆ 固より珍らしき問題に非ず。

It is not an unusual problem to begin with.

1) 人、木石にあらず。

People are not trees or stones.

2) 平氏にあらざれば、人にあらず。

Those who are not of the Taira are not people.

3. 蓋し in my opinion; probably   cf. Ojima

◆ 蓋し三者は支那にて起れる諸の詩派中にありては重要なる地位を占むるが故

に…

Indeed, because the three occupy important positions within the various poetic factions that have arisen in China…

1) 真理というものは、けだし、永遠に古くして、かつ永遠に新しいものではな

かろうか。

Perhaps that which is called truth is eternally old and yet eternally new.

2) 「一期一会」、けだしこれ名言と言えよう。

"One lifetime, one meeting." Truly, this can be called a great saying.

4. ～が故に because ~; due to ~   cf. Taki

◆ 重要なる地位を占むるが故に其の發生以來今日に至るまで之に關する議論多し。

Because they occupy important positions, since their emergence until the present day there have been many debates regarding them.

1) 王であるが故に時として辛い決断も下さなければならない。

Precisely because he is the king, he must sometimes make tough decisions.

2) 事情を知っているが故に、私は彼が苦しむ姿を見るのが耐えられなかった。

Precisely because I knew about the circumstances, I couldn't bear to see him suffer.

5. ～ずして without ~ing   cf. Kano, Naitō, Ojima

◆ [恐るゝ所は…] 立說者の原意を得ずして余輩の獨斷的解釋に流れしもの多からんことを。

[I fear that] there may be much which strays into my own personal interpretation without capturing the original intent of those who made the theories.

1) 風が止むのを待たずして、出発することは危険であろう。

Surely it is dangerous to depart without waiting for the wind to stop.

2) 論語を読まずして、中国の思想は理解できない。

One cannot understand Chinese thought without reading the *Lunyu*.

Note: See Section 8.6.4 in Chapter 1.

6. V 以上（は）once; now that; because it is the case

◆ 若干の文字を集めて一句をつくる以上は其の文字の組立て如何によりて此に句格を生ず。

Once some characters are gathered to form a line, a *kaku* (structure) of the line emerges based on how its characters are put together.

1) いったん始めた以上は、最後まであきらめないつもりだ。

Now that I've started, I don't intend on giving up until the end.

2) 会議で決まった以上は、会社の方針を変えることはできない。

Since it was decided at a meeting, it is not possible to change the company's policy.

7. X を Y とする / 為す regard X as Y; assume; consider
cf. Kano, Matsuura, Naitō, Ojima, Taki, Tanigawa

◆ 各箇人の詩格は多少の相異ありとするも…

Although the poetic structure of each individual differ somewhat from each other…

1) この理論を正しいとすると、我々の考えは間違っていないことになる。

If we take this theory to be correct, it would mean that our thinking is not mistaken.

2) 国連は温暖化問題を最重要課題の一つとなしている。

The UN considers global warming to be a problem of the utmost importance.

Note: See Section 5 in Chapter 1.

8. ～に他 [外] ならず / ならない nothing but ～ cf. Kano, Tanigawa

◆ 箇人につきていへるものに外ならず。

They are none other than [terms] referring to individuals.

1) 成功とは日々の努力の成果に外ならず。

Success is nothing other than the result of daily hard work.

2) 互いに関係が良好であったのは、共通の敵がいたからに他ならない。

Their relationship was good precisely because they had a common enemy.

9. 斯かる such; like this cf. Naitō

◆ かゝる意義に於ての格は…

When used with this kind of meaning, *kaku*…

1) かかる行為は許されない。

Such an action will not be forgiven.

2) かかる慣習は中国に限らず、日本でも行われていたのである。

Such a custom was practiced not just in China but in Japan as well.

10. 宛かも (just) like; (just) as if

◆ 宛かも萬葉集の歌格を用うれば萬葉調を生じ、…

Just like how if one were to use the poetic *kaku* (structure) of the *Man'yōshū*, it would create the *man'yō* rhythm…

1) アメリカで個性が重要視されるのは、あたかも日本で協調性に重きが置かれるのと同様である。

How individuality is viewed with importance in America is just like how weight is placed on cooperativeness in Japan.

2) その人形は宛かも生きているかのようだった。

The doll was as if it were alive.

Chapter 2 Section 7

KANO Naoki 狩野直喜 (1868–1947). Scholar of China with a broad range of research, including Chinese literature, Chinese philosophy, and Dunhuang studies.

After graduating from Tokyo Imperial University (presently, Tokyo University), in 1900 Kano studied abroad in Beijing but was caught up in the Boxer Rebellion and took refuge in the Japanese Embassy.

In 1906, he became a professor at Kyoto Imperial University (presently, Kyoto University), teaching Chinese philosophy, Chinese literature, and Chinese linguistics. In 1910, he headed to Beijing to survey the newly discovered Dunhuang documents.

Starting in 1912 (Meiji 45), Kano studied abroad in Europe, introducing the Sinology of Europe as well as viewing and researching the Dunhuang documents which had gone to France.

The present essay, a lecture he delivered at Kyoto University's literature department, takes the position of placing importance on literature as an expression of the spirit of the times.

Representative works include 『中国哲学史』 *History of Chinese Philosophy* (Iwanami Shoten, 1953) and 『支那学文藪』 *Collection of Sinology Writings* (Misuzu Shobō, 1973).

兩漢文學考

KANO Naoki 狩野直喜 (1964, 78, 88) Ryōkan bungaku kō

兩漢文學の差違

[A] (1) 予が本年の特殊講議題目は兩漢文學考と名け、各週二時間を之に費やす豫定なるが、實は前年度になしたる兩漢學術考の續講に外ならず。本年は東漢の經學に就いて其大體を述ぶる筈なるが、但本年の題目を經學考とせず、文學考としたるは、元來予の講義に出席し之を聴く義務あるは、支那文學科の人人なるを以て、本年は東漢の經學を敍述すると共に、其文學にも言及したしと思ひ、爲めに文學の字を廣義に用ひ、文學考となせり。諸子幸に之を諒せよ。

[B] 一體西漢と東漢とは、其間に王莽の時代が十數年入る丈で、兩者殆んど相從續したるものと見るを得。故に多くの場合には、西漢・東漢と分たずして、唯單に漢といふ。例せば經學に於いても、宋學に對して漢學といひ、文に於いても、六朝・唐・宋文に對して漢文といふ。然れども是れ概括に過ぎたる言葉にして、諸子の知る如く、經學に於いても、文に於いても、西漢と東漢とは大に其趣を殊にするものあり。[C] 何を以てか之れを言ふ。經學に就いて之れを見るに、前年講義にて述べし如く、西漢の博士が學校に於いて學生に授けし經書は、今文を以て書かれたるものなり。東漢に至りても、後に委しく述ぶる如く、學官に立てられたるものは、西漢と何等の差違なく、矢張り西漢に倣うて總べての學制が出來たる事とて、今文の學者が重に博士に採用され、それが各西漢より傳來の家法によりて教授したりしが、博士流の學問以外に、東漢には古文派の學問が盛になつた。

内容質問

(1) 本年の特殊講義は主に何についてですか。

(2) 筆者はなぜ本年の特殊講義の題目を「兩漢文學考」としたのですか。

(3) 西漢と東漢をまとめて単に「漢」ということに対して筆者はどう思っていますか。

(4) 経学は、東漢になってどんな変化が起きましたか。

文法質問

① 最初の段落の「豫定なる」「述ぶる筈なる」「人人なる」の「なる」の意味を文法的に説明しなさい。

② 「なせり」の意味は次のどれですか。
    ❶　なった　　　　　　　　　　　❷　ならされた
    ❸　した　　　　　　　　　　　　❹　なれた

③ 「之」は何を指しますか。本文から最初と最後の三文字を答えなさい。

④ 「概括に過ぎたる言葉」は何ですか。本文の言葉を使って三つ答えなさい。

⑤ 「經書」の修飾部分はどこからですか。最初の三文字を答えなさい。

⑥ 「それ」は何を指しますか。本文の言葉を使って答えなさい。

英訳

Ⓐ 予が本年の特殊講義題目は兩漢文學考と名け、各週二時間を之に費やす豫定なるが、實は前年度になしたる兩漢學術考の續講に外ならず。

Ⓑ 一體西漢と東漢とは、其間に王莽の時代が十數年入る丈で、兩者殆んど相從續したるものと見るを得。

Ⓒ 何を以てか之れを言ふ。

A Practical Guide for Scholarly Reading in Japanese

　勿論この古文學は、西漢の末に劉歆が始めて之れを提唱したけれども、官學に立籠りし博士等より非常に反對され、後彼が王莽に取入りて、其信用を得たる關係よりして、暫時學官に立てられたる事は<u>ありしも</u>、暫らくにして廢せられ、王莽死して再たび漢の天下となり、學制は總べて西漢に則る事となつた。それで、今文學が學官に立てられ、<u>古文學は國家の保護獎勵を受くるといふ事にはならなかつた</u>。然れども縱令劉歆は人物劣等にて取るに足らぬものであつたにせよ、其倡へし古文學なるものは、決して輕視すべきものにあらず。それで或る特別の學者達は熱心に之れを修め、之れを弟子に傳へたり。

　彼等は古文學者といはるる通り、其經書は古文即ち古字を以て書かれ、經書の文字に古今の差ありしが、獨り其れのみならず、所依の經已に同じからず、又經義互ひに異れり。易・書・詩・禮・春秋、皆然らざるはなし。施・孟・梁丘・京房の易と費直・高相の易、歐陽・大小夏侯の書と、孔安國の傳へたる古文尚書、齊・魯・韓三家の詩と毛詩、大小戴・慶氏の禮と孔安國が獻ぜし禮古經と周官經、公羊・穀梁春秋と左氏傳と、其經義同じからざるのみならず、周官經の如き、古文家は周公太平を致すの跡として之を尊べども、今文家は六國陰謀の書として<u>之れ</u>を取らず。

内容質問

(1) 誰がいつ古文学を提唱しましたか。

(2) 古文学はなぜ東漢で「國家の保護奨勵を受くるという事にはならなかった」のですか。

(3) 古文学と今文学はどう違いますか。違いを2つ述べなさい。

文法質問

① 主語「劉歆」の述語動詞を(a)～(i)の中から全て選びなさい。
西漢の末に劉歆が始めて之れを提唱した(a)けれども、官學に立籠りし博士等より非常に反對され(c)、後彼が王莽に取入りて(d)、其信用を得たる(e)關係よりして、暫時學官に立てられたる(f)事はありしも、暫らくにして廢せられ(g)、王莽死して(h)再たび漢の天下となり、學制は總べて西漢に則る(i)事となつた。

② 「ありしも」の意味は次のどれですか。
   ❶ あったが   ❷ あるが
   ❸ あったし   ❹ あるし

③ 「之れ」は何ですか。本文の言葉を使って答えなさい。

英訳

Ⓐ 然れども縦令(たとい)劉歆は人物劣等にて取るに足らぬものであつたにせよ、其倡へし古文學なるものは、決して輕視すべきものにあらず。

清興るに及び、明の性理學の反動として、學問に復古的の傾向を帯び來たり、乾隆以來は純粹なる漢學といふ一の學派が出來た譯であるが、乾隆より嘉慶に至り尤も盛なりしは、賈逵・許愼・馬融・鄭玄といふ如き東漢の古文學者を祖述し、其學說を闡明^{せんめい}にするを目的としたるものにて、嚴密に言へば之れを東漢學⁽¹⁾と稱すべきものなり。それが道光以後になれば公羊學が起り、經學は西漢博士の傳へたるもの尤も信ずべく^①、東漢の學は西漢の學の如く師承明^{あきら}かならず、殊に鄭玄の如きは種々の學派を取入れたるものにて^②、家法もなければ師法もなく、全く經學を毀^きしたるものと、罵倒するものさへ出^いで來^{きた}れり。

内容質問

⑴ 「東漢学」とは何ですか、簡単に説明しなさい。

⑵ 鄭玄が罵倒されたのはなぜですか。

文法質問

① 「信ずべく」の意味は次のどれですか。
- ❶ 信じるべきで
- ❷ 信じてしまって
- ❸ 信じるべきではなくて
- ❹ 信じられなくて
② 「ものにて」の意味は次のどれですか。
- ❶ ものなのに
- ❷ ものの所で
- ❸ ものであって
- ❹ ものによって

両漢文學考 Ryōkan bungaku kō—兩漢文學の差違 Ryōkan bungaku no sai

狩野直喜 KANO Naoki (1964, 78, 88)

Vocabulary

Note: NP=Name of a person, NB=Name of a book, PB=Phonetic borrowing

	本文の語彙	辞書形・漢字	読み方 (現代語表記)	英語
P. 214	予		よ	I (= わたし)
	經學		けいがく	the study of Confucian classics
	〜に就いて		〜について	about; regarding
	諸子		しょし	you (plural)
	幸に		さいわいに	I hope; please do ~
	諒せよ	諒す(る)	りょうす(る)	to acknowledge
	王莽		おう もう	Wang Meng (NP)
	丈 (PB)		だけ	just; only
	相		あい	mutually
	從續したる	從續す(る)	じゅうぞくす(る)	to continue
	見るを得		みるをう	can be seen
	唯單に		ただたんに	simply; just
	然れども		しかれども	although
	概括		がいかつ	generalization; summary
	趣を殊にする		しゅをことにする	to have different views
	今文		きんぶん	1. (written in) the clerical script (modern script) 2. *Jinwen* Classics-Learning (school)
	委しく		くわしく	in detail
	矢張り (PB)		やはり	as expected; also
	家法		かほう	family code
	博士流		はかせりゅう	*boshi* (erudite/academic chair) lineage
	古文		こぶん	1. (written in) the seal script (old script) 2. *Guwen* Classics-Learning (school)
P. 216	劉歆		りゅう きん	Liu Xin (NP)
	立籠りし	立籠る	たてこもる	to barricade oneself

Chapter 2 Section 7 – 兩漢文學考 KANO Naoki 狩野直喜 (1964, 78, 88) Ryōkan bungaku kō

	本文の語彙	辞書形・漢字	読み方 (現代語表記)	英語
P. 216	取入りて	取入る	とりいる	to try to gain someone's favor
	〜關係よりして		〜かんけいよりして	due to 〜; with the influence of 〜
	暫時		ざんじ	for a while
	則る		のっとる	to follow; to obey
	取るに足らぬ		とるにたらぬ	worthless
	のみならず		のみならず	not only... (but also...)
	所依の經		よるところのけい	the original Confucian text they used
	經義		けいぎ	the meaning of the Confucian text
	易		えき	易経 the Book of Changes (NB)
	書		しょ	尚書 the Book of Documents (NB)
	詩		し	詩経 the Book of Odes (NB)
	禮		れい	禮記 the Book of Rituals (NB)
	春秋		しゅんじゅう	春秋左氏伝 Zuo Zhuan (NB)
	然らざるはなし		しからざるはなし	this holds true for all
	施		し	施讎 Shi Chou (NP)
	孟		もう	孟喜 Meng Xi (NP)
	梁 丘		りょう きゅう	梁丘賀 Liang Qiuhe (NP)
	京 房		けい ぼう	京房 Jing Fang (NP)
	費 直		ひ ちょく	Fei Zhi (NP)
	高 相		こう そう	Gao Xiang (NP)
	歐 陽		おう よう	欧陽生 Ouyang Sheng (NP)
	大小夏侯		だいしょうかこう	NP (夏侯勝 and 夏侯建)
	孔 安國		こう あんこく	Kong Anguo (NP)
	齊・魯・韓三家		せ・ろ・かんさんけ	the names of the three Confucian schools: 魯の申公 斉の轅固 燕の韓嬰
	毛詩		もうし	the Book of Odes with Mao's commentary (NB)
	大小戴		だいしょうさい	NP (戴德 and 戴聖)
	慶氏		けいし	NP

221

A Practical Guide for Scholarly Reading in Japanese

	本文の語彙	辞書形・漢字	読み方 (現代語表記)	英語
P. 216	禮古經		れいこけい	NB
	周官經		しゅうかんけい	NB
	公羊・穀梁春秋		くよう・こくりょうしゅんじゅう	春秋公羊伝 Gongyang Zhuan and 春秋穀梁伝 Guliang Zhuang (NB)
	左氏傳		さしでん	春秋左氏伝 (NB)
	周公		しゅうこう	Zhou Gong (NP)
	太平を致す		たいへいをいたす	to create a peaceful society
P. 218	性理學		せいりがく	a school of Neo-Confucianism
	帶び來たり	帶び來たる	おびきたる	to show; to display (a trend, etc.)
	乾隆		けんりゅう	the name of an era 1736−95
	嘉慶		かけい	the name of an era 1796−1820
	尤も		もっとも	most
	賈 逵		か き	Jia Kui (NP)
	許 愼		きょ しん	Xu Shen (NP)
	馬 融		ば ゆう	Ma Rong (NP)
	鄭 玄		じょう げん	Zheng Xuan (NP)
	祖述す		そじゅつす	to succeed Old School Text scholars
	闡明にする		せんめいにする	to clarify
	道光		どうこう	the name of an era
	公羊學		くようがく	the study of Gongyang Zhuan (春秋公羊伝)
	師承		ししょう	transmission from master to disciple
	師法		しほう	masters' teachings
	毀したる	毀す	こわす	to break

222

Expressions

KANO Naoki

---

1. 〜に他[外]ならない／ならず nothing but 〜   cf. Suzuki, Tanigawa

◆ 實は前年度になしたる兩漢學術考の續講に外ならず。

In truth, it is nothing but a continuation lecture from the previous year's "Consideration of Eastern and Western Han Academic Studies."

1) 成功とは日々の努力の成果に外ならず。

Success is nothing other than the result of daily hard work.

2) 互いに関係が良好であったのは、共通の敵がいたからに他ならない。

Their relationship was good precisely because they had a common enemy.

---

2. X を Y とする／為す regard X as Y; assume; consider   cf. Matsuura, Naitō, Ojima, Suzuki, Taki, Tanigawa

◆ 但本年の題目を經學考とせず、文學考としたるは…

However, the reason I did not choose "Consideration of Classics Studies" as this year's title but instead "Consideration of Literature" is…

1) この理論を正しいとすると、我々の考えは間違っていないことになる。

If we take this theory to be correct, it would mean that our thinking is not mistaken.

2) 国連は温暖化問題を最重要課題の一つとなしている。

The UN considers global warming to be a problem of the utmost importance.

Note: See Section 5 in Chapter 1.

---

3. 〜と共に at the same time

◆ 本年は東漢の經學を敍述すると共に、其文學にも言及したしと思ひ…

This year, I want to describe the Eastern Han's study of the classics while at the same time alluding to its literature as well…

1) 妹の唐突な行動が意外であると共に腹立しかった。

My younger sister's sudden behavior was both unexpected and, at the same time, irritating to me.

2) 日が暮れるとともに、男はある種の不安を感じ始めた。

As the sun sank, the man began to feel a kind of anxiety.

4. 〜ずして without ~ing   cf. Naitō, Ojima, Suzuki

◆ 多くの場合には、西漢・東漢と分たずして、唯單に漢といふ。

Often times one simply says Han, without splitting it up into Western and Eastern Han.

1) 風が止むのを待たずして、出発することは危険であろう。

Surely it is dangerous to depart without waiting for the wind to stop.

2) 論語を読まずして、中国の思想は理解できない。

One cannot understand Chinese thought without reading the *Lunyu*.

Note: See Section 8.6.4 in Chapter 1.

5. 〜に対するN　N toward ~; N against ~ / 〜に対して V/ADJ/ADJ-V   cf. Naitō, Ojima, Tanigawa

◆ 例せば經學に於いても、宋學に對して漢學といひ、文に於いても、六朝・唐・宋文に對して漢文といふ。

For example, with regards to the study of the classics, the term Han studies is used in contrast to Song studies, and with regards to writing, the term Han writing is used in contrast to Six Dynasties/Tang/Song writing.

1) 彼の芸術に対する情熱は変わることがなかった。

His passion for art never changed.

2) 政府の経済政策に対して国民の不満が高まっている。

The peoples' dissatisfaction toward the government's economic policies is increasing.

6. 〜如し like ~; look like ~   cf. Naitō, Ojima, Taki, Tanigawa

◆ 諸子の知る如く、…西漢と東漢とは大に其趣を殊にするものあり。

As you are all aware…the Western Han and Eastern Han differ greatly in some aspects.

1) 過ぎたるは及ばざるが如し。

Too much is just like too little.

2) その新人は彗星の如く現れて、その年の全ての賞を独占した。

The newcomer appeared like a comet and monopolized all the awards for that year.

Note: See Section 8.5.7 in Chapter 1.

Chapter 2 Section 7 – 兩漢文學考 KANO Naoki 狩野直喜 (1964, 78, 88) Ryōkan bungaku kō

7. ～事と / になった it has turned out ~; it has been decided ~   cf. Naitō, Ojima

◆ 學制は總べて西漢に則る事となつた。

It became so that the education system was based completely on that of the Western Han.

1) 長い間 入院していた父が、明日ようやく退院できることになった。

It has been decided that my father, who has been hospitalized for a long time, can finally be discharged tomorrow.

2) 次のオリンピックは我が国で開催されることとなった。

It has been decided that the next Olympics will be held in our country.

8. ～にせよ / ～にしても even supporting ~; even though ~   cf. Naitō, Taki

◆ 然れども縱令劉歆は人物劣等にて取るに足らぬものであつたにせよ、其倡へし古文學なるものは、決して輕視すべきものにあらず。

However, even if Liu Xin was an inferior and worthless person, the *Guwen* Classics-Learning that he advocated should never be taken lightly.

1) 何を始めるにせよ、慎重に準備することが肝心だ。

Whatever you are starting, it is important to prepare carefully.

2) たとえ冗談にしても他人を傷つけるようなことを言ってはいけない。

Even if it is a joke, you must not say things which could hurt others.

9. N なるもの = N であるもの so called N; what is called N   cf. Naitō, Taki, Tanigawa

◆ 其倡へし古文學なるものは、決して輕視すべきものにあらず。

The so-called old text learning that he advocated for is in no way something which should be overlooked.

1) 自律性なるものは、日々の努力によって初めて身につくのである。

That which is called autonomy is acquired only through daily hard work.

2) 来年退職したら、SNS なるものに挑戦してみたい。

After I retire next year, I want to challenge myself to use that which is called SNS.

225

A Practical Guide for Scholarly Reading in Japanese

10. 〜に非ず (It) is not 〜   cf. Suzuki

◆ 其倡へし古文學なるものは、決して輕視すべきものにあらず。

The so-called old text learning that he advocated for is in no way something which should be overlooked.

1) 人、木石にあらず。

People are not trees or stones.

2) 平氏にあらざれば、人にあらず。

Those who are not of the Taira are not people.

11. 〜訳だ / である this is why 〜; this means 〜; it is the case that 〜   cf. Matsuura, Naitō, Ojima, Taki, Tanigawa

◆ 乾隆以來は純粹なる漢學といふ一の學派が出來た譯であるが、…

Which is why starting in the reign of Qianlong, a scholarly faction simply called Han Studies emerged…

1) 誰にでも、間違いはあるわけだが、そのあとどう責任をとるかは人それぞれだ。

Of course, everyone makes mistakes, but how you take responsibility afterwards depends on the person.

2) 叔父は学生時代にフランスに留学した。だからフランス語に堪能なわけである。

My uncle studied abroad in France while he was a student. No wonder he is so good at French.

12. X もなければ Y もなし / ない Neither X nor Y

◆ 家法もなければ師法もなく、…

There were no household transmissions nor transmissions from the master…

1) この辺りには道もなければ人影もない。

There is neither a road nor another person around here.

2) だれも見た事もなければ聞いた事もない不思議な花がそこにあった。

There was a mysterious flower which no one had either seen or heard of before.

226

Chapter 2 Section 8

TAKI Seiichi 瀧精一 (1873–1945). Art historian.

After graduating from the philosophy course at Tokyo Imperial University (presently, Tokyo University), Taki became a professor at Tokyo Imperial University in 1914. He lectured on Japanese and East Asian art history and established the foundations for art history as a modern science.

As editor for the art journal 国華 (Flower of the Nation), he published many essays and explanations, among other writings. This not only contributed greatly to the development of our study of art history but also played a large role in educating art hobbyists and introducing East Asian art to foreign countries.

The essay contained in this textbook is from one of his representative works 『文人画概論』 *Outline to Literati Paintings* (Kaizōsha, 1922).

文人畫の原理

TAKI Seiichi 瀧精一 (1922) Bunjinga no genri

　以上に於て文人畫の起源と並に文人畫の流派化の大要を述べたが、それで支那に於ける文人畫なるものゝ成立は大畧說明した積である。前に云つた如く、文人畫が流派化せられない間は、それは文人が畫く畫でさへあれば、どんな畫でも差支ないのである。流派化せられて始めて文人畫に一定の形式が生じて來る譯である。然るにその形式を生ずるに先つて、文人畫に相應しい畫となる爲には、その畫に特殊の原理が出來なくてはならぬ。その原理なるものは、詮じ詰めれば郭若虛の說くが如く、人格を本位として所謂ゆる心印の如くに氣韻の現はれのある事がそれであらう。之を今日の言葉に直して云へば、即ち表現 Expression を眼目とするのである。要するに文人畫の原理は、近頃西洋に起つた藝術上の表現主義と合致するのである。表現主義は心印主義と云ふも同じである。西洋の表現主義を說くものにも種々あるが、例へばクローチエが說く所に依れば、藝術の本義は純眞なる直感に在るので、純眞の直感はそれ自體が即ち表現である。表現を基本とするが故に、藝術は須らく舒情詩的なるべきもので、それには作家の人格から溢れ出でた誠實性がなければならぬと云ふのである。夫故にその主義は丁度文人畫に當篏まるのである。表現派の畫家として有名なるカンディンスキーの唱道する所の内面の音響 (Innerer Klang) と云ふものゝ如きも、郭若虛の云ふ氣韻と頗る似寄つた所がある。そうして見ると文人畫はその主義の上の [sic] 於て、頗る近世的なるものであるかの如くに見える。左樣に近世的なるものが支那に於て古くから開けてゐたと云ふ事は、寧ろ驚くべき事のやうである。

内容質問

(1) 文人画に一定の形式が生じるのはなぜですか。

(2) 文人画にふさわしい画になるための「特殊の原理」とは何ですか。

(3) 筆者は、なぜ文人画の原理が西洋に起こった芸術上の表現主義と合致すると言っていますか。

(4) クローチェは、「藝術」とはどういうものでなければならないと言っていますか。

(5) 文人画が「頗る近世的なるものであるかの如くに見える」のはなぜですか。

文法質問

① 「流派化せられない」の意味は次のどれですか。
   ❶ 流派化しない   ❷ 流派化されない   ❸ 流派化しなかった

② 「それ」は何を指しますか。

③ 「～と云ふ」
   (a) 主語は何ですか。本文の言葉を使って答えなさい。

   (b) 引用はどこからですか。最初の三文字を答えなさい。

④ 「もの」の修飾部分はどこからですか。最初の三文字を答えなさい。

⑤ 「事」の修飾部分はどこからですか。最初の三文字を答えなさい。

英訳

Ⓐ 然るにその形式を生ずるに先つて、文人書に相應しい畫となる爲には、その畫に特殊の原理が出來なくてはならぬ。

A Practical Guide for Scholarly Reading in Japanese

けれども又文人畫の原理が、大體に於て最近の西洋表現藝術の主張と一致するものはあるにしても、文人畫と表現派の藝術とを全く同じものと視る事は出來ない。<u>[A]両者大體に於て主張を同（おなじゅ）うするものがあるとは雖も、尚ほその實際に就（つい）て詳しく分析して考へて見ると、又大いに異ふ所がないとは云へない</u>

5 <u>ので、文人畫は文人畫でおのづから特殊の性質を持つてゐる。</u>

文人畫をその最も發達した時のものに就て見ると、それには更に若干の<u>特(1)殊なる條件</u>がある。先づ第一に文人畫はその性質として職業的ならざるを要するもので、卽ち作家が人の爲めに畫くと云ふよりも、寧ろ自分自身で樂む境涯に於て畫くと云ふ事がなければならん。外からの拘束を受けないで、自

10 身の樂む境涯をその儘（まま）に吐露すると云ふ事がなければならぬ。古の文人高士の技藝は、殊にそうであつたと考へられてゐる。事實に於ては、文人の作る所のもので、時として意外に職業的なるものに近い<u>もの(①)</u>もない事はないが、大體から云へば文人の畫は他人の爲めにするよりも、自分の爲にする點に於て職業的のものとは違はなければならぬ。文人に相應しい文人畫の約束とし

15 ては此<u>職業的でない(②)</u>、自ら樂むの境涯を有すると云ふ事が第一に大切である。倪雲林が友人に答ふる消息の中に、自分の畫いた陳子樫刡源の圖に就て云ふ所を見ると、その文章の中に

*
『僕之所謂畫者。不過逸筆草々。不求形似。聊以自娛耳。』

とあるが、丁度それである。既に表現が主義であるならば、自から（みず）樂むの境

20 涯に在るのは當然だとも云へるかも知れないが、併しそれが特に職業的でない爲（ため）から來るとなると、それには特殊の性質が、伴ふのである。近頃の表現派の藝術の如きは如何に主觀的であつても、強いて（し）それを非職業的のものとすべく要求してはゐない。

230

内容質問

(1) 文人画の「特殊なる條件」とは何ですか。

(2) 「職業的ではない」とはどういう意味ですか。説明しなさい。

文法質問

① 「もの」の修飾部分はどこからですか。最初の三文字を答えなさい。

英訳

A 両者大體に於て主張を同うするものがあるとは雖も、尚ほその實際に就て詳しく分析して考へて見ると、又大いに異ふ所がないとは云へないので、文人畫は文人畫でおのづから特殊の性質を持つてゐる。

---

*『僕之所謂畫者。不過逸筆草々。不求形似。聊以自娯耳。』

訓読:
僕の謂ふ所の畫は、逸筆草々に過ぎず。形似を求めず。聊か以て自ら娯しむのみ。

意味:
私が絵画と申しますのは、筆に任せて乱雑に描いたものにすぎません。（絵画と実際のものの）形を似せようとしたわけでもありません。まあ、自分の楽しみのためにやっているだけのことです。

[What I call painting is no more than something drawn by letting my brush run wild. It is not an attempt to make the painting and real object resemble each other. Well, it's just something I do for my own enjoyment.]

A Practical Guide for Scholarly Reading in Japanese

文人畫の原理 Bunjinga no genri
瀧精一 TAKI Seiichi (1922)

Vocabulary

Note: NP=Name of a person, NB=Name of a book, PB=Phonetic borrowing

	本文の語彙	辞書形・漢字	読み方 (現代語表記)	英語
P. 228	文人畫		ぶんじんが	a literati painting
	積 (PB)		つもり	intention
	差支ない (PB)		さしつかえない	have no difficulty; may do; will do
	然るに		しかるに	however
	先つて		さきだって	before
	相應しい		ふさわしい	appropriate
	詮じ詰めれば		せんじつめれば	in short
	郭 若虛		かく じゃくきょ	Guo Ruoxu (NP)
	本位		ほんい	standard; principle
	所謂ゆる		いわゆる	so-called; so to speak
	心印		しんいん	*xinyin* (imprint of the mind) to understand with the heart; not by thinking with the brain
	氣韻		きいん	*qiyun* (grace; elegance)
	卽ち		すなわち	that is to say
	眼目		がんもく	the main point
	クローチエ		クローチェ	Benedetto Croce (NP)
	溢れ出でた	溢れ出でる	あふれいでる	to overflow
	夫故に		それゆえに	because of that
	丁度 (PB)		ちょうど	just; exactly
	當篏まる (PB)		あてはまる	to be applicable
	カンディンスキー		カンディンスキー	Wassily Kandinsky (NP)
	頗る		すこぶる	very
	左様に (PB)		さように	like that
	寧ろ		むしろ	rather
P. 230	主張を同うする		しゅちょうをおなじゅうする	to have the same view
	尚ほ		なお	still

232

Chapter 2 Section 8 – 文人畫の原理 TAKI Seiichi 瀧精一 (1922) Bunjinga no genri

	本文の語彙	辞書形・漢字	読み方 (現代語表記)	英語
P. 230	〜に就て		〜について	about; regarding
	職業的		しょくぎょうてき	occupational
	境涯		きょうがい	circumstances
	その儘 (PB)		そのまま	as it is
	吐露する		とろする	to express
	高士		こうし	man of noble character
	倪雲林		げい うんりん	Ni Yunlin (NP)
	消息		しょうそく	a letter; news
	陳子樫		ちん しけい	Chen Zijing (NP)
	剡源		えん げん	Yan Yuan (NP)
	併し		しかし	however
	強いて		しいて	forcibly

233

TAKI Seiichi

Expressions

1. N なるもの = N であるもの so called N; what is called N   cf. Kano, Naitō, Tanigawa

◆ 支那に於ける文人畫なるもの〻成立は大畧説明した積である。

I think I have generally explained the birth of that which is called literati paintings in China.

1) 自律性なるものは、日々の努力によって初めて身につくのである。

That which is called autonomy is acquired only through daily hard work.

2) 来年退職したら、SNSなるものに挑戦してみたい。

After I retire next year, I want to challenge myself to use that which is called SNS.

2. ～て始（初）めて only after ～   cf. Ojima

◆ 流派化せられて始めて文人畫に一定の形式が生じて來る譯である。

Thus, only after the creation of factions did literati paintings have a set form for the first time.

1) 病気になってはじめて、健康のありがたみがわかる。

It is not until you get sick that you realize the value of good health.

2) 苦労して初めて人の気持ちがわかるようになった。

After going through hardship, I understood others' feelings for the first time.

3. ～訳だ / である this is why ～; this means ～; it is the case that ～   cf. Kano, Matsuura, Naitō, Ojima, Tanigawa

◆ 文人畫に一定の形式が生じて來る譯である。

Thus, only after the creation of factions did literati paintings have a set form for the first time.

1) 誰にでも、間違いはあるわけだが、そのあとどう責任をとるかは人それぞれだ。

Of course, everyone makes mistakes, but how you take responsibility afterwards depends on the person.

2) 叔父は学生時代にフランスに留学した。だからフランス語が堪能なわけである。

My uncle studied abroad in France while he was a student. No wonder he is so good at French.

Chapter 2 Section 8 – 文人畫の原理 TAKI Seiichi 瀧精一 (1922) Bunjinga no genri

4. 〜如し like ~; look like ~   cf. Kano, Naitō, Ojima, Tanigawa

◆ 郭若虚の説くが如く、人格を本位として所謂ゆる心印の如くに氣韻の現はれのある事がそれであらう。

It is likely what Guo Ruoxu talked about, the appearance of *qiyun* (grace) like a so-called *xinyin* (imprint of the mind) based on the standard of [the artist's] personality.

1) 過ぎたるは及ばざるが如し。

Too much is just like too little.

2) その新人は彗星の如く現れて、その年の全ての賞を独占した。

The newcomer appeared like a comet and monopolized all the awards for that year.

Note: See Section 8.5.7 in Chapter 1.

5. X を Y とする / 為す regard X as Y; assume; consider   cf. Kano, Matsuura, Naitō, Ojima, Suzuki, Tanigawa

◆ 表現Expressionを眼目とするのである。

It takes expression as its focus.

1) この理論を正しいとすると、我々の考えは間違っていないことになる。

If we take this theory to be correct, it would mean that our thinking is not mistaken.

2) 国連は温暖化問題を最重要課題の一つとなしている。

The UN considers global warming to be a problem of the utmost importance.

Note: See Section 5 in Chapter 1.

6. 〜が故に because ~; due to ~   cf. Suzuki

◆ 表現を基本とするが故に、藝術は須らく舒情詩的なるべきもので…

Precisely because it takes expression as its foundation, art should be lyrical…

1) 王であるが故に時として辛い決断も下さなければならない。

Precisely because he is the king, he must sometimes make tough decisions.

2) 事情を知っているが故に、私は彼が苦しむ姿を見るのが耐えられなかった。

Precisely because I knew about the circumstances, I couldn't bear to see him suffer.

A Practical Guide for Scholarly Reading in Japanese

7. 須らく it is essential that; by all means; in all cases; ought to do

◆ 表現を基本とするが故に、藝術は須らく舒情詩的なるべきもので…

Precisely because it takes expression as its foundation, art should be lyrical…

1) 学生はすべからく学業に専念するべきだ。

Students ought to focus on their studies.

2) 「男すべからく強かるべし」という言い方は、現代社会に合うだろうか。

Is the saying that "men ought to be strong" really appropriate for modern society?

8. 寧ろ rather; rather than otherwise cf. Naitō, Tanigawa

◆ 左様に近世的なるものが支那に於て古くから開けてゐたと云ふ事は、寧ろ驚くべき事のやうである。

It seems rather surprising that something so modern emerged in China so long ago.

1) 疲労が溜まっているので、明日の日曜日は遊びに行くよりもむしろ家で休みたい。

My exhaustion has built up, so tomorrow, Sunday, instead of going out, I'd rather rest at home.

2) 徳川家康は政治家と言うより寧ろ策士であったと言えようか。

Perhaps it could be said that TOKUGAWA Ieyasu was more of a strategist than a politician.

9. ～にせよ / ～にしても even supporting ~; even though ~ cf. Kano, Naitō

◆ 最近の西洋表現藝術の主張と一致するものはあるにしても、文人畫と表現派の藝術とを全く同じものと視ることは出來ない。

Even though there are overlaps with the assertions of the recent western expressionist art, literati paintings and the art of the expressionists cannot be viewed as exactly the same.

1) 何を始めるにせよ、慎重に準備することが肝心だ。

Whatever you are starting, it is important to prepare carefully.

2) たとえ冗談にしても他人を傷つけるようなことを言ってはいけない。

Even if it is a joke, you must not say things which could hurt others.

236

10. ～と（は）雖も even ~; even though ~ cf. Naitō

◆ 両者大體に於て主張を同うするものがあるとは雖も、…

Even though there are some assertions between the two which are more or less the same...

1) その推論は当らずと雖も遠からずであろう。

That conjecture, although not exactly correct, is perhaps not too far off.

2) 如何に天才と雖も、一人の手でこれを造り上げることは不可能に近い。

No matter how genius one may be, it would be close to impossible for just one person to create this.

11. ～点に於て in terms of ~; in regard to ~ cf. Naitō

◆ 大體から云へば文人の畫は他人の爲めにするよりも、自分の爲にする點に於て職業的のものとは違はなければならぬ。

Generally speaking, literati paintings are not done for the sake of others but rather for oneself, and in this regard they must be different from professional works.

1) 両者はあらゆる点において意見が一致している。

Their opinions coincide in every aspect.

2) 品質の点においては、この商品に勝るものはない。

In terms of quality, there is nothing better than this product.

12. 如何に～とも / ども / ても / でも no matter how ~ cf. Naitō, Tanigawa

◆ 近頃の表現派の藝術の如きは如何に主觀的であつても、強いてそれを非職業的のものとすべく要求してはゐない。

No matter how subjective (things like) the recent expressionists' art may be, they do not forcibly demand it to be non-professional.

1) いかに本物に見えようとも、偽物はやはり偽物だ。

No matter how much it looks like the real thing, a fake is a fake.

2) 人生の道はどんなに険しくとも、笑いながら生きようと思う。

No matter how rough the path of life is, I want to live smiling.

237

A Practical Guide for Scholarly Reading in Japanese

練習問題解答

Answers

中国史の時代区分問題をめぐって—現時点からの省察—
Chūgokushi no jidaikubun mondai o megutte
—Genjiten kara no shōsatsu—
TANIGAWA Michio PP. 101–138

P. 103

▶内容質問

(1) 本文で述べられている重要な２つの説の関係は今どのような状態にありますか。

両説は平行線をなしたまま膠着した状態である。
The two theories are locked in a stalemate, as if running in parallel lines.

(2)「大方の読者はお考えであろう」で、読者が「何を」考えているだろうと言っていますか。

どうして今頃、時代区分問題を取り上げるのだろうかという疑問。
Why the author is still bringing up the problem of periodization now.

(3)「自らを持してゆずらず」とは、ここではどういう意味ですか。

両説が時代区分問題についてお互い妥協しないということ。
The two theories do not compromise with each other over the periodization problem.

▶文法質問

① 「大方の読者はお考えであろう」で、敬語を使っているのはなぜですか。

読者に話しかけて引き込もうとしているから。
The text is addressing the reader, directly in order to draw them in.

② 「その理由」は何を指しますか。

かつて両説の間に交わされた論戦が今では行われなくなった理由。
That the debate once exchanged between the two theories is no longer active.

③ 「今日」の修飾部分はどこからですか。最初の三文字を答えなさい。そのよ

④ 「問題」の修飾部分はどこからですか。最初の三文字を答えなさい。時代区

⑤ 「点」の修飾部分はどこからですか。最初の三文字を答えなさい。時代区

▶英訳

Ａ 戦後しばらくの間は、歴史をいかに発展的にとらえるかが重要なモチーフであったために、時代区分問題が大いに論議されたが、そのような、いわば歴史主義的な関心がうすれた今日では、当然時代区分論への情熱も低下したと考えられる。

For a while after the war, the question of how to understand history in terms of developments became a prominent motif in scholarship, so the problem of periodization was hotly debated. However, now that such a historicist interest has faded, fervor toward debating periodization has naturally declined as well.

P. 105

▶内容質問

(1) なぜ両説の間の論戦が行われなくなったと筆者は考えていますか。以下、正しいものに○、正しくないものに✕をつけなさい。

❶（○）歴史主義的な関心が少なくなったから

❷（✕）全時代を見通すような問題がもっと大切になったから

❸（○）両説の論戦が一種の膠着状態になったから

❹（✕）両説は今までも影響しあうことはなかったから

(2) 何が「周知の事実」ですか。

『史学雑誌』が毎号巻末に附載する文献目録も、「中国一般」「中国古代」「中国中世」「中国近現代」の四つの項目で中国史関係論文を分類し、古代と中世の唐宋の間で区切っていること
The fact that the bibliography at the end of each issue of *Shigaku Zasshi* divides papers relating to Chinese history into the four categories of "General China," "Ancient China," "Medieval China," and "Modern and Contemporary China," thereby drawing the line between the ancient and medieval periods at the transition from Tang to Song.

(3)「要するに〜おもわれるのである」で筆者が言いたいことは何ですか。次の❶〜❹の中から最も正しいものを選びなさい。

❶ 中国史研究者は時代区分に全く関心がなかった。
❷ 時代区分の問題は常に歴史家の議論の中心である。
❸ 歴史家は何らかの形で時代区分を意識している。
❹ 時代区分説に対する研究者の理解は共通している。
Answer: ❸

▶文法質問

① 「そのため」は何を指しますか。

両説が自らを持してゆずらず、それぞれの体系と学派を形づくってきたため
That both theories upheld themselves without compromise and each formed their own systems and scholarly factions.

② 「この問題」は何を指しますか。

中国史の時代区分問題
the problem of the periodization of Chinese history

③ 「傾向」の修飾部分はどこからですか。最初の三文字を答えなさい。この問

④ 「共通理解」の修飾部分はどこからですか。最初の三文字を答えなさい。何らか

238

練習問題解答 – Answers

⑤「成果」の修飾部分はどこからですか。最初の三文字を
答えなさい。私自身

P. 107

▶内容質問

⑴「軌を一にする」とは、ここではどういう意味ですか。

時代区分のしかたを統一させること
to unite the different periodization methods

⑵「つねに二説併記から始めなければならない」のは、な
ぜですか。

中国史では時代区分に関して異なる説が二つあって、そ
れぞれを説明する必要があるから。
Because there are two different theories of periodization
in Chinese history, and there is a need to explain both of
them.

⑶「このような学問の根本におけるくいちがい」とは何を
指しますか。

中国史に対する学問方法や、現代日本人の中国に対する
理解方法におけるくいちがい
Discrepancies in the method of scholarship taken
towards Chinese history and the understanding of China
held by modern Japanese people

▶文法質問

①「意識」の修飾部分はどこからですか。最初の三文字を
答えなさい。それを

②「それ」は何を指しますか。本文の言葉を使って答えな
さい。時代区分

③「それら」は何を指しますか。本文の言葉を使って答え
なさい。日本史や西洋史

④「問題」の修飾部分はどこからですか。最初の三文字を
答えなさい。中国史

▶英訳

Ａ それらの分野でも、時代区分の実際には諸説があって、
なかなか軌を一にすることが難しいのかも知れないが、
しかしともかくも、古代といい、中世といえば、ことさ
らに注釈を加えなくても、そこにほぼ共通した時代観念
を想定することができる。

In those fields too, there are actually various theories
of periodization which can be difficult to reconcile.
Nevertheless, terms such as "ancient" or "medieval"
conjure up an essentially common conceptual
understanding of a certain time period without need for
further elaboration.

P. 109

▶内容質問

⑴「この凝固した状態に生きた血流を通わす」とはどうい
う意味ですか。

既成の説が対立する根拠は何かを問い、両説の相違点を

深く見つめ、この凝固したままの対立を一歩前進させる
こと
to question the basis for the opposition of the existing
theories, carefully observe their differences, and move
the current stalemate one step forward

⑵ 何が「至難のわざ」ですか。また、それはどうしてか説
明しなさい。

両者の相違点をできるだけ深く、公平に見つめること
筆者はこれまでそのうちの一方の立場をとってきたか
ら、それは難しいことだ。
to perform the task of carefully observing the differences
between the theories in a fair manner
It is difficult because the author has thus far been a
supporter of one theory

▶文法質問

①「そうした立場」は何を指しますか。本文の言葉を使っ
て答えなさい。

既成の説にとらわれない立場

②「この作業」は何を指しますか。

両説の相違点をできるだけ深く見つめること
to perform the task of carefully observing the differenccs
between the theories

③「学説」の修飾部分はどこからですか。最初の三文字を
答えなさい。今世紀

④「方法」の修飾部分はどこからですか。最初の三文字を
答えなさい。中国史

⑤「主張した」の主語は何ですか。本文の言葉を使って答
えなさい。内藤湖南

⑥「それじたい」は何を指しますか。本文の言葉を使って
答えなさい。中国史の時代区分法

⑦「そこ」は何を指しますか。

内藤説に対置された説
the theory placed in opposition to that of Naitō

▶英訳

Ａ 以上のような意味をもった時代区分説の対立状態が今日
凝固したままであることは、個々の研究の進展にも影響
していないであろうか。というのは、このような状況は、
個々の研究者をして事象を自由に、トータルに考えるこ
とを躊躇させるおそれなしとしないからである。

We have seen how this stalemate between competing
periodization theories holds broader significance, but
does this situation affect the progress of individual
research? I fear that it may make individual researchers
hesitant to think about phenomena freely and
comprehensively.

(Lit. As for the fact that the conflicting theories of
periodization in the sense described above is still in the

239

A Practical Guide for Scholarly Reading in Japanese

state of stalemate even today, doesn't it affect the progress of individual research? I fear that it may make individual researchers hesitant to think about phenomena freely and comprehensively.)

P. 111

▶内容質問

(1) A 説、B 説で中心的な役割を担ったのは、それぞれ誰ですか。

A 説は内藤湖南、B 説は歴史学研究会
Theory A: Naitō Konan
Theory B: the Historical Science Society of Japan

(2) A 説と B 説の時代区分に関する相違は、何だと筆者は言っていますか。二つ答えなさい。

1. 10 世紀以降を、A 説は近世、B 説は中世とする。
From the 10th century onward is considered to be early modern under theory A but medieval under theory B.

2. 3 ～ 10 世紀を、A 説は中世時代、B 説は古代の延長とする。
The 3rd through 10th centuries are considered to be the medieval period under theory A but an extension of the ancient period under theory B.

▶文法質問

① 「こと」の修飾部分はどこからですか。最初の三文字を答えなさい。十世紀

② 「その内容」は何を指しますか。

十世紀前後に起こった中国史上決定的な社会変化の内容
the substance of the decisive societal changes in Chinese history which occurred around the 10th century

③ 「性格理解」の修飾部分はどこからですか。最初の三文字を答えなさい。十世紀

④ 「これ」は何を指しますか。本文の言葉を使って答えなさい。佃戸制

⑤ 「第一の問題」の修飾部分はどこからですか。最初の三文字を答えなさい。十世紀

⑥ 「この部分」は何を指しますか。本文の言葉を使って答えなさい。
三世紀前後の時期に中国史上の画期を設けるかどうかという点

P. 113

▶内容質問

(1) なぜ A 説は六朝・隋唐時代を中世としましたか。

この時代に貴族政治が盛行したから。
Because aristocratic rule was at its height during this period.

(2) 岡崎は貴族階級と軍閥勢力についてどのような見解を

持っていますか。

貴族階級は軍閥帝王に対して優位であったという見解
the view that the aristocratic class held a superior position over the military factions and the emperor

(3) P. 112 と P. 114 を読んで、次のことを言ったのは誰か、(A)〜(E)から選びなさい。複数回答あり。

❶ （ C ） 漢から六朝に至る時代転換の本質を景気変動であると考えた
❷ （ C ） 九品官人法の分析を行った
❸ （B, C） 大土地所有の研究を行った
❹ （ B ） 「時代格」という用語を用いてそれぞれの時代を特徴づけた
❺ （C,D,E） 中世的集落とされる塢と村の実態を究明した
❻ （ A ） 貴族階級と軍閥勢力が互いに結びついて貴族制国家を作ったと考えた

(A) 岡崎文夫　　(B) 宇都宮清吉　　(C) 宮崎市定
(D) 那波利貞　　(E) 宮川尚志

▶文法質問

① 「概念」の修飾部分はどこからですか。最初の三文字を答えなさい。近世の

② 「このような時代の変転」は何を指しますか。

古代の君主独裁政治が自らを貫徹できず、後漢中期あたりから第二次的貴族政治の段階へはいること
how the absolute monarchy of the ancient period could not sustain itself and gave way to the second stage of aristocratic rule around the middle of the Later Han

③ 「こと」の修飾部分はどこからですか。最初の三文字を答えなさい。複雑を

④ 「この両者」は何を指しますか。本文の言葉を使って答えなさい。貴族階級と軍閥勢力

P. 115

▶内容質問

(1) 岡崎は湖南の見解が正しいことをどのように証明しようとしましたか。

湖南の見解を歴史の展開の中で立証しようとした
He attempted to show the validity of Konan's view within the development of history.

(2) 「時代格」の意味は何ですか。一番近いものを下から選びなさい。

(A) その時代の特徴
(B) その時代の経済的発展段階
(C) その時代に生きる人達の人格
(D) その時代に起きた歴史的出来事
Answer: (A) その時代の特徴

▶文法質問

① 「研究」の修飾部分はどこからですか。最初の三文字を答えなさい。貴族（あ

練習問題解答 – Answers

② 「それら」は何を指しますか。本文の言葉を使って答え
なさい。湖南の六朝中世説が与えた影響

③ 「こと」の修飾部分はどこからですか。最初の三文字を
答えなさい。そのこ

④ 「もの」の修飾部分はどこからですか。最初の三文字を
答えなさい。漢から

⑤ 「もの」の修飾部分はどこからですか。最初の三文字を
答えなさい。秦漢の

⑥ 「こと」の修飾部分はどこからですか。最初の三文字を
答えなさい。そこに

▶英訳

Ⓐ 宮崎の九品官人法の分析は、学会に多大の影響を与えた
が、これもまた六朝の官僚制がその内実においては貴族
制であることを実証したものであった。これらの他、思
想史・宗教史の分野にいたるまで、湖南の六朝中世説が
与えた影響は広汎であり且つ深刻である。

Miyazaki's analysis of the nine-rank system had great
influence on the academy, and this too was something
which proved that the bureaucratic system of the Six
Dynasties was aristocratic in essence. Not only in this
but extending to the fields of the history of thought and
religion, the influence of Konan's Six Dynasties medieval
theory was broad and profound.

P. 117

▶内容質問

(1) B説が３世紀以後を古代とみなす根拠は何ですか。二つ
答えなさい。

　1. 六朝期の大土地所有制が主として奴隷制経営にもとづ
　　いていたこと
　　The system of large land ownership during the Six
　　Dynasties period was primarily rooted in slavery.

　2. 唐代均田農民の課役負担のうち徭役のそれがことに過
　　重であったこと
　　Among the tax burdens placed on farmers under the
　　Tang equal field system, corvee labor was especially
　　burdensome.

(2) 西島は、漢代の基本的階級関係とは何だと言っています
か。
　専制的な皇帝権力と小農民との間を結ぶ直接的関係
　a direct relationship between the autocratic authority of
　the emperor and small farmers

▶文法質問

① 「の」の修飾部分はどこからですか。最初の三文字を答
えなさい。B説が

② 「それ」は何を指しますか。本文の言葉を使って答えな
さい。負担

③ 「新説」の修飾部分はどこからですか。最初の三文字を
答えなさい。専制的

④ 「両者」は何を指しますか。本文の言葉を使って答えな
さい。皇帝権力と小農民

▶英訳

Ⓐ しかしまた民の側は、国家権力を媒介として共同体の成
員たりえているので、純然たる自由民ではない。このよ
うな皇帝権力と人民との支配関係は、個別人身的支配と
いう用語で表現される。皇帝権力は人民のひとりひとり
を、何ものをも介在させることなく直接に人身的に支配
した、というのである。

On the other hand, as for the people, they could become
members of a collective body with state authority as
an intermediary and were thus not purely free peoples.
This kind of relationship of control between imperial
authority and the people is expressed by the term
"individual personal control." The implication is that
imperial authority directly and personally controlled
each individual without any mediation.

P. 119

▶内容質問

(1) 堀敏一は北魏以後の均田体制をどのように見ていました
か。

　（北魏以後の均田体制は）国家権力が秦漢以来の個別人
　身的支配を再編しようとしたものであると見ていた。
　He saw it (the equal-field system from the Northern Wei
　onward) as an attempt by state authority to reorganize
　the individual personal control in place since the Qin
　and Han.

(2) B説における古代のメルクマールは何ですか。本文の言
葉を使って答えなさい。
　国家の小農民に対する個別人身的支配

▶文法質問

① 「もの」の修飾部分はどこからですか。最初の三文字を
答えなさい。国家権

② 「見る」の主語は何ですか。本文の言葉を使って答えな
さい。堀敏一

③ 「時代転換」の修飾部分はどこからですか。最初の三文
字を答えなさい。A説が

④ 「後者の面」は何を指しますか。本文の言葉を使って答
えなさい。
　（豪族の）郷里社会の共同体秩序の維持者という性格

⑤ 「再建する」の主語は何ですか。本文の言葉を使って答
えなさい。国家

▶英訳

Ⓐ これが均田制、三長制等々のいわゆる均田体制である。

241

A Practical Guide for Scholarly Reading in Japanese

そしてこの体制のもとで豪族（貴族）階級は寄生官僚として転身延命することになったというのである。

This is what is known as the equal-field system, encompassing the equal-field system, the three-heads system, and others. Under this system, the aristocrat class transformed into and lived on as parasitic bureaucrats.

P. 121

▶内容質問

(1) B 説の古代のメルクマールは、漢から六朝にかけてどうなりましたか。

（B 説の古代のメルクマールである国家の小農民に対する個別人身的支配体制の原理は）漢から六朝に至って変革しなかった。

It (= theory B's marker/*merkmal* for the ancient period, the principle of the system of individual personal rule toward the small scale farmers of the state) did not undergo change from the Han to the Six Dynasties period.

▶文法質問

① 「その枠組み」は何を指しますか。本文の言葉を使って答えなさい。個別人身的支配

② 「これ」は何を指しますか。

九品官人法をどのように理解するのか
how to understand the nine-rank system

③ 「それら」は何を指しますか。本文の言葉を使って答えなさい。堀による幾つかの論考

④ 「等級」の修飾部分はどこからですか。最初の三文字を答えなさい。同郷人

⑤ 「これ」は何を指しますか。本文の言葉を使って答えなさい。郷品

▶英訳

Ⓐ 漢から六朝への過程を中心にしてみた場合、A・B両説の理解には以上のようにいちじるしい差異があるが、しかし両説が対象としてとり上げる歴史事象はさほどかけはなれたものでなく、むしろ、同一事象に対する見方の相違が、時代区分上の相違につながっているのである。

When focusing on the transition from the Han to the Six Dynasties, the understandings of Theories A and B differ greatly as observed above, but the historical phenomena they discuss are not so different. Rather, differences in interpretation of the same phenomena lead to differences in periodization.

Ⓑ 九品官人法は、宮崎によって解明されたように、郷品と官品の対応関係にもとづいて運用される、貴族主義的官吏登用法である。

As Miyazaki demonstrated, the nine-ranks system was an aristocratic method of employing officials which was operated upon the basis of the relationship between village ranks and official ranks.

P. 123

▶内容質問

(1) P. 120 と P. 122 を読んで、堀の九品官人法の解釈が書いてあるところはどこですか。本文から最初と最後の三文字を答えなさい。

「九品官」から「（の一面）である」まで

▶文法質問

① 「現実」の修飾部分はどこからですか。最初の三文字を答えなさい。漢帝国

② 「このような意味」は何を指しますか。本文の言葉を使って答えなさい。中央集権の強化を計る（ということ）

③ 「このような豪族勢力」は何を指しますか。本文の言葉を使って答えなさい。

地方で実力をにぎっている豪族勢力

④ 「目的」の修飾部分はどこからですか。最初の三文字を答えなさい。人材を

▶英訳

Ⓐ この立法の趣旨 (…) は甚だ良かったのであるが、当時は社会に貴族的ムードが横溢していた折なので、この新法は忽ち骨抜きにされ、反って貴族制を擁護する防波堤と化してしまった。

The intent of this law was fine, but at the time society was overflowing with an aristocratic mood. As a result, the new law was immediately dismantled and, on the contrary, became a barrier protecting the aristocrat order.

P.125

▶内容質問

(1) 堀は国家権力の主体についてどのように主張していますか。

（貴族勢力の実力を認めつつも）主体は貴族主義ではなく、あくまで国家の側にあると主張している。

He argues (while recognizing the abilities of the aristocratic powers) that the agency of state authority lay with the state, not with aristocratic rule.

(2) 「承認」とは何を承認することですか。本文の言葉を使って具体例を答えなさい。占田・課田法、給客制等々

(3) 以下の文は A 説（宮崎）か B 説（堀）か答えなさい。

❶ （堀） 九品官人法は、国家意思が貴族勢力に対抗し、これを取り込んだ制度である。

❷ （宮崎） 当時の社会全体が貴族主義に染まっているため、国家の政策も貴族化する傾向にあった。

❸ （宮崎） 当時の社会の本質は貴族主義にあった。

❹ （宮崎） 国家権力は貴族主義の規定を受けなければならなかった。

❺ （堀） 貴族は実力はあったが、主体は国家の側にある。

❻ （堀） 国家権力は土地私有制や給客制を規制していた。

練習問題解答 – Answers

▶文法質問

① 「この両者」は何を指しますか。本文の言葉を使って答えなさい。国家意志と貴族勢力

② 「これ」は何を指しますか。本文の言葉を使って答えなさい。貴族勢力

③ 「傾向」の修飾部分はどこからですか。最初の三文字を答えなさい。国家の

④ 「これ」は何を指しますか。本文の言葉を使って答えなさい。貴族主義 / 貴族勢力

⑤ 「その規定」は何を指しますか。本文の言葉を使って答えなさい。貴族主義 / 貴族勢力の規定

⑥ 「占田・課田法」の修飾部分はどこからですか。最初の三文字を答えなさい。当時の

⑦ 「給客制等々」の修飾部分はどこからですか。最初の三文字を答えなさい。私的従

⑧ 「承認」の修飾部分はどこからですか。最初の三文字を答えなさい。ひとつ

▶英訳

Ⓐ これを敷衍していえば当時の社会の本質は貴族主義にあり、国家権力はこれに比べれば相対的な位置にあって、その規定を受けざるをえなかった、ということになるであろう。

Extending this argument, one might arrive at the conclusion that the essence of society at the time was aristocratic order and that even the authority of the state was positioned relative to it and inevitably bound by it.

P. 127

▶内容質問

(1) B 説では六朝の国家権力をどう捉えていますか。

貴族権力から自立した権力で、小農民の対局にある一種の階級
an authority which had gained independence from aristocratic authority and formed a sort of class in opposition to the small scale farmers

(2) 筆者は、A 説において貴族政治、君主独裁政治といった概念がどのような観点から生まれたと述べていますか。

ヨーロッパ史との類比の意識であり、差異あるものを比較する意識はそれほど強くない。中国とヨーロッパは、文明の進歩の上で、大局的には同じ歩みを歩むのだという観点。
They come from an effort to draw analogies with European history, while the effort to contrast things with differences is not so strong. In other words, they come from the point of view that, on a macro-level, China and Europe walked the same path of civilizational progress.

▶文法質問

① 「こと」の修飾部分はどこからですか。最初の三文字を答えなさい。六朝社

② 「こと」の修飾部分はどこからですか。最初の三文字を答えなさい。B 説が

③ 「そこ」は何を指しますか。

A 説が世界史的見地から試みてきた中国史の時代区分
the periodization of Chinese history attempted by theory A from the viewpoint of world history

④ 「それ自身」は何を指しますか。本文の言葉を使って答えなさい。中国史の発展

▶英訳

Ⓐ 周知のように、湖南は中国史の発展を一本の樹にたとえた。それ自身一個の世界史を形成しているという意味である。この立場からすれば、中国とヨーロッパとは、文明の進歩の上で、大局的には同じ歩みを歩むのである。貴族政治、君主独裁政治等々の概念は、まさにこのような観点から導き出された文化史的概念に他ならない。

As is widely known, Konan compared the development of Chinese history to a tree, meaning that it itself forms an individual world history. From this standpoint, in terms of the progress of civilization, China and Europe walk the same path on a macro level. Concepts such as aristocracy or absolute monarchy are none other than cultural historical concepts derived from this viewpoint.

> 中国古典詩のリズム—リズムの根源性と詩型の変遷—
> Chūgoku kotenshi no rizumu—Rizumu no kongensei to shikei no hensen—
> (五)四言詩 Shigonshi
> MATSUURA Tomohisa PP. 139–149

P. 141

▶内容質問

(1) 四言詩が中国詩の中で最も古くて基本のものであるという根拠は何か、2 つ答えなさい。

1. 中国で一番古い詩集の『詩経』が四言を基本としているから。
Because the oldest poetry anthology in China, the *Shijing*, uses the four-syllable form as its fundamental form.

2. 中国語のリズムの基本単位が二音節であり、それを重ねた四言句が詩句の基本となるから。
Because the basic unit of the rhythm of the Chinese language is two syllables, so a four-syllable line composed of two such units becomes the foundation for lines in poetry.

(2) 何が「まったく疑問の余地がない」のですか。

四言詩が中国詩の詩型の中で最も古く、かつ最も基本的なものであるということ

243

That among the forms of Chinese poetry, the four-syllable form is the oldest and most fundamental.

▶文法質問

① 「それ」は何を指しますか。本文の言葉を使って答えなさい。二言句

② 何が「必然の結果」なのですか。本文の言葉を使って答えなさい。四言句が詩句の基本となること

P. 143

▶内容質問

(1) 『詩経』の「桃夭」と唐詩の「寿和」に共通する点は何ですか。本文の言葉を使って答えなさい。

（四言詩の）リズム

(2) 「四言詩」の形式の特徴は何ですか。3つ答えなさい。

   1. 一句四字である。
   There are four characters in a line.

   2. 原則として一句の第二字・第四字が節奏点（リズムの強調点）である。
   In principle, the second and fourth characters in a line are *sessō* points (the emphasis points of the rhyme).

   3. 一句が上下に二字ごとに二分され、一首全体としては二字一拍の二拍子となる。
   Each line is split into top and bottom halves of two characters, and the poem as a whole has a rhythm of two characters to one beat.

(3) 松浦は四言詩のリズムの性格をどう見ていますか。

きわめて均質的で、変化が少ない。
It is extremely uniform and monotonous.

▶文法質問

① 「もの」の修飾部分はどこからですか。最初の三文字を答えなさい。きわめ

② 「それ」は何を指しますか。本文の言葉を使って答えなさい。
人為的な休止(ポーズ)

▶英訳

Ⓐ むろん、視覚的あるいは内容的な判断から、句末の、詩句と詩句との間には、より大きな人為的な休止(ポーズ)（あるいは延長(フェルマータ)）を入れて読むのが普通であるが、それは韻律構造として本来的に内在するものとは異なるため、一首全体の、リズムとしての均質性は左右されない。

It is normal to deliberately insert a longer pause (or fermata) between verses in consideration of visuals or context. That pause, however, is not part of the inherent rhythmical structure, so the rhythmical homogeneity of the overall poem remains unaffected.

P. 145

▶内容質問

(1) 「こうした均質性」のプラス（＝長所）とマイナス（＝短所）は何ですか。

プラス：安定感、重厚さ、簡潔性が生まれる。
Plus: It creates stability, depth, and simplicity.

マイナス：平板、単調となる。
Minus: It becomes plain and monotone.

(2) 四言詩の詩型は魏晋以降、どのように使われたか、2つ答えなさい。

   1. 『詩経』の補遺（詩経で抜けたものを補うものとして）として使われた。
   to supplement what is missing from the *Shijing*

   2. 古代風の詩風、内容、表現感覚が意図される場合に使われた。
   when aiming for an ancient style, content, or feeling of expression in poetry

(3) 何が「中心的な詩型となりえなかった」のですか。また、その理由は何ですか。

四言詩。単純明快すぎるから。
the four-syllable form
It was too simple and too clear.

▶文法質問

① 「最も安定したものであり」の主語は何ですか。

四言詩の均質性
the uniformity of the four-syllable form

② 「こと」の修飾部分はどこからですか。最初の三文字を答えなさい。古代風

封建制度と家族道徳 Hōken seido to kazoku dōtoku
OJIMA Sukema PP. 151–163

P. 153

▶内容質問

(1) 孔子の社会思想は「周の封建制度」の何を是認しましたか。

（周の封建制度の）形式を是認した。
He approved of the form (of the feudal system of Zhou).

(2) 封建制度における権力服従の関係が社会の秩序を維持できないのはなぜですか。

権力の推移によって下剋上という現象を引き起こすから。
Because shifts in authority trigger the phenomenon of those below toppling those above.

(3) 殷の相続法は、周に至ってどのように変わりましたか。

殷では子供だけでなく弟たちも王位を継ぐことができたが、周では嫡長だけが王位をつぐことができるようになった。

練習問題解答 – Answers

Under the Yin, not only sons but also younger brothers could inherit the throne, but under the Zhou it became limited to only eldest sons.

⑷「父の位を襲う」とはどういう意味ですか。

父（＝王）の位を受け継ぐこと
to inherit the father's (king's) position

▶文法質問

①「これ」は何を指しますか。本文の言葉を使って答えなさい。周の封建制度

②「これ」は何を指しますか。本文の言葉を使って答えなさい。従来の封建制度

③「道徳」の修飾部分はどこからですか。最初の三文字を答えなさい。孔子が

④「その基調」とは何の基調ですか。本文の言葉を使って答えなさい。周の封建制度の基調

⑤「こと」の修飾部分はどこからですか。最初の三文字を答えなさい。これら

P. 155

▶内容質問

⑴ 同姓不婚とは何ですか。

同姓の親戚同士の結婚を禁じること
forbidding marriage between relatives of the same surname

⑵ 同姓不婚の制度によって、王と異姓（もともと王の親戚ではない諸侯）の関係がどう変わりましたか。

異姓の諸侯も婚姻によって王と結合された（＝家族関係を持つこととなった）。それにより、王は異姓の諸侯に対しても血族関係と同様な服従関係を強いることができるようになった。
Lords with different surnames also came to hold familial ties with the king through marriage. Because of this, the king became able to force lords with different surnames into relationships of submission identical to those with blood relatives.

▶文法質問

①「もの」の修飾部分はどこからですか。最初の三文字を答えなさい。後世の

②「服従関係」の修飾部分はどこからですか。最初の三文字を答えなさい。同姓の

③「この難関」は何を指しますか。

異姓の諸侯に対して、同姓の諸侯と同じく家族制度にもとづく服従関係を強いることができないこと
being unable to force lords with different surnames into relationships of submission based on the familial system in the same way as lords with the same surname

④「それ」は何を指しますか。

同姓不婚の制度（が維持されていること）
(upholding) the system of forbidding marriage between same surnames

⑤「準ぜしめた」の意味は次のどれですか。

❶「準ずる」ことをさせた　　❷「準ずる」ことをした
❸「準ずる」ことをされた　　❹「準ずる」ことをさせられた
Answer: ❶

準ぜ	V 準ず, *MIZEN*
しめ	AUX しむ (causative) *RENYŌ*
た	AUX た (perfective) *SHŪSHI*

The modern Japanese auxiliary verb た originates from たり of classical grammar losing the り. It expresses completion.

▶英訳

Ⓐ 同時に同姓の諸侯相互の間も家族制度を以て律せらるることとなった。

At the same time, they began to use the familial system to regulate mutual interactions between feudal lords with the same surname as well.

P. 157

▶内容質問

⑴ 同姓不婚の習俗はその後どのように受け継がれますか。

王族だけでなく卿士大夫、さらに庶人階級にまで広げられ、文化の発展とは関係なく今日まで中国社会を支配してきた。
It spread beyond nobility to officials and even commoners and controlled Chinese society up until the present day regardless of cultural developments.

⑵ 筆者は、周の封建制度の精神的基礎はどこにあると言っていますか。本文の言葉を使って答えなさい。

家族道徳

▶文法質問

①「こと」の修飾部分はどこからですか。最初の三文字を答えなさい。この原

② 筆者によると、何が「過言ではない」のですか。

周の封建制度の拠って立つ精神的基礎がその家族道徳に存するということ
that the spiritual foundation of the feudal system of the Zhou lies in family values

▶英訳

Ⓐ 周の封建制度を道徳的に維持せんが爲めには、その家族道徳を鞏固なものにしなければならぬ。

In order to morally preserve the feudal system of Zhou, it was necessary to solidify family morals.

A Practical Guide for Scholarly Reading in Japanese

> 概括的唐宋時代觀 Gaikatsuteki Tō-Sō jidai kan
> NAITŌ Konan PP. 165–198

P. 167

▶内容質問

(1) 「かゝる區劃法」はどのような区画法ですか。

唐宋、元明清など朝代による時代区画法
the method of periodization based off of dynasties, e.g. the Tang-Song, Yuan-Ming-Qing, etc.

(2) 湖南が、(1)の歴史区画法を「改むる必要がある」と言っているのはなぜですか。

歴史特に文化史的に考察すると、実は意味をなさない語だから。(たとえば唐代は中世の終末に属し、宋代は近世の発端である。)
Because those words do not actually mean anything when considered in the context of history, especially cultural history (for example, the Tang lies at the end of the medieval period, whereas the Song marks the beginning of the early modern).

(3) 湖南は、中世と近世の文化の状態は「如何なる點に於て異る」と言っていますか。

(政治上よりいえば)貴族政治が廃頽して君主独裁政治が起こったこと
(With regards to politics) Aristocratic rule declined and gave way to absolute monarchy.

▶文法質問

① 「それ」は何を指しますか。

唐宋時代という言葉は、歴史特に文化史的に考察すると意味をなさないということ
how the word "Tang-Song Period" does not have meaning when considered in the context of history, especially cultural history

② 「状態」の修飾部分はどこからですか。最初の三文字を答えなさい。支那の

③ 「事」の修飾部分はどこからですか。最初の三文字を答えなさい。貴族政

④ 「これ」は何を指しますか。

李延壽が朝代にかかわらず各家の人を祖先から子孫まで続けて纏まれる伝を書いたこと
how Li Yanshou wrote comprehensive biographies of each subject from their ancestors to their descendants, without concern for the dynasty

▶英訳

Ⓐ 此時代の支那の貴族は、制度として天子から領土人民を與へられたといふのではなく、其家柄が自然に地方の名望家として永續したる關係から生じたるもので、所謂郡望なるものゝ本體がこれである。

The aristocrats of China at this time did not systematically receive land and subjects from the emperor. Rather, the social standing of aristocratic families naturally arose from their long-standing prominence in the provinces. This is the essence of the class known as the prefectural gentry.

P. 169

▶内容質問

(1) この時代の貴族政治において、高い官職に就くのはどのような人でしたか。貴族　aristocrats

(2) 君主独裁政治においては、何が変わりましたか。当てはまるものをすべて選びなさい。

❶ 君主一人が、国家の権力の根本を有することとなった。
❷ 家柄としての特権がなくなったが、高い官職に就くことができた。
❸ 貴族が廃頽して、君主と人民が近接し、人民が君主を選ぶことになった。
❹ 高い官職は、第一流の貴族たちに占領されていた。
❺ 君主だけが、高官たちを任命できることになった。
Answer: ❶ ❺

▶文法質問

① 「これ」は何を指しますか。

天子の位置　the position of the emperor

② 「これ」は何を指しますか。

家柄番付　ranking of family standings

▶英訳

Ⓐ ことに天子の位置は尤も特別のものにて、これは實力あるものゝ手に歸したるが、天子になつても其家柄は第一流の貴族となるとは限らない。

The standing of the emperor was especially peculiar, for although the throne fell in the hands of those with competence, even if one became emperor his family's social standing would not necessarily be elevated to that of a first-rate aristocrat.

P. 171

▶内容質問

(1) 孟子の引用はどこからどこまでですか。最初と最後の5字を記しなさい。

「卿に異姓の」から「取り換へる」まで

▶文法質問

① 「これ」は何を指しますか。本文の言葉を使って答えなさい。君主

② 「かゝる事」とは何を指しますか。

君主の親戚である貴族たちは、君主に不都合があれば諫めて、(君主が)言うことを聞かなければ君主を取り替えるということ
how noble relatives would admonish the emperor when he did something inconvenient and replace him if he did not listen

246

練習問題解答 – Answers

③「かゝる場合」とは何を指しますか。

君主が臣民全体の代表となる場合
When the ruler becomes the representative of all subjects.

④「其然る」の「其」は何を指しますか。

君主は臣民全体の代表者ではなくて、君主自身が絶対権力の主体となったこと
That the ruler was not the representative of all subjects but made himself the agent of absolute power.

P. 173

▶内容質問

(1)「一種の矛盾した状態をあらはした」のはいつの時代ですか。それはなぜですか。元代

元朝はまだ貴族政治の状態だったのに、近世的国家の支那の上に立つこととなったため
the Yuan
Because the Yuan dynasty was still under aristocratic rule yet came to stand above China, which had formed an early modern state.

(2)「天子が臣下の上奏に對する批答なども、極めて友誼的で、決して命令的でない」のはいつの時代ですか。それはなぜですか。唐代

唐代では大官が皆貴族出身で、貴族は天子の命令に絶対に服従したのではないから。
the Tang
Because during the Tang the major officials were all of aristocratic origin, and aristocrats did not totally submit to the emperor's orders.

▶文法質問

①「これ」は何を指しますか。

元代のみはすこぶる異例がある事
how the Yuan dynasty alone has extreme exceptions

②「これ」は何を指しますか。

中書省（の案文）
the Palace Secretariat (their proposals)

▶英訳

Ⓐ 然るに明清時代になりては、批答は全く従僕などに對すると同様、ぞんざいな言葉遣ひで命令的となり、封駁の權は宋以後益々衰へ、明清に在りては殆んどなくなつた。

However, in the Ming and Qing periods, imperial responses came to use crude words and take on a commanding tone, in the same way that one might address servants. The power of remonstrance declined more and more beginning in the Song and had almost disappeared in the Ming and Qing.

P. 175

▶内容質問

(1)「かくの如き變化」とは、どのような変化ですか。

君主の権力が強くなり、宰相など大官の発言力が弱まっ

たこと。
how the emperor's authority increased while that of the prime minister and other major officials weakened

(2) 天子の権力は、唐代、宋代、明清で、どのように変化しますか。弱い方から順番に述べなさい。

唐代→宋代→明清

(3)「定策國老門生天子」という諺は何を表していますか。正しいものを選びなさい。

❶ 宦官が権力を失って、天子の生徒になること
❷ 宦官の権力が強くなって、天子は宦官に従うようになったこと
❸ 宦官が天子の家族から選ばれるようになること
Answer: ❷

▶文法質問

①「俤」の修飾部分はどこからですか。最初の三文字を答えなさい。天子を

②「習慣」の修飾部分はどこからですか。最初の三文字を答えなさい。天子と

③「もの」の修飾部分はどこからですか。最初の三文字を答えなさい。殆ど君

④「其勢力」は何を指しますか。

宦官の勢力　the influence of the eunuchs

P. 177

▶内容質問

(1) 宋代に至って、君主と人民の関係はどのようになり、政治の形はどのように変わりましたか。

君主と人民と直接に相対するようになり、近世的政治の状態となった。
The relationship between the emperor and the people became direct, therefore arriving at the condition of early modern politics.

▶文法質問

①「大に趣を異にするやうになつた」の主語は何ですか。

（君主独裁政治の時の）人民の地位と財産上の私権
the status and private rights to property of the people (under absolute monarchy)

②「かくの如き意義」とは何を指しますか。

隋唐の代に、人民を貴族の手から解放して、国家の小作人のごとく扱う制度が作られたが、事実は政治の権力は貴族にあった。そのため、農民は貴族団体の小作人という状態にあった。
During the Sui and Tang, the people were freed from the grasp of aristocrats and placed under a new system which treated them as tenant farmers of the state, but in reality, political authority lied with the aristocrats. This meant the condition of farmers was that of tenant farmers of aristocrat groups.

247

A Practical Guide for Scholarly Reading in Japanese

③「此制度」とは何ですか。

　唐代の租・庸・調の制度
the tax system of the Tang (i.e., 租・庸・調)

④「端緒」の修飾部分はどこからですか。最初の三文字を答えなさい。土地に

⑤「意味」の修飾部分はどこからですか。最初の三文字を答えなさい。人民の

⑥「の」の修飾部分はどこからですか。最初の三文字を答えなさい。貴族の

P. 179

▶内容質問

(1)「科擧は其方法が矢張依然として貴族的なりしが、これも宋の王安石時代から一變した」とありますが、どのように変わりましたか。正しい文を全て選びなさい。

　❶ 帖括を経義に変え、詩賦を策論に変えて、人格主義から実務主義に改めようとした。
　❷ 科挙の試験で政治上の意見を書かせることがなくなった。
　❸ 合格者数が急増した。
　❹ 一般庶民は官吏となることができなくなった。

Answer: ❶ ❸

▶文法質問

①「方法」の修飾部分はどこからですか。最初の三文字を答えなさい。人格試

②「これ」は何を指しますか。本文の言葉を使って答えなさい。

　經義は經書の中の義理に關して意見を書かせ、策論は政治上の意見を書かせたこと

③「遊戯」の修飾部分はどこからですか。最初の三文字を答えなさい。單に一

④「なった」の主語は何ですか。本文の言葉を使って答えなさい。策論

P. 181

▶内容質問

(1)「この黨派の弊害」とは何ですか。

　政治上の意見が党派を作る主要なる目的となったこと
Political views became the primary goal in creating a faction.

(2) 経済の「著しき變化」において、正しいものを全て選びなさい。

　❶ 唐代に「開元通宝」の鋳造が行われ、貨幣の流通が著しく増えた。
　❷ 宋代にも銅銭があったが、絹布、綿なども貨幣のかわりに用いられた。
　❸ 紙幣は宋代から初めて用いられるようになった。
　❹ 宋代には紙幣を多く発行したため、物価の変動が激しくなった。

⑤ 元の時代には紙幣と銅銭の両方が作られた。
⑥ 貨幣経済が盛んになったのは宋代からである。
❼ 銀は貨幣として使われなかった。
❽ 銭の数え方は時代によって変化した。

Answer: ❹ ⑥ ❽

▶文法質問

①「これ」は何を指しますか。

　宋代になってから、著しく政治上の主義が朋党の上に表われた事
how during the Song, differences in political beliefs strongly appeared along factional lines

②「目的」の修飾部分はどこからですか。最初の三文字を答えなさい。黨派を

③「其利用」とは何を指しますか。

　紙幣の利用　the use of paper currency

④「其ため」とは何を指しますか。

　紙幣の発行高が非常の額に上ったため
how the amount of paper currency printed reached an extremely high amount

P. 183

▶内容質問

(1)「此傾向」とは、どのような傾向ですか。

　銀が貨幣として重要な位置を占めるようになってきた傾向
the trend of silver coming to occupy a prominent position as a currency

(2) 銭の数え方は宋代からどのようになりましたか。

　重量で数える方法から、個数で数えるように変わった。
It changed from being counted by weight to being counted by number of pieces.

(3)「學術文藝の性質も著しく變化して來た」とありますが、経学では何が変わりましたか。

　唐の初期までは昔から伝え来た説を変えることができなかったが、唐の中頃からは自分の意見を言えるようになり、宋代では自己の見解で新解釈を施すのが一般的となった。
Through the early Tang, long held theories could not be changed, but starting from the mid-Tang scholars became able to voice their own opinions, and in the Song it became normal to apply new interpretations to the texts based on one's own reading.

▶文法質問

①「と」の修飾部分はどこからですか。最初の三文字を答えなさい。宋代に

②「の」の修飾部分はどこからですか。最初の三文字を答えなさい。元の伯

③「かくの如き試み」とは何ですか。

　旧説を変える事　changing old theories

248

練習問題解答 – Answers

▶英訳

Ⓐ 元の伯顏が南宋を滅ぼして北京に歸る時に、南宋の庫から收得した銀を、北京に運ぶために一定の形に鑄造したのが、今日の元寶銀の始めだといはれて居るから、宋末には餘程流通をしたものと見える。

When Boyan of Yuan vanquished the Southern Song and was on his way back to Beijing, it is said that he cast the silver obtained from the Southern Song's vaults into a particular shape in order to transport and that this is the origin of today's *yuanbao*. This suggests that silver circulated widely at the end of the Song.

P. 185

▶内容質問

(1)「一時は貴族的の文學が一變して、庶民的のものにならんとした」のはなぜですか。

形式が自由となり、俗語などを用いて自由に表現するようになったから。

Because the form became free and writers became free in expression with the use of slang and such.

▶文法質問

①「事」の修飾部分はどこからですか。最初の三文字を答えなさい。古來の

②「發達して來た」の主語は何ですか。本文の言葉を使って答えなさい。(詩餘卽ち)詞

P. 187

▶内容質問

(1)「唐と宋の時代に於いて、あらゆる文化的生活が變化を來したので」とありますが、どのような分野ですか。本文の言葉を使って、具体的に３つ述べなさい。

文學、藝術、音樂

▶文法質問

①「もの」の修飾部分はどこからですか。最初の三文字を答えなさい。從來貴

②「もの」の修飾部分はどこからですか。最初の三文字を答えなさい。平民よ

③「變化した」の主語は何ですか。本文の言葉を使って答えなさい。音樂

④「所」の修飾部分はどこからですか。最初の三文字を答えなさい。歴史を

▶英訳

Ⓐ 五代を中心として、以前の畫は、大體は傳統的の風格を重んじ、畫は事件の說明として意味あるものにすぎざりしが、新らしき水墨畫は、自己の意志を表現する自由な方法をとり、從來貴族の道具として、宏壯なる建築物の裝飾として用ゐられたものが、卷軸が盛んに行はれる事となり、庶民的といふ譯ではないが、平民より出身した官吏が、流寓する中にも、これを携帶して樂しむ事が出來る種類のものに變化した。

These transformations in painting occurred largely around the time of the Five Dynasties. In contrast to previous paintings which generally valued traditional styles and only served as explanations for the events which they depicted, the new ink paintings employed a free method of expressing one's own will. Rather than decorating grand buildings as tools of aristocrats, with the rise of scrolls, paintings became something that, while not popular per se, were carried around and enjoyed by government officials of commoner origin while traveling.

格調・神韻・性靈の三詩說を論ず Kakuchō, shin'in, seirei no sanshisetsu o ronzu—緒言 Chogen
SUZUKI Torao PP. 199–212

P. 201

▶内容質問

(1) 中国の詩の歴史で大切な３つの詩説とは何ですか。本文の言葉を使って答えなさい。格調、神韻、性靈

(2) 筆者はなぜそれらの３つの詩説を論じますか。

３者、それぞれの説の主張がまだ全て明らかになっていないから

None of the three theories' assertions have been completely clarified yet.

▶文法質問

①「其」は何を指しますか。本文の言葉を使って答えなさい。

格調・神韻・性靈

②「之」は何を指しますか。本文の言葉を使って答えなさい。

格調・神韻・性靈

③「未だ明白ならざるものあり」は何について言っていますか。

格調・神韻・性靈、それぞれの主張

respective assertions of 格調 *getiao*, 神韻 *shenyin*, and 性靈 *xinglin*

▶英訳

Ⓐ 然れども此等の詩說、詩派は獨り支那本土に於て流行せしのみならず、順次に本邦にも傳來し今日に至るも猶ほ消長の跡を絶たず、或は將來亦た然るべし。蓋し三者は支那にて起れる諸の詩派中にありては重要なる地位を占むるが故に其の發生以來今日に至るまで之に關する議論多し。

However, these poetry theories and schools were not only popularized in China itself but also gradually introduced to Japan, where their influence has seen constant decline and rise continuing to the present day and perhaps into the future as well. Due to the important positions occupied by these three theories in the various poetry

249

A Practical Guide for Scholarly Reading in Japanese

schools of China, there have been a great many debates regarding them since the time of their conception down to the present day.

B 恐るゝ所は由來説明的態度を取ること少き支那の詩説に向ひて、立説者の原意を得ずして余輩の獨斷的解釋に流れしもの多からんことを。

I only fear that, since Chinese poetry theories generally do not take an explanatory stance, I may sway toward my own arbitrary interpretations without grasping the original intent of their proponents.

P. 203

▶内容質問

(1)「格」の普通語と特別語の（詩における）意味は何ですか。

普通語の意味：骨格、体格という意味。
normal meaning: framework, physique
詩における特別の意義：文字の組み立て方、または、句の組み立て方。組み立て様式。
special meaning in poetry: the arrangement by which characters or phrases are assembled

(2) この章の目的は何ですか。

格調、神韻、性霊の普通の言葉としての意味と特別な意義を説明すること
to explain both the everyday and special meanings of the terms 格調 getiao, 神韻 shenyin and 性霊 xinglin

▶文法質問

①「もの」の修飾部分はどこからですか。最初の三文字を答えなさい。支那に

②「もの」の修飾部分はどこからですか。最初の三文字を答えなさい。一本一

▶英訳

A 之を詩派に名るに及びて普通語と全然異なるには非れども少しく特別の意義を有するに至る。

When used as the names of poetry schools, these (=the three terms) are not completely different from their regular usage, but they have somewhat special meanings.

B 乃ち骨格は一本一本の骨が或る工合ひに組立てられて一定の形體を爲すものをいふ。

In other words, skeletal structure refers to a set structure (framework) formed from individual bones put together in a certain way.

P. 205

▶内容質問

(1) 律詩は格詩とどう違いますか。

律詩は近体詩（音声の規則に従う）。格詩は古体詩（音声の規則に従わない）。
律詩 lüshi follows phonetic rules; 格詩 geshi does not follow phonetic rules.

(2) 趙執信が清の王漁洋を笑ったのはなぜですか。

王漁洋が「格詩」を「律詩」と誤解したから。
Wang Yuyang mistook 格詩 geshi for 律詩 lüshi.

▶文法質問

①「之」は何を指しますか。本文の言葉を使って答えなさい。
詩格

②「詩篇」の修飾部分はどこからですか。最初の三文字を答えなさい。漢魏齋

③「それ」は何を指しますか。

唐代の或る時期に於る何等かの共通の組み立て方
some common way of constructing [a poem] in any given period of the Tang Dynasty

④「詩」の修飾部分はどこからですか。最初の三文字を答えなさい。後世、

▶英訳

A 各箇人の詩格は多少の相異ありとするも之を一定の時代に限りて見るときは其時代に共通せる詩格を有することあり。

Although the poetic structure of each individual differ somewhat from each other, when looking at a particular time period, the time period can have a poetic structure which is common to it.

B 律詩に對して聲音の規則に從わざる詩を時として「格詩」といふことあり。

In contrast with lüshi, poems which do not follow the rules of tonal prosody are sometimes called geshi.

C 律詩に對する格詩は近體詩に對する古體詩といふに同じ。

Comparing geshi poetry to lüshi poetry is analogous to comparing ancient style poetry to modern style poetry.

P. 207

▶文法質問

①「こと」の修飾部分はどこからですか。最初の三文字を答えなさい。漢魏の

②「其」は何を指しますか。本文の言葉を使って答えなさい。
格と調

▶英訳

A 格と調とは本來二事なれども一定の詩格には必ず一定の音調を伴隨し二者離る可らざる關係あり。

Kaku and chō are fundamentally two different things, but a certain shikaku always accompanies a fixed onchō, giving them an inseparable relationship.

B 其の不可離の關係にあるによりて格と調とは連稱せられて此に『格調』として用ゐらる。是格調の普通の意義なり。

250

練習問題解答 – Answers

Because of their inseparable relationship, *kaku* and *chō* are combined to be used as "*Kakuchō*." This is the normal meaning of *kakuchō*.

兩漢文學考 Ryōkan bungaku kō — 兩漢文學の差違 Ryōkan bungaku no sai
KANO Naoki PP. 213–226

P. 215

▶内容質問

(1) 本年の特殊講義は主に何についてですか。

東漢の経学　the classics studies of Eastern Han

(2) 筆者はなぜ本年の特殊講義の題目を「兩漢文學考」としたのですか。

この講義を聞く（義務のある）のは中国文学科の学生なので、東漢の経学だけでなく文学にも言及したいから。
The students attending (the ones required to) the lecture are from the Chinese Literature department, so the author wants to discuss not only the classics studies of Eastern Han but also literature.

(3) 西漢と東漢をまとめて単に「漢」ということに対して筆者はどう思っていますか。

経学においても文においても西漢と東漢は大きく異なる。
With regards to both classics studies and literature, the Western and Eastern Han differ greatly.

(4) 経学は、東漢になってどんな変化が起きましたか。

古文派の学問が盛んになった。
The scholarship of the Guwen school rose to prominence.

▶文法質問

① 最初の段落の「豫定なる」「述ぶる筈なる」「人人なる」の「なる」の意味を文法的に説明しなさい。

意味は「である」
断定の助動詞「なり」(nominal に接続するので)
MJ: である
Function: AUX (copular) (following a nominal)

②「なせり」の意味は次のどれですか。

❶ なった　　　　　　❷ ならされた
❸ した　　　　　　　❹ なれた
Answer: ❸

③「之」は何を指しますか。本文から最初と最後の三文字を答えなさい。「本年は」から「なせり」まで

④「概括に過ぎたる言葉」は何ですか。本文の言葉を使って三つ答えなさい。漢、漢學、漢文

⑤「經書」の修飾部分はどこからですか。最初の三文字を答えなさい。西漢の

⑥「それ」は何を指しますか。本文の言葉を使って答えなさい。今文の學者（博士）

▶英訳

Ⓐ 予が本年の特殊講義題目は兩漢文學考と名け、各週二時間を之に費やす豫定なるが、實は前年度になしたる兩漢學術考の續講に外ならず。

I named this year's special lecture series "Eastern and Western Han Literature Studies," which I plan to spend two hours per week on, but it is actually (nothing but) a continuation of last academic year's lecture series "Consideration of Eastern and Western Han Academic Studies."

Ⓑ 一體西漢と東漢とは、其間に王莽の時代が十数年入る丈で、両者殆んど相從續したるものと見るを得。

The Eastern and Western Han can be viewed as essentially continuous, except for the short era of Wang Mang which lasted a little more than ten years.

Ⓒ 何を以てか之れを言ふ。

What do I mean by this? (Let me explain.)

P. 217

▶内容質問

(1) 誰がいつ古文学を提唱しましたか。

劉歆が西漢の末に提唱した。
Liu Xin advocated it at the end of the Western Han.

(2) 古文学はなぜ東漢で「國家の保護奬勵を受くるという事にはならなかった」のですか。

東漢になると学制はすべて西漢のものに戻り、今文学が学官に任命されたから。
Because in the Eastern Han the education system completely reverted to that of the Western Han, and those of New Text learning were appointed to scholarly posts.

(3) 古文学と今文学はどう違いますか。違いを２つ述べなさい。

1. 古文学の経書は古文で、今文学は今文で書かれている。
The classic texts of *Guwen* Classics-Learning are written in old writing (the seal script), while those of *Jinwen* Classics-Learning are written in modern writing (the clerical script).

2. それぞれの学問の根拠としている経書の注釈書が異なる。
The commentaries of the classics which form the basis of their scholarship are different.

▶文法質問

① 主語「劉歆」の述語動詞を(a)〜(i)の中から全て選びなさい。

西漢の末に劉歆が始めて之れを提唱したけれども、官學に立籠りし博士等より非常に反對され、後彼が王莽に取入りて、其信用を得たる關係よりして、暫時學官に立て

251

A Practical Guide for Scholarly Reading in Japanese

られたる事はありしも、暫らくにして廢せられ[g]、王莽死して再たび漢の天下となり、學制は總べて西漢に則[i]る事となつた。

Answer: (a), (c), (d), (e), (f), (g)

② 「ありしも」の意味は次のどれですか。

   ❶ あったが   ❷ あるが
   ❸ あったし   ❹ あるし

Answer: ❶

③ 「之れ」は何ですか。本文の言葉を使って答えなさい。
周官經

▶英訳

Ⓐ 然れども縦令劉歆は人物劣等にて取るに足らぬものであつたにせよ、其倡へし古文學なるものは、決して軽視すべきものにあらず。

However, even if Liu Xin was an inferior and worthless person, the Guwen Classics-Learning that he advocated should never be taken lightly.

P. 219

▶内容質問

(1) 「東漢学」とは何ですか、簡単に説明しなさい。

東漢の古文学者の学説を受け継いで、さらに発展させようとした学派の学問

The scholarship of a faction which aimed to succeed and develop the Guwen Classics scholars of the Eastern Han and elucidate their theories.

(2) 鄭玄が罵倒されたのはなぜですか。

種々の学派をとり入れて家法もなく師法もなく、それまでの経学の規則を破ったから。

Because he broke existing rules of classics studies by incorporating various scholarly factions and having neither family codes nor masters' teachings.

▶文法質問

① 「信ずべく」の意味は次のどれですか。

   ❶ 信じるべきで   ❷ 信じてしまって
   ❸ 信じるべきではなくて   ❹ 信じられなくて

Answer: ❶

② 「ものにて」の意味は次のどれですか。

   ❶ ものなのに   ❷ ものの所で
   ❸ ものであって   ❹ ものによって

Answer: ❸

文人畫の原理 Bunjinga no genri
TAKI Seiichi PP. 227–237

P. 229

▶内容質問

(1) 文人画に一定の形式が生じるのはなぜですか。

文人画が流派化されたから。
Because factions of literati paintings were born.

(2) 文人画にふさわしい画になるための「特殊の原理」とは何ですか。

人格を本位として、いわゆる心印の如くに気韻の現れのあること。
With the artist's character as the basis, it is an expression of *qiyun* (grace) like a so-called *xinyin* (pure senses).

(3) 筆者は、なぜ文人画の原理が西洋に起こった芸術上の表現主義と合致すると言っていますか。

文人画の原理が、表現 Expression を眼目とするから。
Because the principle of literati paintings takes expression as its focus.

(4) クローチェは、「藝術」とはどういうものでなければならないと言っていますか。

叙情詩的でなければならない。そして作家の人格から溢れ出でた誠実性がなければならない。
It must be lyrical and have a sincerity flowing out from the artist's character.

(5) 文人画が「頗る近世的なるものであるかの如くに見える」のはなぜですか。

郭若虚の言う「気韻」と、カンディンスキーの提唱する「内面の音響」が似ているから。
Because the *qiyun* (grace) of Guo Ruoxu and "Innerer Klang" of Kandinsky are similar.

▶文法質問

① 「流派化せられない」の意味は次のどれですか。

   ❶ 流派化しない ❷ 流派化されない ❸ 流派化しなかった
Answer: ❷

② 「それ」は何を指しますか。

文人画にふさわしい画となるための特殊な原理
a particular principle in order to be befitting of literati paintings

③ 「～と云ふ」

   (a) 主語は何ですか。本文の言葉を使って答えなさい。
     クローチェ
   (b) 引用はどこからですか。最初の三文字を答えなさい。
     藝術の

④ 「もの」の修飾部分はどこからですか。最初の三文字を答えなさい。表現派

⑤ 「事」の修飾部分はどこからですか。最初の三文字を答えなさい。左様に

▶英訳

Ⓐ 然るにその形式を生ずるに先つて、文人畫に相應しい畫となる爲には、その畫に特殊の原理が出來なくてはならぬ。

However, before such a form could be produced, the paintings needed to exhibit a particular principle in order to be befitting of literati paintings.

252

練習問題解答 – Answers

P. 231

▶内容質問

(1) 文人画の「特殊なる條件」とは何ですか。

職業的でないこと。　It must not be professional.

(2)「職業的ではない」とはどういう意味ですか。説明しなさい。

人のためではなく自分で楽しむために描くこと
It must be created not for the purpose of others but for one's own enjoyment.

▶文法質問

① 「もの」の修飾部分はどこからですか。最初の三文字を答えなさい。意外に

▶英訳

Ⓐ 両者大體に於て主張を同うするものがあるとは雖も、尚ほその實際に就て詳しく分析して考へて見ると、又大いに異ふ所がないとは云へないので、文人畫は文人畫でおのづから特殊の性質を持つてゐる。

Although they more or less share the same view, careful analysis and consideration reveals major differences between the two. Thus, literati paintings have their own unique characteristics.

253

Bibliography

Fogel, J. A. and Jōo, F. (2017) *Japanese for Sinologists*, University of California Press.

Hasegawa, Y. (ed.) (2018) *Japanese: A Linguistic Introduction*, Cambridge University Press.
Online ISBN:9781316884461
DOI: https://doi-org.ezproxy.cul.columbia.edu/10.1017/9781316884461

Hasegawa, Y. (2012) *The Routledge Course in Japanese Translation*, Routledge.
eBook ISBN9780203804476
DOI: https://doi-org.ezproxy.cul.columbia.edu/10.4324/9780203804476

McGloin, N., Endo, M., Nazikian, F. and Kakegawa, T. (2014) *Modern Japanese Grammar: A Practical Guide*, London and New York, Routledge.

Makino, S. and Tsutsui, M. (1986) *A Dictionary of Basic Japanese Grammar*, Tokyo: The Japan Times.

Makino, S. and Tsutsui, M. (1995) *A Dictionary of Intermediate Japanese Grammar*, Tokyo: The Japan Times.

Makino, S. and Tsutsui, M. (2008) *A Dictionary of Advanced Japanese Grammar*, Tokyo: The Japan Times.

Shirane, H. (2005) *Classical Japanese, A Grammar*, Columbia University Press.

Image Providers

Imperial Rescript of Education: The University of Tokyo Archives 東京大学文書館

An Encouragement of Learning: Noda Public Library 野田市立興風図書館

TANIGAWA Michio: Kawai Institute for Culture and Education 河合文化教育研究所

MATSUURA Tomohisa: Kenbun Shuppan 研文出版

OJIMA Sukema: Kochi City Haruno Local Museum 高知市春野郷土資料館

NAITŌ Konan: Chikuma Shobo 筑摩書房

SUZUKI Torao: Tsubame-shi Chozen House Archives Museum 燕市長善館史料館

KANO Naoki: Kyoto University Archives 京都大学文書館

TAKI Seiichi: Ochanomizu University お茶の水女子大学

Index Chapter 1

A

ateji 当て字 Chinese character(s) used for its phonetic sound **37**, 38

B

ba ば conditional expression 'if/when' 20
ba ば hypothetical/logical connections 71
ba'ai 場合 conditional expression 'in the case of' 21
bakari ばかり marks the subject 8
beshi べし AUX advice; appropriateness;
    potential; intentional; speculative; command 47, 54, 55, 59, **63**

D

da だ AUX copular **4**, 23
dake だけ marks the subject 8
de aru である AUX copular 4
de motte でもって particle equivalent phrase 32
demo でも marks the subject 8
desu です AUX copular 4
de wa では compound particle 29
do ど concessive connections 73
dōkei igi go 同形異義語 Japanese-Chinese homographs 39
domo ども concessive connections 73
dō'on igi go 同音異義語 Japanese-Chinese homophones 40

F

fukubun 複文 complex sentence 10

G

ga が conjunctive particle 18
ga が subject marker 5, **6**
gotoshi ごとし AUX comparative 65

H

hodo ほど marks the subject 8

I

izen-kei 已然形 perfective form 47

J

jodōshi 助動詞 auxiliary verb 54
jūbun 重文 compound sentence 10
jutsugo 述語 predicate 5

255

A Practical Guide for Scholarly Reading in Japanese

K

kagiri 限り conditional expression 21

ka-gyō henkaku katsuyō カ行変格活用 *k*-row irregular conjugation 48

kami ichidan katsuyō 上一段活用 upper one-grade conjugation 48, **49**

kami nidan katsuyō 上二段活用 upper two-grade conjugation 48, **49**

kanbun 漢文 *kanbun*; literary Chinese 42, **85**, 86

kango 漢語 Chinese compounds; Chinese words 86

keiyōdōshi 形容動詞 adjectival verb; *na*-adjective 4, 12, **52**

keiyōshi 形容詞 adjective; *i*-adjective 4, 12, **51**

keri けり AUX recollective 56

ki き AUX recollective 56

kokuji 国字 kanji made in Japan 37

ku-katsuyō ク活用 *ku*-type conjugation of ADJ in Classical Japanese 51

M

made まで marks the subject 8

mai まい AUX negative speculative; negative intentional 69

meirei-kei 命令形 imperative form 47

mizen-kei 未然形 imperfective form 47

mo も concessive connections 73

mo も represent the subject 7

mu む AUX speculative; intentional; circumlocution 67

N

na-gyō henkaku katsuyō ナ行変格活用 *n*-row irregular conjugation 48

nado など marks the subject 8

nara なら conditional expression 20

nari なり AUX copular 58

nari-katsuyō ナリ活用 *nari*-type conjugation of ADJ-V in Classical Japanese 52

ni に causal, concessive, simple connections 75

ni atatte にあたって particle equivalent phrase 35

ni hanshite に反して particle equivalent phrase 33

ni oite に於いて particle equivalent phrase 30

ni taishite に対して particle equivalent phrase 33

ni totte にとって particle equivalent phrase 31

ni wa には compound particle 29

ni yotte によって particle equivalent phrase 34

no の subject marker 6

no da のだ sentence-ending expression 23

no darō ka のだろうか sentence-ending expression 23, **24**

no dewa nai ka のではないか sentence-ending expression 23, **24**

no motode のもとで particle equivalent phrase 34

nu ぬ AUX perfective 60

256

O

o を causal, concessive and simple connections......................................75

o ba をば compound particle..30

o megutte をめぐって particle equivalent phrase........................35

o motte をもって particle equivalent phrase........................32

o shite をして indirect object marker for the causative sentence..........................67, **85**

R

ra-gyō henkaku katsuyō ラ行変格活用 *r*-row irregular conjugation..........................48

raru らる AUX passive, potential, honorific, spontaneous..........................64

rekishiteki kana zukai 歴史的仮名遣い historical *kana* system/orthography..............42

rentai-kei 連体形 attributive form........................47, **80**

renyō chūshihō 連用中止法 the suspended form method; listing..........................14

renyō-kei 連用形 continuative form........................47

ri り AUX perfective........................60

ru る AUX passive, potential, honorific, spontaneous..........................64

S

sa-gyō henkaku katsuyō サ行変格活用 *s*-row irregular conjugation..........................48

sae さえ marks the subject........................8

shi し listing form........................16

shika しか marks the subject........................8

shiku-katsuyō シク活用 *shiku*-type conjugation of ADJ in Classical Japanese..........51

shimo ichidan katsuyō 下一段活用 lower one-grade conjugation..........................48, **49**

shimo nidan katsuyō 下二段活用 lower two-grade conjugation..........................48, **49**

shimu しむ AUX causative........................66

shinjitai 新字体 simplified kanji characters........................38

shite して causal, concessive and simple connections........................77, 78

shugo 主語 subject........................**5**, 6, 7, 8, 9

shūshi-kei 終止形 final form........................47

T

tanbun 単文 simple sentence........................10

tara たら conditional expression........................20

tari たり AUX copular........................58

tari たり AUX perfective........................60

tari-katsuyō タリ活用 *tari*-type conjugation of ADJ-V in Classical Japanese..............52

te-form て-form listing........................11

temo ても concessive conjunction........................21

to と conditional expression........................20

to kangae rareru と考えられる sentence-ending expression........................23, **25**

to kangaeru と考える sentence-ending expression........................23, **24**

to omou と思う sentence-ending expression........................23, **24**

to omowareru と思われる sentence-ending expression........................23, **25**

257

A Practical Guide for Scholarly Reading in Japanese

to shite　として　particle equivalent phrase 31

tokoro　(V)所　nominalization of verbs...86

tokoro to naru　所と為る　passive expression...86

tomo　とも　concessive conjunction...21, **73**

W

wa　は　topic marker; represent the subject 6

X

X o Y to suru　X を Y とする　defining expression..28

X to yū Y　X という Y　'Y called X'...17

Y

yodan katsuyō　四段活用　*Yodan* (fourth grade) conjugation 48

Z

zu　ず　AUX　negative...55

258

Index (Expressions)

A

aete　敢えて 133

atakamo <toki atakamo>　（時）恰も 196

B

~ bakari de wa naku <~ bakari de naku>　〜ばかりで（は）なく 162

D

N de aru mono <N naru mono>　N であるもの/N なるもの 138, 194, 225, 234

E

~ eru <~ uru>　得る 137, 194

G

~ gatai　〜がたい 147

~ ga yueni　〜が故に 211, 235

~ gotoshi　〜如し 135, 162, 195, 224, 235

I

V ijō <V ijō wa>　V以上（は） 148, 211

ikani ~ tomo <ikani ~ domo, ikani ~ temo, ikani ~ demo>
　如何に〜とも/ども/ても/でも 133, 196, 237

imasara　今更 132

K

~ kagiri　〜限り 134

kakaru　斯かる 193, 212

kakute wa　かくては 160

katsu　且つ 136, 147

kedashi　蓋し 160, 210

~ koto to natta <~ koto ni natta>　〜事と/になった 162, 197, 225

M

X mo nakereba Y mo nashi <X mo nakereba Y mo nai>
　X もなければ Y もなし/ない 226

~ monono　〜ものの 132, 148

~ moto yori　固より 210

mushiro　寧ろ 134, 197, 236

N

~ nagara　〜ながら 149

N naru mono <N de aru mono>　N なるもの/N であるもの 138, 194, 225, 234

~ ni arazu　〜に非ず 210, 226

~ ni hoka naranai <~ ni hoka narazu>　〜に他（外）ならない/ならず 138, 212, 223

259

A Practical Guide for Scholarly Reading in Japanese

~ ni kagirazu ～に限らず 137
~ ni seyo <~ ni shitemo> ～にせよ/～にしても 195, 225, 236
~ ni shitemo <~ ni seyo> ～にしても/～にせよ 195, 225, 236
~ ni suginai ～に過ぎない 198
~ ni taishite V/ADJ/ADJ-V <~ ni taisuru N>
 ～に対して V/ADJ/ADJ-V/ ～に対する N 136, 161, 194, 224
~ ni taisuru N <~ ni taishite V/ADJ/ADJ-V>
 ～に対する N/ ～に対して V/ADJ/ADJ-V 136, 161, 194, 224

O

X o Y to suru <X o Y to nasu> X を Y とする/為す......133, 147, 160, 193, 212, 223, 235
~ osore ga aru ～恐れがある 136

S

subekaraku 須らく 236

T

~ te hajimete ～て始(初)めて 161, 234
~ ten ni oite ～点に於て 193, 237
~ to iedomo <~ to wa iedomo> ～と(は)雖も 196, 237
~ to ittemo kagon de wa nai ～と謂(言)っても過言ではない....................163
toki atakamo <atakamo> (時)恰も 196
~ to tomoni ～と共に 223
~ tsutsu ～つつ 135

U

~ uru <~ eru> ～得る 137, 194

W

~ wake da <~ wake de aru> ～訳だ/である 134, 148, 163, 197, 226, 234
~ wake ni wa ikanai ～訳には行かない 135, 198

Y

Vpot yō (Vpot) よう 132, 149

Z

~ zaru o enai ～ざるを得ない 137
~ zu shite ～ずして 161, 195, 211, 224

260

Auxiliary Verb Conjugations

Follows MIZEN

		MIZEN	RENYŌ	SHŪSHI	RENTAI	IZEN	MEIREI	Function
1	る	れ	れ	る	るる	るれ	れよ	Passive Potential Honorific Spontaneous
2	らる	られ	られ	らる	らるる	らるれ	られよ	
3	す	せ	せ	す	する	すれ	せよ	Causative Honorific
4	さす	させ	させ	さす	さする	さすれ	させよ	
5	しむ	しめ	しめ	しむ	しむる	しむれ	しめよ	
6	ず	◯ ざら	ず ざり	ず ◯	ぬ ざる	ね ざれ	◯ ざれ	Negative

7	じ	◯	◯	じ	じ	じ	◯	Negative
								  speculative
								Negative
								  intentional

8	む	◯	◯	む	む	め	◯	Speculative Intentional Circumlocution
9	むず	◯	◯	むず	むずる	むずれ	◯	Intentional Speculative
10	まし	ましか ませ	◯	まし	まし	ましか	◯	Counterfactual speculative
11	まほし	◯ まほしから	まほしく まほしかり	まほし	まほしき まほしかる	まほしけれ	◯	Desire

Follows RENYŌ

		MIZEN	RENYŌ	SHŪSHI	RENTAI	IZEN	MEIREI	Function
12	き	(せ)	◯	き	し	しか	◯	Recollective
13	けり	けら	◯	けり	ける	けれ	◯	
14	つ	て	て	つ	つる	つれ	てよ	Perfective
15	ぬ	な	に	ぬ	ぬる	ぬれ	ね	
16	たり	たら	たり	たり	たる	たれ	たれ	
17	けむ	◯	◯	けむ	けむ	けめ	◯	Past speculative
18	たし	◯ たから	たく たかり	たし	たき たかる	たけれ	◯	Desiderative

A Practical Guide for Scholarly Reading in Japanese

Follows SHŪSHI

		MIZEN	RENYŌ	SHŪSHI	RENTAI	IZEN	MEIREI	Function
19	べし	(べく) べから	べく べかり	べし ○	べき べかる	べけれ ○	○	Advice Appropriateness Potential Intentional Speculative Command
20	らむ	○	○	らむ (らん)	らむ (らん)	らめ	○	Present speculative
21	らし	○	○	らし	らし	らし	○	Supposition
22	めり	○	に	ぬ	ぬる	ぬれ	ね	Supposition
23	まじ	(まじく) まじから	まじく まじかり	まじ	まじき まじかる	まじけれ	○	Negative speculative
24	なり	○	(なり)	なり	なる	なれ	○	Hearsay

Follows RENTAI/N

		MIZEN	RENYŌ	SHŪSHI	RENTAI	IZEN	MEIREI	Function
25	なり	なら	なり に	なり	なる	なれ	なれ	Copular

Follows N

		MIZEN	RENYŌ	SHŪSHI	RENTAI	IZEN	MEIREI	Function
26	たり	たら	たり と	たり	たる	たれ	たれ	Copular

Follows IZEN of YODAN/MIZEN of SAHEN

		MIZEN	RENYŌ	SHŪSHI	RENTAI	IZEN	MEIREI	Function
27	り	ら	り	り	る	れ	れ	Perfective

Follows RENTAI, N, P (の/が)

		MIZEN	RENYŌ	SHŪSHI	RENTAI	IZEN	MEIREI	Function
28	ごとし	(ごとく)	ごとく	ごとし	ごとき	○	○	Comparison